Naughb

Also by Sami Timimi:

Pathological Child Psychiatry and the Medicalization of Childhood

Naughty Boys
Anti-Social Behaviour, ADHD and the Role of Culture

SAMI TIMIMI

palgrave
macmillan

MT

First published 2005 by
PALGRAVE MACMILLAN
Houndmills, Basingstoke, Hampshire RG21 6XS and
175 Fifth Avenue, New York, N.Y. 10010
Companies and representatives throughout the world

PALGRAVE MACMILLAN is the global academic imprint of the Palgrave
Macmillan division of St. Martin's Press, LLC and of Palgrave Macmillan Ltd.
Macmillan® is a registered trademark in the United States, United Kingdom
and other countries. Palgrave is a registered trademark in the European
Union and other countries.

ISBN 1–4039–4511–x paperback

This book is printed on paper suitable for recycling and made from fully
managed and sustained forest sources.

A catalogue record for this book is available from the British Library.

Library of Congress Cataloging-in-Publication Data

A catalog record for this book is available from the Library of Congress.

10   9   8   7   6   5   4   3   2   1
14 13 12 11 10 09 08 07 06 05

Printed in China

3/7/06

Contents

Preface

Some years ago as a trainee in child psychiatry, I saw in my clinic a 'naughty' boy who started crying when I asked him if he missed his absent father. In the supervision session my consultant asked me whether I had checked for symptoms of childhood depression because 'tearfulness' might indicate that he is 'suffering from depression'. I hadn't. I naively assumed that his crying was because he was understandably unhappy and not because he was suffering from an illness. I thought that there were reasons for children like this young boy presenting as they did and that my task was to explore and try and understand the links between a person's history, emotional state and subsequent behaviour.

For many years I struggled with making a connection between the behaviours children in clinic were presenting with and the diagnoses being given to them. For the pre-adolescents the bread and butter work is naughty boys – boys who will not conform to what adults want them to be. I kept seeing these referrals describing 'monstrous', 'bizarrely behaved', 'out of control' children, then I would see them in clinic and they would behave like angels. Many of the descriptions I heard reminded me of my own children and myself when I was a boy. I looked for answers in the child psychiatric literature, trying to work out what these diagnoses meant. The more I looked, the less sense these diagnoses made. I asked my colleagues to explain to me what diagnoses like attention deficit hyper-activity disorder (ADHD), conduct disorder and Asperger's syndrome were, what was going on physically in these children, and how they 'knew' which child had a conduct disorder caused by family problems as opposed to ADHD caused by an immature frontal lobe (in other words a physical problem in the development of the brain). They couldn't explain this to me and didn't know how to differentiate physical from emotional or other environmental causes. The best they could come up with was 'it must be so'. Shockingly, I realized that the whole profession is built on subjective opinion masquerading as fact. To find answers I started to look at the literature of other disciplines and other branches of science.

This was an eye opener. All I have done so far is a dip into a small bit of the huge and diverse literature of other disciplines and of critical psychiatry perspectives. It was quickly apparent to me that there is no serious engagement with other disciplines' perspectives and therefore no serious debate within my chosen profession – child-and-adolescent psychiatry. It has left me with the impression that, as child psychiatry gained confidence in itself in the latter quarter of the last century, doctors' status was enough to allow the accelerating medicalization of childhood problems, which child psychiatry as a profession has been promoting, to go un-debated and unchallenged. Our professional theory base has become simplistic, context-deprived and as a result disconnected and alienating. Furthermore, this intellectual poverty goes unrecognized because our cultural status and power allows us the luxury of ignoring our critics. Child psychiatry has been on a backward slide into the medical model, enabling it to create new pseudo-medical specialities like 'neuro-developmental psychiatry', which have given the profit-motivated drug industry the ideal tools for exploiting the medicalization of childhood problems. That the number of children getting child psychiatric (and the so-called neuro-developmental) diagnoses and psychotropic drugs is increasing cannot be disputed (see Chapters 2 and 5). This, in my opinion, has been doing terrible things to children, particularly in the West, and has not made any positive impact on the problem of anti-social behaviour in the young.

So why is this happening? This book is an exploration of that process. To try and get a handle on what is happening means looking at how culture shapes our understanding of childhood problems and how to deal with them. By putting a cultural perspective at the centre of our thinking we can also begin to understand how culture shapes the experience of childhood, child rearing practices and the institutions (including child-and-adolescent mental health) that deal with children.

This is not an anti-child psychiatry book, but it is critical. Although many practitioners find it very hard to accept criticism and have a strong need to maintain their powerful status unquestioned, I have experienced most of my colleagues as genuinely concerned with trying to do the best for their patients. The problem lies not with individual practitioners so much as with the institutionalization of Western cultures' hostility towards children. We have much to learn about looking after children from cultures that the West views as more 'primitive'. Of course non-Western cultures have their own problematic dynamics such as those of patriarchy and class (e.g. the caste system in India), but they also have much to teach us not only in terms of more child friendly values, beliefs and practices, but also in terms of what professionals, like myself, who work with children could do to enrich their ways of working with naughty boys and their families.

Summary of Content and Themes

Throughout the book I try to integrate perspectives from a variety of disciplines including psychiatry, psychology, sociology, anthropology, critical psychiatry/psychology, cultural studies, philosophy, psychoanalysis and politics together with experiences from my personal and professional life. Some of the key themes that I examine are: cross-cultural differences in child rearing patterns, the medicalization of problematic boys with labels such as ADHD, regulatory discourses in developmental psychology and medicine, the moral panic about boys in the West, Western market economies' covert hostility to children, good and bad clinical practices in relation to boys defined as 'troublesome' and their families and Post-modernism, modernism and self reflexivity in clinical practice.

In the first half of the book I show how culture influences the way we define what is considered to be a normal or deviant childhood. I then show how increasingly medicalized meanings are given to children's perceived deviance. Following this I explore how, once we have defined certain behaviours as problematic and given them a particular meaning, culture influences how we go about seeking to solve this perceived problem. I then examine the role that the political and cultural value systems have in promoting and censoring certain types of behaviour amongst children. To illustrate the theoretical points I make in the first four chapters, the fifth chapter focuses on a modern medical invention which has been promoted by the pharmaceutical industry – that of ADHD.

In the last three chapters I show how an understanding of the cultural and political dynamics discussed in the earlier chapters opens the door to many new ways of looking at and trying to solve the problem of naughty boys in the clinical setting and society more generally. Bringing a cultural perspective into the centre of our thinking greatly enriches the potential number of therapeutic models that can be used to help and influence children, their families, social institutions such as schools, and even policy makers. I reflect on how all professionals working with children need to examine their own values and beliefs. Our professional values, beliefs and practices have an enormous impact not only on the children we deal with directly, but also more broadly on our common cultural ways of view-ing and dealing with issues such as those of boys' anti-social behaviours.

In the first chapter, I examine how our definition and understanding of what is a normal or deviant childhood depends on the cultural context. The idea that there is one universal way to define what is a normal/abnormal child is shown to be both unscientific and unhelpful. When faced with a particular behaviour our understanding of the significance of that behaviour is arrived at by viewing it through a cultural prism which helps us decide whether this behaviour is first of all to be considered a problem and secondly what meaning should be given to it. I illustrate this by examining both the vertical evidence (how definitions of childhood have changed over time) in Western culture and the horizontal evidence (the different ways of conceptualising childhood that different cultures have). Following this I examine how modern, Western culture has been particularly influential in its ability to discount alternative ideas and beliefs about the nature of childhood and child rearing. Given the global power of Western culture this has meant that a particular culture's vision of childhood is being imposed on the rest of the world.

In the second chapter I explore how modern Western beliefs about childhood have led to an increasingly medicalized way of viewing children and their problems. This has resulted in a massive rise in the number of medical diagnoses and the amount of psychiatric medication being given to boys in the West. I explore the impact that culturally invented fields such as developmental psychology and developmental psychopathology have had on the way we understand children and point out the alternatives to Western ideas about child development. I examine how the eugenic movement developed and influenced a social discourse that said mental ill health was the product of faulty genes and that to improve the health of society these faulty genes need to be got rid of. I point out that one of the main factors that made the eugenic philosophy acceptable for such a long period was the fact that respected members of the public (doctors) were arguing that social problems were the result of individuals having genetic disorders. Successfully medicalizing social issues opened the door to the use of medical 'remedies' to deal with social ills. I point out with examples how much of the same philosophy underlies current medical approaches to dealing with naughty boys. Finally, I examine the role of the pharmaceutical industry that has cynically manipulated this trend in order to open up new and bigger markets for their products.

In the third chapter I explore the influence of culture on the process of deciding how to solve the problem of naughty behaviour. I include summaries of interviews with several colleagues who grew up in developing countries and who are now doctors. They reflect on their experiences in relation to both how naughtiness was dealt with in their community and their experience as doctors in the UK being asked to deal with behaviour problems in children. I explore the approaches different cultures use to deal with naughtiness including: discipline and punishment (carrot and stick), acceptance and encouraging emotional expression, developing a value system, developing self-esteem, independence and mastering emotions, the role of religion and the supernatural, medication, the role of schools and education, the role of Governments and other approaches. This chapter illustrates that just as culture has a central role to play in how we define and give meaning to a problem, it also has a central role to play in the process of how we go about seeking a solution to that problem.

In the fourth chapter I argue that culture, by promoting particular sets of values, beliefs and practices, encourages certain types of behaviours and discourages others. I argue that Western culture has a set of values, beliefs and practices that encourages more anti-social behaviour amongst children when compared to many non-Western cultures. Under the headings of lessons from India and South Asia, lessons from Arabs and the Middle East, and lessons from Central and Southern Africa, I show how the beliefs, values and practices in these particular cultures provides a more coherent and nurturing framework that can result in less anti-social behaviour in young boys. I then examine the effect of contemporary, Western culture on children's behaviour and show how free market values such as freedom, independence and competitiveness have infiltrated deeply into the institutions that deal with raising children, from family to Government. This has resulted in Western societies being ambivalent and indeed hostile towards children, with boys often absorbing the anti-social values that are a central feature of the Western market economy value system. I also discuss how boys in the West are able to use positively the cultural resources available to them.

In the fifth chapter I examine the medical diagnosis of ADHD. I look at the history behind the diagnosis of ADHD and illustrate how the growth in the popularity of this diagnosis mirrors certain cultural dynamics that has resulted in the diagnosis being ideally placed to be used (or rather misused) to respond to the growing cultural anxiety about children and their development. I examine the scientific evidence for the existence of this disorder and show why this disorder can only be understood as a cultural invention rather than a medically valid condition. In my critique of the ADHD diagnosis, I point out the physical, psychological and social dangers to children and their families, which the growing use of this diagnosis and the medications accompanying it present. I show that there are alternative ways of helping these children in clinical practice and present the results of an audit I have done on the use of medication in children who could be diagnosed as having ADHD and who have been under my care, to illustrate that non-medication-centred ways of working with these children and their families are available, practical and workable.

In the last three chapters I explore how a cross-cultural perspective can be used to allow access to multiple theoretical frameworks and diverse clinical approaches that can help us deal more effectively with the problem of naughty boys. In the sixth chapter I explore how changing the meaning given to a behaviour problem can make a difference to how we deal with it. I illustrate how certain aspects of boy behaviour that have come to be labelled as abnormal can be normalised. Following this, I show how we can reframe the meaning of particular behaviours and experiences. I then discuss how to go about noticing and amplifying strengths within children and their families, changing meanings in the system (e.g. a child's school) and deconstructing the role of the expert. Case material is presented throughout the chapter to illustrate the ideas being discussed.

In the seventh chapter I explore how a cultural perspective can enable access to a huge range of possible approaches that can be used to try and help change problem behaviours. I discuss, summarise and critique the research literature on a variety of commonly and not so commonly used approaches in Western clinical practice including: the use of medication, teaching parenting skills, therapy with the child, family therapy approaches, other Western inspired therapies and incorporating non-Western ideas.

In the eighth and final chapter I explore the question of what cultural values, beliefs and therefore practices we take into our work and how this then affects not only the clients we directly deal with, but also the local community and its institutions. I reflect on the creative tension that can result from the conflict between modernist and post-modernist approaches to clinical practice. Science can never be value-free. It develops within a social dynamic and reflects historically developed interests of particular powerful groups. I show how deeply imbedded white, middle-class, male colonialist values are in Western child mental health ideology. These values are not debated within child-and-adolescent psychiatry. Our profession's cultural power also means we are undermining better systems by exporting this colonial ideology globally. I suggest we need a radical rethink that puts a cultural perspective at the centre, in order for us to develop a more socially aware set of values, beliefs and practices. I provide some concrete suggestions as to how to influence the local discourse in a positive way and discuss my own value system and how this impacts on my clinical work.

The Limitations of this Book

This book has been written within a context of living in a Western society that presents non-Western cultures as being oppressive to both women and children. The bias of this book reflects my wish to provide an antidote to this negative stereotyping. This means that some of my exploration of non-Western cultures may itself appear stereotyped (albeit in a more positive direction) and to have glossed over the problems of male violence in those societies. My intention is not to fall into the trap of over-generalization and essentializing of cultures or, for that matter, genders. Those who have read my first book (Timimi, 2002) will be aware of the frequency with which I encountered clinicians with negative stereotypes of 'others' particularly in relation to culture and class. In arguing for a more positive appraisal of these 'others' I am mindful that together with limitations of time and space, I have not fully explored the diversity of within-group differences. These differences are further complicated by the impact of colonialism and globalization on local politics, economies and cultures, which has further skewed their own development both through integration into and through opposition to these powerful global forces.

On the problem of patriarchy I essentially agree with Kovel (2002) who argues that the bifurcation of gender relationships has set up male dominance from hunter–gatherer societies onwards and that capitalism with its history of institutionalized dominance, violence and control is the most advanced form of male dominance. With highly masculine values shaping Western global dominance the phrase 'people in glass houses shouldn't throw stones' comes to mind when we in the West criticize other culture's patriarchy and violence to women and children. This does not excuse what happens in other cultures, nor does it mean that non-Western cultures should be absolved of their own responsibilities by blaming (correctly) the harsh conditions of living their populations often experience, which is caused by Western political and economic domination. But before we lecture others we need take a hard look at ourselves. I hope this book helps with that.

Acknowledgements

To my wife, Kitty, my children, Michelle, Lewis and Zoe, my parents, brothers, my extended family, and my friends for their enduring love, support and friendship without which writing would not be possible. To the UK Critical Psychiatry Network for their invaluable help in supporting my critical stance. To my employers, the Lincolnshire Partnership NHS Trust, for allowing me the time to research and write.

To the following individuals who have helped by giving me material and/or pointing me in the right direction (in no particular order): Hawar Gollany, Qaiser Zaidi, Samuel Ted-Aggrey, Joanna Moncreiff, Jon Jureidini, Priscilla Alderson, Jonathan Leo, David Cohen, Lady Margaret McNair, Brian Daniels, Kitty Timimi, Bakir Timimi, Mary Timimi, Hazim Timimi, Jackie Scott-Coombes, Andrew Wade, Carl Cohen, Charles Whitfield, Duncan Double, Eia Asen, Bob Johnson, Pat Bracken, Rhodri Huws, Janice Hill, Begum Maitra, Sue Parry, Phil Thomas, Graham Vimpani and Jaak Panskepp.

To my wife, Kitty, for her help with typing, and administrators Sue and Lou for their help with the final preparations and printing.

To all the children and families I've worked with who have taught me so much.

Chapter 1

Is This Boy Naughty?

Undoubtedly, the aspiration for rationality and universalism is not the product of the modern world. Not only has rationality always accompanied human action, but the universal concept of the human being, transcending the limits of his or her collective membership (in a race, a people, a gender, a social class) had already been produced by the great ideologies... However, despite this, universalism had remained only a potential before the development of European capitalism, because no society had succeeded in imposing itself and its values on a worldwide scale.

AMIN, 1988: 72

The Influence of Culture on Problem-defining

When should a child's behaviour be defined as 'naughty'? Before we can begin to explore the problem of naughty boys we must first get a handle on what we mean by 'naughty'. This requires putting culture at the heart of our thinking, as the process of giving meaning to behaviours and events is a cultural one, shaped by the contexts in which we live. Culture can be defined as 'The peculiar and distinctive way of life of a group, the meanings, values and ideas embodied in institutions, in social relations, in systems of belief, in customs, in the uses of objects and material life... the "maps of meaning" that make things intelligible to its members' (Clarke *et al.*, 1975: 10).

Some years ago I used to do fortnightly visits to a school for children with special needs in East London. My role was to discuss individual children with the staff, advise them and help select cases that might be suitable for referral to our child-and-adolescent mental health department. One day when I was carrying out an observation on a particular child in the playground I was, at the same time, chatting to one of the teachers.

1

She told me that a few years earlier the school had decided to change its policy on aggression and violence amongst the pupils, such that it was now less tolerant towards it. She told me that ever since they had become more intolerant of aggression amongst the pupils, the number of exclusions, including permanent exclusions, had risen dramatically (particularly amongst boys). It seems that a policy change created a new set of 'naughty boys', rather than the boy's behaviour deteriorating dramatically. In this chapter I wish to explore this question of problem defining further. How do our beliefs and practices influence our definition of naughty children in general and naughty boys in particular? After all the meaning we give these behaviours will have a huge influence on how we then deal with them.

As Durkheim (1925) explained, a society can neither create nor recreate itself without at the same time creating an ideal. To decide that certain behaviours on the part of our children are deviant requires a value judgement. What a society then judges as good or bad for its children depends on what it intends to make of them and the model to which it wants them to conform. Coles (1986) argues that as children grow into the value system of any given culture, they are absorbed and moulded by that culture's vision of what they should become, thus a nations politics becomes the child's everyday psychology.

To understand how deviance (in this case naughtiness) is defined, we must also examine what is considered to be a 'normal' childhood. Every culture defines what it means to be a normal child, how children should look and act, what is expected of them and what is considered beyond their capabilities. Any given society may not explicitly discuss or even acknowledge their particular definition, but they will act on their assumptions in their dealings with children (Calvert, 1992). Definitions of childhood vary not only between cultures but also within cultures over time. This means that a culture's definition of 'naughtiness' varies not only between cultures but also within cultures over time. Therefore, I start by exploring how concepts of normal/deviant childhood and child rearing have changed over time in Western culture (vertical evidence) and then examine how concepts of normal/deviant childhood and child rearing vary between cultures (horizontal evidence).

Visions of Childhood in Western History

The immaturity of children is a biological fact of life. The ways in which this immaturity is understood and made meaningful is a fact of culture

(La Fontaine, 1979; Prout and James, 1997). To understand modern Western notions of childhood deviance I wish to first examine the historical changes that have taken place in Western culture's ideological beliefs regarding normal childhood and child rearing.

While Aries's *Centuries of Childhood* (1962) was not the first book to put forward a critique of universalistic notions of childhood (in other words the idea that there is one 'true' way of defining normal childhood), his thesis had a major impact on social sciences, particularly because of the boldness of its basic assertion that in Medieval society the idea of childhood did not exist. Norbert Elias had already anticipated Aries's arguments in his book *The Civilizing Process* (Elias, 1939), in which Elias argues that visible difference between children and adults (psychologically and socially) increases in the course of the (as Elias saw it) 'civilizing' process. However, Aries goes further and illustrates the profound variability of human society's attitudes and practices concerning child rearing and childhood, not just by examining the exotic or, the so-called, primitive societies, but by referring to the familiar Western European past. Aries argued that the modern conception of childhood as a separate life stage emerged in Europe between the fifteenth and eighteenth centuries at the same time as modern bourgeois notions of family, home, privacy and individuality were developing. Aries asserted that before the fifteenth century children past the dependent age of infancy were conceived and depicted simply as miniature adults. Aries is not saying that this is necessarily a bad thing, if anything he is suggesting the reverse, that modern Western culture insists on a period of quarantine (e.g. through education) before allowing subjects to join society. Even if we modify Aries's bold thesis and acknowledge that every known society has concepts and practices that in some respect marks off children from adults the importance of his book is the understanding that there are many forms of childhood and that they tend to be socially and historically specific.

Each historical period has created a novel version of the child. The developing images of childhood are not simply abandoned over time but as Hendrick (1997) argues fragments from each period are incorporated into the succeeding period's ideas of childhood. Concepts of childhood, normality, deviance and child rearing practices are neither timeless nor universal but instead rooted in the past and reshaped in the present.

In medieval Europe, child rearing was seen as being a mother's responsibility for the first seven or so years of life (Cunningham, 1995). However, during the Renaissance period in fifteenth-century Italy, the emphasis began to change with the father–child relationship now being seen as the most crucial in child rearing. It was then seen as the fathers' responsibility to choose and hire a wet nurse, to watch over their children's development and to thoughtfully interpret their child's actions so as to understand and shape their future destiny. In addition a new stress was being placed on early learning and here too it was fathers who were given the primary role in teaching and maintaining their authority through love and punishment where necessary, although the role of corporal punishment was increasingly de-emphasized as the fifteenth century progressed (Cunningham, 1995).

An influential writer at this time was Dutchman Desiderius Erasmus (see *Collected Works of Erasmus*, Vol. 25, 1985). Erasmus placed considerable emphasis on early education and attacked those who, in his view, allowed children to be pampered by their mothers or wet nurses out of a false spirit of tenderness. He encouraged fathers to take control of their children's (in particular their son's) upbringing, in order to develop their child's character in a way that would, in his view, bring them closer to reflecting the divine. At this time Protestant belief in Europe was beginning to emphasize the importance of the family which was viewed as a microcosm of church and state; both in the sense that in its internal government it should mirror those larger institutions and in the sense that the family should be a nursery for both church and state, training the young for its service (Hill, 1997). The analogies and metaphors used in books of this period are not ones of natural growth, but of horticulture, of preparing soil, rooting out weeds and training young shoots in the direction you want them to go, with the belief left to themselves that children will go bad. With the increasing emphasis on the importance of guiding children from an early age, new schools for educating children into becoming good Christians were founded (Cunningham, 1995).

Relieved by infant baptism of the obsession with original sin, Catholic parents were not so immediately brought face to face with the question of their child's salvation. Moreover the strain within Protestantism, which had elevated the father within the household, was in part due to the removal of the authority of the priest as the intermediary between god and man. Within Catholicism this of course did not happen. There was therefore less pressure within Catholic families for the family to become a min-church in itself (Hill, 1997). There was, however, a growing emphasis within Catholicism too, on the duties of parents towards their children. At the same time children were expected to love their parents; however, the emphasis on the nuclear family as the primary location for affectionate bonds appears to lag behind in catholic thinking compared to protestant thinking (Cunningham, 1995).

A new attitude towards children began to emerge in the late seventeenth century and early eighteenth century in Europe. The story of European childhood in the eighteenth century is framed by the writings of John Locke at its beginning and Jean-Jack Rousseau and the Romantic Movement towards its end. During this century more and more people began to see childhood not just in terms of preparation for something else, whether adulthood or heaven, but as a life stage to be valued in its own right. In 1693, Locke published *Some Thoughts Concerning Education* (see *The Clarendon Edition of the Works of John Locke*, 1989), which included an attack on the idea of infant depravity and portrayed children as a *tabula rasa* or blank slate to be moulded into shape by adults. However, this was with respect to ideas only, not to abilities and temperament. Locke recurrently returns to the issue of corporal punishment, stating that he sees little use for this except in children who display obstinacy or rebellion, for he was convinced that a child must become used to submitting his will to the reason of others. Although Locke was not revolutionary in relation to child rearing methods, he carried an authority unmatched by his predecessors. In addition it is widely agreed that Locke began the process of viewing children as individuals (Sommerville, 1982; Cunningham, 1995; Hardyment, 1995).

During the eighteenth century the ongoing debate about the child's nature, between harsh discipline and tolerant affection, heated up. At one extreme Methodists like John Wesley urged parents to break the will of their children to bring it into subjugation of the parents and then God, and at the other extreme stood Rousseau, author of the influential *Emile* (1762), who argued that children should be viewed with a new understanding and affection (Sommerville, 1982; Hardyment, 1995). In *Emile*, Rousseau captured the imagination of Europe with his validation of nature, espousing the natural goodness of children and criticizing what he saw as the corrupting effects of certain kinds of education. Rousseau argued that nature wanted children to be children before they were men and urged educators to allow children to develop in a more naturalistic and unconstrained manner. He attacked the traditions of the time that encouraged fathers to take charge of child rearing, insisting that father's ambition and harshness are a hundred times more harmful to a child than the blind affection of mothers. Rousseau asserted that children have a right to be happy in childhood and even goes on to suggest that childhood may be the best time of life. With the Rousseau-inspired 'romantic movement' gaining a foothold in popular culture by the end of the eighteenth century, mothers regained the predominance they held in the middle ages, child rearing again becoming a predominantly female occupation. By the end of the eighteenth century the romantics had adopted the concept of original innocence derived from Rousseau and used it to investigate the self. Poets and other writers used these new ideas to protest against the experience of society. This did much to provide children with an identity, not just of naturalness but also of significance for evolution and society itself (Hendrick, 1997).

The reaction to the French revolution with the suppression of liberties and the impact of the industrial revolution, with its demand for free labour, then pushed adult–child relations in the opposite direction to that promised by the romantic's aspirations. Optimistic notions of childhood soon found themselves pitted against the weight of the evangelical revival with its belief in original sin and the need for redemption. By the beginning of the nineteenth century, evangelists were advising parents to teach their children that they are sinful, polluted creatures and were warning them of the dangers of treating children as if they were innocent (Hendrick, 1997). Discussion on the meaning of childhood in an industrializing and urbanizing nation was now very much the work of evangelicals who produced their own agenda for child welfare reform. The evangelicals promoted the notion of a domestic ideal with an emphasis on home, family, duty, love and respect (Heasman, 1962; Davidoff and Hall, 1987). The one notable surviving idea from the romantic ideal that the evangelicals had grasped and used for their own purposes was the concept that childhood was a state of being that was fundamentally different from adulthood.

Prior to the nineteenth century there were few voices raised against child labour. For most children, labouring was held to be a condition that would teach them numeracy, economics, social and moral principles (Hendrick, 1997). This view would soon be challenged. During the course of the nineteenth century a new construction of childhood was being put together where the wage-earning child would no longer be considered to be the norm. Instead childhood would soon be seen as constituting a separate and distinct life stage that required protection and fostering through school education. There are several explanations for this fundamental change. The scale and intensity of exploitation of children appalled many and the scale and intensity of the industrialization process itself equally appalled these critics. The plight of the factory child became symbolic of the profound and confusing changes that were occurring in Western society. The campaigners for reform had their roots in the eighteenth-century psychological, educational and philosophical developments and wished to promote a childhood that they considered more suitable for a civilized and Christian nation. With the growth of the first mass working-class political movements that were also complaining about the brutalization and dehumanization of their children, the middle and upper classes became concerned about the unstable conditions, and issues relating to public order became matters of national security (Pearson, 1983; Rosman, 1984; Davidoff and Hall, 1987). As the century moved on, the growing economic success of industrial capitalism resulted in a growing demand for a semi-skilled, skilled and educated workforce, lessening the economic need for child labour and increasing the demand for education (Zelizer, 1985).

Although Rousseauean, romantic and evangelical understandings of childhood all had parts to play in the reformers campaigns there were more specific arguments against child labour, which were developed during this period and which also pointed to the child's special character. First was the emergence of the view that child labour was not free labour (Cunningham, 1991). It followed from this that child labour was different from adult labour and as a basic principle of capitalist, political economy at that time was that labour had to be free and therefore able to make its own contracts with employers, this distinguished child labour from adult labour. Secondly, many reformers from the late eighteenth century onwards associated child labour with slavery and looked to the anti-slavery movement of the period to draw analogies (Cunningham, 1991). The effect of the comparison of child wage earners to slaves furthered the view that their condition rendered them unfree. The third factor in the debate was the fear that the natural order of parents, and particularly fathers in supporting their children, was being inverted through the demand for child labour in factories at the expense of adult males. This led to a fear in the ruling classes that the neglect of children could easily lead, not only to damnation of souls, but also to a social revolution (Pearson, 1983; Cunningham, 1991). The growing influence of the campaigners coupled with the fears of the ruling classes thus led to the first piece of effective legislation in 1833 in the United Kingdom, which prohibited selective employment of children under nine and limited the working day to 8 hours for those aged between 9 and 13 (Cunningham, 1995). Although initially making little difference in practice, the ideal situation had been formulated and posed and for the rest of the century, reformers, educationalists, politicians and social scientists strove to make real the ideal through two further reconstructions: the reformed juvenile delinquent and the compulsorily schooled child.

By the mid-nineteenth century many of the middle-class reformers were using a concept of childhood that was at odds with what they saw as the childhood of the poor and the neglected. Their intention was to make these children conform to a middle-class notion of a properly constituted childhood, characterized by a state of dependence (Pearson, 1983). This movement took the romantic approach to childhood, fused it with evangelical convictions to produce an image of the innocent child who needed to be given protection, guidance, love and discipline in the family, the family referred to now being the nuclear family. Where poor parents failed to rear such a child it was determined that parental discipline for delinquents should be provided by reformatory schools (Carpenter, 1853; Pinchbeck and Hewitt, 1973; Pearson, 1983). Young 'delinquents', and by implication all those other 'neglected' working-class children, were exhibiting features which were the reverse of what the reformers desired to see in childhood. Thus, children had to be restored to the 'true' position of childhood (Manton, 1976). In order to understand the significance of these developments it has to be remembered that the movement to create a separate order of juvenile justice emerged from the debate on child labour, the economic and political upheavals of the nineteenth century and the increasing popularity of school as a means of class control (Hendrick, 1997). Consequently, the writings of the reformers reflect their convictions about the nature of social order at a time when the middle classes were anxious about what it deemed was rebellious and aggressive attitudes and behaviour from those young people (and their parents) who frequented the streets of urban areas (May, 1973). The question facing politicians at that time was how to build a healthy, co-operative society with a cohesive social fabric to replace the perceived chaos and immorality of that time (Pearson, 1983; Selleck, 1985). A new conception of juvenile delinquency, and with it a new way of defining an ideal childhood, was seen as part of the answer (May, 1973).

In their approach to reforming the juvenile delinquent many made the implicit assumption that in the long run only education would prevent the dangerous classes from continually reproducing their malevolent characteristics. The birth of the idea of 'willing obedience' through education was another step towards the coming of age of industrial democracy where the idea of 'rule by consent' was to become the norm (Pearson, 1983). For the reformers the idea of effective schooling now became paramount. The reconstruction of the factory child through the prism of dependency and ignorance was a necessary precursor to mass education in that it helped prepare opinion for shifts in the child's identity from wage earner to school pupil and for a reduction in the income of working-class families that would result from the loss of the child's earning. It further paved the way for an important new development – that of introducing the state into the parent–child relationship. Not only had the reformers put aside the financial hardships many working-class families would suffer as a result of the ending of the child labourer, but in addition they depicted the parents of such families as collaborators in the exploitation of their own children and so introduced a new way regulating family feeling too; if children were useful and produced money, they were not being properly loved (Zelizer, 1985).

The new school system threw aside the child's knowledge that was derived from their parents, community, peer group and personal experience and instead demanded a state of ignorance. It required upon the pain of punishment, usually physical, a form of behaviour accompanied by a set of related attitudes, which reinforced the child's dependence and vulnerability, and, in terms of deference towards established authorities, its social class (Humphries, 1981). The wage-earning child was no longer a proper child and therefore had to be made innocent of such adult behaviour. School also reinforced the idea of the child as being in need (e.g. of learning and of particular forms of discipline). It also further institutionalized the separation of children from society, confirming upon them a separate identity; their proper place now being in the classroom (Hendrick, 1992, 1997). When in the late nineteenth century the church and state began to enforce schooling, signs of opposition from parents began to surface in many Western countries. Much of this opposition was not to education itself, but to the syllabus, the system of controls and the fines given for non-attendance. At the same time enforced school attendance was seen by many children as depriving them of the opportunity of contributing to the family budget, a task many viewed with pride (Cunningham, 1995). However, by the dawn of the twentieth century the principle of compulsory education for all was well established in most Western nations.

By the late nineteenth century, partly under the impact of schooling and partly as a result of growing concern about poverty and its possible political consequences, a prolonged and unprecedented public discussion about the physical and the mental condition of children began (Sutherland, 1984). One development above all others turned children into attractive research subjects, namely the opportunities afforded to investigators by mass schooling. School made children available to professionals like sociologists, psychologists and doctors, all of whom sought to do scientific surveys of pupils (Sutherland, 1984). Now children found themselves being examined under the influence of science, whose main institutional forum was the 'child study movement'. Mass schooling revealed the extent of mental and physical handicap amongst pupils which, together with a growing anxiety about racial degeneration and the effects of poverty, led a variety of professionals and middle-class parents to become anxious about the quality of the child population leading to a great interest in the subject of human development (Wooldridge, 1995).

The 'child study movement' developed in the late nineteenth century, from two important organizations. The first, the 'child study association', argued for a scientific study of individual children by psychological, sociological and anthropometric methods and for the examination of the normal as well as the abnormal (Keir, 1952). The emphasis of this association was on the individual child, to try and gain an insight into the processes involved in the unfolding of the human mind. The second group was the more medically orientated 'childhood society' formed largely under the influence of the British Medical Association and whose main interest lay in studying the mental and physical condition of children, with a special emphasis on racial characteristics (Wooldridge, 1995). These child study organizations helped popularize the view that a child's normal development was marked by stages and that there were similarities between the mental worlds of children and, the so-called, primitives (Woolridge, 1995).

By the early twentieth-century child welfare was achieving a new social and political identity, with a shift in emphasis toward maximizing children's potential (Baistow, 1995). This was thought politically, to be in the national interest. At that time in Western society policy was being developed that stressed the importance of national efficiency with an emphasis on education, racial hygiene, responsible parenthood, social purity and pre-ventative medicine (Hendrick, 1994). In each of these areas the state was becoming more interventionist through legislation. Both the state and charitable welfare organizations were now making a number of assumptions mainly derived from the rise of 'psycho-medicine', about what constituted a proper childhood. There was a growing concern with children's rights and an assumption that it was the state alone that could enforce these rights (Cunningham, 1995). Protecting children and their rights was in harmony with the larger purposes of the state, which was of securing the reproduction of a society capable of competing in the harsh conditions of the twentieth century (Cunningham, 1995). These developments not only consolidated the idea that childhood is a period essentially different to adulthood and marked by vulnerability that required protection but also began the trend towards a universalized idea of childhood. Children in middle-class Western society were viewed as approaching this new ideal for childhood, with other childhoods (e.g. in colonized countries) being seen as primitive and uncivilized.

The inter-war period saw further significant refinements of the con-ceptualization of childhood through the influence of early developmental psychology and the psychiatrically dominated child guidance movement (Hendrick, 1994, 1997; Woolridge, 1995). A properly functioning family was deemed essential for mental health and the role of the mother in rearing emotionally balanced children was emphasized. Children were now being viewed through a more psychological lens with their inner life of emotions, fantasies, dreams, instincts and unconscious conflicts being explored. A more understanding, liberal and tolerant attitude towards children was encouraged by European professionals (Rose, 1985). By the 1930s, child guidance clinics had become important propagandist institutions through radio talks, popular publications and lectures that promoted certain views of happy families and happy children which were dependent upon a new tolerance of and sympathy for the child (Rose, 1985).

Following the traumas of the Second World War and the evacuation process for children in Britain, prominence began to be given to the effects of early separation of young children from their mothers. This construction was reinforced by the development of attachment theory by the British psychoanalyst Bowlby (1969, 1973). The evacuation was to reveal the extent of urban poverty and slum housing, the tenacity of ordinary working-class families in sticking together and the existence of what was coming to be known as the 'problem family'. Evacuation, it was claimed, had shone a torchlight into the darkest corners of urban Britain and was revealing frightening implications for racial efficiency, emotional stability and post-war democracy (MacNicol, 1986; Inglis, 1990; Holman, 1995). Separation, it was now claimed, produced an affectionless character that was the root cause of anti-social behaviour (Bowlby 1969, 1973).

In North America, the pre-Second World War view was that relations between parents and children were seen primarily in terms of discipline and authority. This pre-war paradigm, grounded in behaviourism, stressed the importance of forming habits of behaviour necessary for productive life and warned against too much affection (particularly from mothers) towards children, believing that this led to passive and unproductive individuals (Watson, 1928). During the Second World War anxiety about the impact on children of discipline and authority began to be expressed, the concern being that 'despotic' discipline could lead to the sort nightmare society that Nazi Germany represented. Scholarly and professional discourses that spoke about the child as an individual and which favoured a more democratic approach to child rearing, encouraging 'humane' disciplining of the child through guidance and understanding, became increasingly popular in political circles and everyday culture (Jenkins, 1998). The resulting culture of 'permissiveness' represented an ideological response to the Second World War and public distaste for anything smacking of authoritarianism. In addition, whilst the pre-war model prepared children for the workplace within a society of scarcity, the post-war model prepared them to become pleasure-seeking consumers within a prosperous new economy. 'Fun morality' began to emerge, where fun far from being taboo (as it was in the pre-war years) became obligatory (Wolfenstein, 1955). This post-war 'permissiveness' model saw parent–child relations increasingly in terms of pleasure and play and parents were now advised to relinquish traditional authority in order for the children to develop autonomy and self-worth.

With the birth of the welfare state in the United Kingdom, citizens now had a right to free social and health services. This deliberate democratization of citizenship began with an eye on sustaining a healthy and growing population as well as a fear of the effects of the growth of communism throughout Europe and nationalism throughout the empire. New rights for children were enshrined in the Children Act of 1948 in Britain, which established local authority children's departments and emphasized a preference to boarding out children in foster families rather than residential homes, returning children in care to their natural parents and proceeding to adoption where appropriate. It also suggested that the publicly cared child should now be treated as an individual who has rights and possessions (Hendrick, 1994, 1997).

Contemporary Childhood

By the time we reach the end of the twentieth century a perception of a new moral crisis in childcare and child development is evident. In certain quarters there is a belief that childhood has been eroded, lost or has suffered a 'strange death' (Jenhs, 1996). For example Postman (1983) claimed that childhood is disappearing, mainly through the influence of television but also by the use of child models in advertising, the tendency of children's clothes to resemble adult fashions, the increasing violence of juvenile crime and the gradual replacement of traditional street games by organized junior sport leagues. He claimed that the child, having gained access to the world of adult information, had been expelled from the garden of childhood. This concern with the end of 'innocence', important features of which are the sexualization of childhood, the commercialization of childhood and the blurring of boundaries between adulthood and childhood such that children have increasing access to the adult world of information and activity, is reflected in a huge number of book titles promoting this view. Books such as *Children Without Childhood* (Winn, 1984), *Stolen childhood* (Vittachi, 1989), *There are no Children Here* (Kotlowitz, 1991), *The Rise and Fall of Childhood* (Sommerville, 1982), *Children in Danger* (Garbarino *et al.*, 1992) and of course *The Disappearance of Childhood* (Postman, 1983), all suggest that with the invasion of the adult world into the space of childhood, childhood innocence has been lost. The blurring of boundaries between our current notions of normal childhood and normal adulthood has been exploited by the market economy's drive to open up new markets resulting in children becoming 'adultified' and adults becoming 'childified' (Aronowitz and Giroux, 1991). In such a context the idea of 'childhood innocence' comes to be viewed nostalgically as something belonging to the past, an idea that many politicians from a variety of persuasions then use for their own purposes (e.g. to talk about returning to traditional family values) (Jenkins, 1998).

At the same time there has been a growing concern that children themselves have become the danger with the children being viewed as deviant and violent troublemakers despite coming from a generation who are perceived to have been given the best of everything (Alcock and Harris, 1982; Seabrook, 1982). Thus by the end of the twentieth century our vision of childhood in the West is a polarized one: in one pole we have victimized 'innocent' children who need rescuing, and in the other pole we have impulsive, aggressive, sexual children who are a threat to society. Just as children are polarized, so are parents who are now set impossible standards by the child savers, many finding themselves marginalized, as potentially abusive parents, by child welfare professionals (Scheper-Hughes and Stein, 1987). Being viewed as a 'normal' child and a 'normal' parent has arguably become harder than ever to achieve.

The common thread through both these visions of 'childhood at risk' and 'children as the risk' is the suggestion that modern society has seen a collapse of adult authority (morally and physically). This collapse is reflected in the growth in parental spending on children and the endless search by parents for emotional gratification to their children (Zelizer, 1985; Cunningham, 1995).

Much of the concern about this perceived crisis of childhood centres on boys, particularly the 'children as risks' point of view. Boys are underachieving in schools, more likely to be involved in violence, to be bullied or act as a bully, to be registered as having special needs, to be expelled from school, to abuse substances and to commit suicide (*Times magazine*, 30 March, 1996; *British Medical Journal*, 1995; Hey *et al.*, 1998). The increase in these psychosocial problems, particularly amongst boys, has been put down to a number of reasons, including lack of male role models for boys at school, a lack of clear goal setting and poor management at schools, economic changes effecting boys (especially working-class boys), a crisis of masculinity, incompatibility of the behaviour styles of boys with modern schooling, the impact of feminism and a breakdown in family stability (Cohen, 1998; Hey *et al.*, 1998; Jackson, 1998; Kryger, 1998; Pollack, 1998).

A major tenet of contemporary children's rights and welfare thinking is that childhood should be a carefree, safe, secure and happy phase of human existence (Sommerville, 1982). Under capitalism the foundation for productive work in the family has been eroded, extended family has fallen into decline and the nuclear family and smaller family units (such as the single parent household) have emerged (Qvortrup, 1985). With economic specialization and the advance in complex technologies, children have become less useful materially and schools have become the training ground, the place for containing and shaping childhood for future productive work. As child welfare has developed hand in hand with these future goals for children in modern, industrialist, capitalist society, so child welfare has focused on improving the home environment, scrutinizing parenting practices and improving the productivity of the schooling system (Boyden, 1997).

As increasing concerns are voiced about children's development, so fingers have pointed towards the role of the family, particularly mothers, the genetic make-up of the child (see Chapter 2) and the nature of schooling environments. Judgements about abnormal childhoods and family forms have become harsher such that parents feel evermore closely scrutinized and many are anxious that they will be accused of child abuse (Winn, 1984; Barlow and Hill, 1985; Morgan, 1987; Boyden, 1997).

The character of school life in Western society has changed. Towards the end of the twentieth century, capitalist countries have responded to the changing needs of their economies by restructuring their education systems. Common features of this process has been: centralizing control, a decrease in expenditure on education, greater use of marketing principles, increase in privatization and links with the corporate sector, deskilling of the teaching force (through greater technicalization of teaching), and a reorganization of teacher education (Davis, 1992). By the turn of the century a declining manufacturing sector has resulted in an increasing demand for an educated workforce and so schools are under greater pressure to increase the number of pupils gaining educational qualifications and moving on into higher education and are subject to constant monitoring by the government. With fewer 'traditional' jobs available to boys at the end of their schooling, the link between self-esteem and academic achievement is greater than that at any time in the past (Frosh *et al.*, 2002). Corporal punishment has been abolished in most Western countries (in UK state schools this happened in 1986) and there is a perception that modern schools are ruled by out-of-control boys in violent gangs. The rates of exclusion from mainstream schooling in the United Kingdom for boys has increased fourfold in the 10 years from 1986 (Hey *et al.*, 1998). With the introduction of league tables to compare school performances and the poor levels of resource for schools resulting in large classes, together with a philosophy highly influenced by Western psychology of positive encouragement, independent learning and a high emphasis on verbal skills, boys' underachievement has become very visible. There has been a paralleled growth in special needs provision within the school and boys have consistently dominated this special needs provision in the United Kingdom (Cooper *et al.*, 1991; Hay *et al.*, 1998).

The nature of the discourse within special needs practice has been dominated by the disciplines of medicine and psychology. The adherence of these two fields to measuring physical and mental competence in order to determine normality has invariably conveyed assumptions about the nature of deviance and failure (Hay *et al.*, 1998). Thus current special needs practice tends to rest on 'within child' explanations of any difficulties (Ainscow and Tweddle, 1988), with medical and psychological labels attached to individuals who have failed to measure up to or conform to the current expectations of children's in-school behaviour. In junior schools these labels consistently focus on children (predominantly boys) who are perceived to have difficulties in their reading ability or who show 'acting out' behaviour (Daniels *et al.*, 1998).

Whilst parents are feeling the pressure to constantly scrutinize their practices in order to measure up to the high expectations from the authority breakdown discourse and to quell the anxiety from the child welfare discourse, schools have also had to respond to these dual pressures. The result at the individual child level has been a mushrooming of individual child explanations, locating the cause of the problems within individual children and the development of a new reconstruction of childhood which I term the 'genetically predetermined child' and which I shall explore in the next chapter.

The Story so Far

I have taken a brief look at the history of childhood in Western society over the past five centuries, to illustrate how our ideas of what constitutes a normal childhood (and therefore a deviant one) has changed over time in a way that reflects changing political and social circumstances. This illustrates that the interpretation of what normal or deviant childhood and child rearing practices are depends partly on what has gone before and partly on the social and political circumstances of the time. Times of social and political uncertainty or crisis seem to accelerate these transformations.

I then explored some of the anxieties influencing the way Western society currently conceptualizes normal and deviant childhood. The discourse about children being vulnerable and the growth of the child's rights movement sits on the opposite side of the same coin as the discourse about children themselves being the risk. The coin in this instance is the growing concern that there has been a breakdown in adult authority within modern, Western society. This has put enormous pressure and, at times, intolerable anxiety on to parents and schools who have used the well established individualized, medical/psychological within-child framework to try and divert the perceived blame for things 'going wrong' onto individual children who thus become a convenient scapegoat group onto whom many of our fears about impending chaos can be projected. This has led to a growth in the popularity of the genetically predetermined vision of childhood and a widening in the notion of disability within children as a way of trying to deal with this cultural anxiety.

Problem-defining Patterns in Non-Western Cultures

As well as visions of normal and deviant childhood changing within cultures vertically over time, many differences can be seen horizontally, that is between different cultures, at the same time. Broadly speaking, the predominant difference between non-Western and Western approaches to children is that in many non-Western cultures infancy tends to be more indulgent and prolonged with adulthood arriving earlier. Thus, in Western cultures the search for evidence of independence, self-reliance and self-control starts more or less as soon as you are born. In non-Western cultures you are more likely to encounter more immediate gratification of perceived needs and an encouragement towards emotional dependence with the child. As the child grows older in Western culture, independent thinking, verbal communication and emotional expression are encouraged. Physical labour and the acceptance of duties and responsibilities do not occur until much later in Western Cultures as opposed to many non-Western cultures, to the extent that a new phase in children's development emerged, a phase between childhood and adulthood, which we call adolescence. In many non-Western cultures adolescence as a clear life stage with its own culture is not apparent with physical labour, duties and responsibilities as well as an early introduction to spiritual life already apparent before the onset of puberty.

An African Childhood

Most Africans of both sexes assume that children are an unmixed blessing to their parents and their kin groups. Among the Agrarian societies of sub-Saharan Africa, children of legitimate marital unions are universally wanted. The desire for children in Africa has its roots in the economic, social and spiritual goals of the parents (Bronfenbrenner, 1994). Children, to the benefit of the family, can perform many tasks. In adulthood, children are expected to provide for aging parents with a level of security and protection that could not be expected from others. The defence of collective resources, such as land and cattle, requires able-bodied people. Children are necessary to provide their parents with the proper burial and to perform appropriate rituals. Africans often feel enhanced by the sense that their progeny will continue to expand after they have died. In local thinking childbearing often becomes the final common pathway for diverse human motives, confirming wealth, security, prestige and immortality, all of which are valuable for the prospective parents (LeVine *et al.*, 1994). Children clearly have an important role to play for the family well beyond that of emotional gratification of a parent.

The significance of children in much of African society transcends purely material reality; it touches the spiritual being and most intimate aspects of the culture. Being born is often thought of in terms of the category of passage. To come into this world is to leave the world beyond. It is to be in transit, to change one's state. Being born here means dying 'up there' and at the end of life the opposite is true; to die here is to be born 'up there'. The body represents the most transitory element of the person. However, far from being looked upon as a prison, it is seen as an instrument through which one communicates with others and participates in the life of this world that is basically good. The body is a means of self-expression whose maturation allows the personality to emerge from the other world, and whose decline forces the personality to return to that other world (Erny, 1981). Childhood therefore, like old age, constitutes an intermediate or transitory stage, a period of progress. While the child tries to free himself from the control of the other world the old man prepares himself to return. At each stage of development the child gets further and further away from the world of his origin and as this happens the group makes a gesture of acceptance and proceeds by means of rites and rituals to integrate the child into the world of the living. The first appearance of the child is often celebrated by taking him/her outside to the yard, to the small alleys of the village, to the crossroads, to the marketplace, that is to those points of social life that shapes the human world (Erny, 1981). By being weaned the child severs the psychological umbilical cord that has hitherto bound him to the maternal figure. With the appearance of the second dentition there appears in the body an adult element which signifies that the time has come for the child to begin to participate fully in the common tasks and to receive clan and tribal marks. With the onset of sexual maturity, the person becomes capable of procreation, which is to say of fulfilling that social function of ensuring the continuity of the group (Erny, 1981). Although the rites of passage from one stage to another differs from one ethnic group to another, they have a common aim, to integrate the child into his community and to give him the place that he will occupy as a person during different stages of his/her development.

African ontology rests essentially on the idea of force, in other words it views spiritual life as being dynamic. For example, for the Bambara man, in his childish, uncircumcised condition he remains infected with a congenital vice called '*wanzo*', which fouls the spirit, covers it as if by a veil and blocks the knowledge of both one's self and God. In a sense all human development can then be looked upon as a struggle against the *wanzo*. The rite of circumcision lends help to this struggle by making part of the *wanzo* flow into the earth with the blood and by provoking through pain the illumination and purification of the spirit. In this view of life, force constitutes the very essence of being and the integration of the child in the cosmos is realized analogically, not only at the level of thought but also at that of a dynamism which sees everything as connected. Thanks to the child, the living can hope to enjoy the prerogatives attached to the ancestral state to be joined to the future generations of the social group. The child is a mediating force, a dynamic link that strengthens the alliance ritually concluded between lineages at the time of the marriage between two of their members, he is the connecting link between the member's wife's family and that of the husband. He is the proof that the exchange has been successful (Erny, 1981).

In traditional Africa, the kinship system regulates most of the social relations. The individual cannot be conceived of as an autonomous element for they are completely dependent and bound up with others. The centre of gravity of the organization of kinship is not found at the level of the married couple or the individual but at the level of the extended family and the lineage. Children are therefore educated to have regard to the life they are destined to lead within the family and as members of a group in which the incentives to social action ought to take priority over those that are personal.

These overarching principles reflect in the attitudes and expectations many African parents have of their children and consequently their child rearing methods. These differences are illustrated in LeVine *et al.*'s study (1994) comparing attitudes, values and practices of childcare amongst the Gusii tribe in Kenya with that of white, American, middle-class parents in Boston (LeVine *et al.*, 1994).

What LeVine *et al.* (1994) demonstrated in their study is that Gusii parents have very different attitudes, beliefs and practices with regard to childhood and child rearing when compared to middle-class American parents. This partly relates to the differing goals each hold. For Gusii parents the primary concern is with survival, health and physical growth of the child, whereas for the American parents the main goal is behavioural development of the child and his/her preparation for education. Whereas American parents are orientated towards promoting active engagement, for example using toys and proto-conversations with an infant, for the Gusii parents the attention is directed towards protection, soothing and keeping the infant safe from 'over-stimulation'. Whereas American mothers play with and talk to their children, a Gusii mother can depend on her children and other older children of the family to provide her toddler with opportunities for rich social interaction. Whereas American child rearing emphasizes the importance of praise for building self-confidence, Gusii child rearing believes praise can ruin a child and lead to immorality. Whereas American parents believe promoting fear in the child unhealthy, Gusii parents believe it to be important for a child to acquire fear not only of physical hazards but of imaginary creatures that are then used to frighten a child into compliance. Whereas for American mothers talking to their child is considered essential for healthy development, for Gusii mothers conversations between her and her children are not encouraged or expected. Whereas American parents encourage independence from an early age, for example by putting babies to sleep in separate beds from their parents, Gusii parents would find it strange that mothers would permit their child so little access to their body even when they are in the house together. Whereas American parents may consider that using an unsupervised child for infant day care as a type of neglect, Gusii parents would be appalled at the slow or casual responsiveness of American mothers to the crying of young infants. As LeVine *et al.* point out (1994: 256),

Thus each culture's model of care constitutes a moral and pragmatic position from which the others practices can be devastatingly criticized as misguided, ineffective and even immoral...practices of the Gusii and the American white middle-class represent strategies and scripts aimed at different goals, each of which makes (or did make) moral and pragmatic sense in its own context.

Major cultural differences in many indigenous African concepts of child rearing are apparent almost everywhere you look. Much of traditional African education consisted of observation, imitation and explanation. In contrast to Western education, which emphasizes cognitive learning and achievement through rational explanation and acquisition of facts, in much of traditional African teaching explanation is sparingly provided. Observation and imitation were so insisted upon that a child who asked too many questions was frowned upon. For traditional Africa, if one can see, hear, feel, smell and taste, one cannot help but learn. With this attitude you are not educated for life or through life but life itself is education. Many Africans thus see Westerners as simple minded precisely because of their habit of asking too many questions and uttering too many unnecessary things (Erny, 1981).

An Aboriginal Childhood

In traditional Aboriginal thinking children do not start to live at birth or even at conception, as they are believed to pre-exist in the form of spirit children (Hamilton, 1980). When they 'catch' a mother they are transformed into human babies who then need to pass through a number of stages before they reach adulthood. These stages are not expressed chronologically; instead they are based on what children are observed to do as they grow older. Childhood is thought to end before puberty and girls are expected to have a sexual experience before their first menstruation. For Aborigines the new baby is not classified as a child, instead they are called by the same term given to the unborn child. At this stage no distinction is made with regard to gender. The term 'child' is not usually used until the baby begins to smile at about 3–8 weeks of age and this term then remains as the generic term throughout childhood until the child is about 9–12-years old (Hamilton, 1980).

In the first six or so months of life babies are characterized as 'fat and happy', from about 6–18 months they are referred to as 'clinging', from then to about 3-year old children are described as 'the frightened one', as the child may have to give up the mother's breast and body and come to terms with having a new sibling. At this stage the child starts to move into their peer group but often appears distressed and unhappy. Then up until about five years of age, the child is called 'the cheeky one', with the child being expected to want to touch everything and be where the action is. After about five years of age gender differences in expect-ations become more apparent, with boys joining in the play of older groups of boys, and girls learning to become obedient and helpful to their mothers. From this age on children are referred to as 'all the children', perhaps the equivalent in English of the 'kid mob'. Somewhere between 9 and 12 years of age childhood comes to an end with boys being seized for circumcision and girls being claimed by their husbands. After circumcision boys go to the 'bachelors camp'. They can continue to visit their families but should be restrained in the presence of their sisters. Girls can expect to remain with their parents for a period after their marriage. In more traditional Aboriginal society once a girl's breasts has developed she can no longer remain single. At this stage in Aboriginal child development there is a sudden and massive change in the child's life as the world of *wura* (man) and *gama* (woman) claim them (Hamilton, 1980).

The 'fat and happy' child exists in a sleepy apparently rhythm-less world. They are in constant physical contact with others, frequently fed, allowed to sleep whenever they wish and carers make every effort to insure that babies never cry. No one complains about the inconvenience babies cause and no one makes a special fuss of them. During the 'clinging' stage, Aboriginal child rearing practices are governed by the principle of never interfering in the child's activities until it, or another child, indicates distress. Children are never expected to sleep on their own. Toys do not distract children's exploratory drives and although they are often denied freedom of movement at this stage, they usually live in an environment rich in social contact. Young children are allowed to be as temperamental and demanding as they wish. From about five years of age onwards, boys become part of the 'kid mob', spending time with groups of boys who are free to accompany elders on a hunt or food gathering, or to just roam around amusing themselves. According to Hamilton (1980), these groups do not have the quality of gangs as is familiarly encountered in Western society. They do not bind their members, have regular leaders or give their group an identity (such as a name). Within the group little bickering or quarrelling is found and a strong ethic of sharing and co-operation exists with older boys often taking it upon themselves to look after the younger ones (Hamilton, 1980). Children are rarely made to feel a burden or inconvenience for their parents, and in return children often help by running errands within a settlement or by acting as a go-between passing goods and information between individuals who share a relationship. Normal everyday behaviour of children is not usually divided into 'good' or 'bad' behaviour nor are there moral tales about good or bad children and so children grow up without having to think about themselves and their behaviour in terms of goodness or badness (Hamilton, 1980).

Traditional Aboriginal culture is not as concerned as Western culture with the business of child development. Aborigines tend to be neither amazed nor anxious about their children's development, accepting each transition when it occurs. There is no timetable for development to which Aborigines expect their children to conform and they do not seem particularly interested in comparing their own children with their siblings or other family's children. While European parents might find themselves waiting with their heart in their mouth as their youngster climbs a tall tree, the Aboriginal parent will observe this in a relaxed manner neither encouraging nor discouraging such behaviour. Just as they assume that a baby knows best what it wants, so the adult assumes that the child is the best judge of his/her own abilities and skills. There is an attitude of basic trust in the child and basic trust in the physical world of the child. With regard to displays of aggression by children, the response of most Aboriginal adults is a passive one. Adults being attacked by a child will either ignore this, laugh at the child or at worst swear at the child. Little in the way of active overt attempts to control such aggression is made. Rarely are behaviours such as tantrums, aggression or minor theft viewed as a problem (Hamilton, 1980).

Each child is exposed from early on to certain stereotypes that function to explain certain behaviours. This is a system of 'role-types' characterized by the predominance of certain emotional and social responses. For example the statement 'she/he is wild' of an aggressive child does not merely describe her/his passing state but places her/him in a system of classification that puts the child in the same category as saltwater, poisonous yams and rough weather. Most Aborigines would see no need to attribute motives to these behaviours when that behaviour merely conforms to the expectations of a member of that class (Hamilton, 1980).

A South Asian Childhood

South Asian culture, Particularly within Hindu religion, emphasizes the closeness of a child to their mother, a relationship that is often viewed in an idealized manner. Early child rearing is usually conducted in an atmosphere of indulgence, physical closeness, common sleeping arrangements and immediate gratification of physical and emotional needs. Holme (1984: 117) summarizes some of the differences between the Indian and English way of caring for infants thus,

> A child in India is hardly ever alone. Babies are carried around by their mothers, and it is a common sight to see a girl, even as young as six with a younger brother ... children play with other children much more than they do with objects ... a regular bedtime is virtually unknown. They tend to play or sit listening to the older members of the family until they drop off to sleep, younger ones probably in their mothers lap ... children learn to respect their parents because they see them showing respect to their parents.

Whereas a European may use phrases such as 'bringing up' or 'child rearing', the equivalent in traditional Indian culture are phrases that imply protecting and nurturing, such as 'going with the child's nature' (Kakar, 1994). There is a basic difference in attitude towards children and their importance to a family and community. The task of child rearing is viewed as a family task with adult responsibility and acceptance for this role rather than a focus on 'normal' development of the individual. This often leads to what many describe as a 'prolonged babyhood' when compared with Western culture, with an overriding attitude that children are there to be loved for just being, rather than for doing the right things (Kumar, 1992). This period, however, does not last forever, often being disrupted by the birth of a new sibling or the phenomena of the 'second birth'. This occurs at about four or five years of age when the expectations placed upon children radically change (Carstairs, 1957). At these ages gender roles often become more starkly demarcated, with girls being given more household chores and boys being expected to show more socially responsible behaviour.

Children in South Asian culture grow up in an extended family system. This often means that there is a large amount of psychosocial diffusion in family roles. Thus, a father has to be restrained in the presence of his own sons in the interests of being able to divide his support equally between his own sons and his brother's sons (Kakar, 1978). Similarly many mothers will refer not only to their own biological offspring but also to offspring of sisters-in-law, sisters and even friends as 'my children' (Trawick, 1990).

A marked preference for sons over daughters exists in many traditional South Asian families. Sons are necessary to complete some religious rituals and are also more economically valuable as they become the parent's source of economic support in later life (Kakar, 1979; Dosanji and Ghuman, 1996). Once the child passes four or five years of age, new often-inflexible standards of absolute obedience and conformity to familial and social standards are imposed especially for boys (Kakar, 1979; Segal, 1991). There is little conscious attempt made to train children to be independent as it is understood in the West. For the rest of their growing years children are encouraged to honour their elders and their role is viewed as that of bringing honour to their family by exhibiting good behaviour, high achievement and contributing to the well-being of the extended family. Children are often expected to be dependent emotionally and socially on their parents throughout the parent's lives (Segal, 1991; Dosanji and Ghuman, 1996).

Religion continues to play an important part in the process of rearing children and most South Asian families stress the importance of religion in their family's life and have a deep desire to pass religious beliefs and practices on to their children (Akhtar, 1993; Ghuman, 1994). Most South Asian parents expect their children to remain loyal to their value system and prize high achievement. Many are critical of schools where teachers are felt to be too friendly to pupils, where there is a poor record on discipline and where they feel not enough homework is given (Ghuman, 1980; Dosanji and Ghuman, 1996).

An Arab Childhood

In Arab and Middle-Eastern societies, the values beliefs and practices of Islam have heavily influenced traditional child rearing. In Islam the child is seen as a crucial generational link in the family unit, the key to its continuation, tying the present to the past and to the future. As with South Asian attitudes, child rearing practices here foster behaviour orientated towards interdependence as opposed to individuation and independence. Within their kin group, children receive an identity, affection, discipline, role models, and economic and social support from birth until death; in exchange the family requires conformity and loyalty from all members.

The importance of children within Islam can be summarized by one of the prophet Mohammed sayings, 'When a man has children he has fulfilled half of his religion, so let him fear god for the remaining half' (Fernea, 1995: 2). Early indulgence of babies and demand breast-feeding are widely shared ideals. Emotionally and physically affectionate behaviour towards infants and young children is highly visible from friends and relatives as well as parents (Fernea, 1995). Young children are encouraged to express their emotions as opposed to being under pressure to develop self-control over such feelings. By Western standards the behaviour of parents, particularly that of mothers towards their offspring would be considered enmeshed and intrusive (Timimi, 1995). Toilet training tends to start early, often before the age of one, on the other hand breast-feeding may well continue for a number of years, although the birth of a sibling may result in abrupt weaning. Socialization for important societal norms of behaviour begins almost as soon as a child is deemed to be conscious of others. These norms include a respect for religion, for food, for the kin group, hospitality to guests and above all respect for and obedience to the authority of the parents (Fernea, 1995). Small children are taught the names and relationship of the members of her/his kinship and many can recite their genealogies on both sides of their family going back some five or so generations (Fernea, 1965).

As the child grows older, differences in gender role expectations become apparent. Girls are expected to share responsibility for younger siblings and household chores, whereas boys are given more responsibilities outside the home, such as caring for animals or helping run errands in a family business.

One of the important goals of child rearing for Muslim parents is that of instilling the capacity to 'reason' which is felt to be necessary for the development of self-discipline, politeness and conformity, which is needed for successful adult life. These aimed for values are summarized in some of the sayings of the prophet Mohamed, for example, 'Cherish your children. Treat children with a view to inculcating self-respect in them. Verily a man teaching his child manners is better for him than giving one bushel of grain in alms.' (Khan, 1965: 41) and 'Be gentle to your children the first seven years and in the following seven be firm' (Kennedy, 1977: 75).

In Arab and other so-called honour and shame societies the importance of responsibility, reputation of the group and the maintenance of the public image runs through the daily discourse. Honourable as opposed to shameful behaviour is one of the strongest values for which children are socialized (Fernea, 1995). Thus parents often categorize their children's behaviour as 'honourable' or 'shameful'. Fernea (1995) summarizes the cultural ideals enshrined in Middle-Eastern and Arab culture as

> The primacy of the group over its individual members; the importance of children, especially sons, to continue and maintain the group; the values of honour, morality, religiosity, generosity, hospitality, respect for parents

(especially the father) and responsibility for their care in old age; strong masculine and feminine identity and the primacy of male over female in terms of
authority; the division of labour by sex and age; the idea of *adab* (manners or
good behaviour) to develop a child who is *mu'addab* who would become an
adult who was honourable and conformed to the norms of the group.
(Fernea, 1995: 11)

Thus in many Middle-Eastern families, when puberty arrives it is
expected that conflicts between the individual's personal aspirations and
familial needs are resolved predominantly in the interests of the latter
(Timimi, 1995). Arab and Middle-Eastern families are sometimes characterized as being dominated by hierarchy and ambivalence as opposed
to autonomy and conflict that characterize the Western nuclear family
(Davis and Davis, 1989).

A Far Eastern Childhood

In Far Eastern societies the family is also considered to be the basic unit
of society (Xantian, 1985) and central to self-identity (Hsu, 1985). Many
of the basic beliefs and values that inform child rearing practices have
been heavily influenced by the teachings of Confucius, which date back
to the fifth century BC (Meredith and Abbott, 1985). Confucius teaches
that individuals need to value the collective of the family and take
responsibility in community affairs (Schneider *et al.*, 1997). Traditional
extended family systems provide not only material security, but also the
psychological security of ancestral lineage (Chu, 1985). This philosophical
attitude has led to the development of various practical and educational
practices when it comes to the task of bringing up children. Childhood
stories, often with religious underpinnings, are regularly told to children
from a young age. These stories stress the importance of family and family
interdependence (Lau, 1996).

These attitudes mean that self-realization is not seen as being as
important as the development of broader social responsibility (King and
Bond, 1985). Boys in particular are expected to show obedience throughout
their life to the authority of their father (Hsu, 1983; Wolf, 1996).
This can mean that boys are obliged to continue making a financial
contribution to their parents even after they have left the family home
(Argyle, 1982). With the obligation of individuals to learn how to sustain
harmony with the social order, the idea of an individual defined completely
apart from their environment becomes a foreign notion. Thus the

unremitting work many children show, be this academically or physically, may have less to do with the competitiveness of the self-seeking individual seen in Western society than the incorporation into the self of a high-achieving society (Kojima, 1984).

A Recap

The more you examine how different cultures and the same culture over time views 'normal' childhood, the more difficult it becomes to know what is meant by a normal childhood. This means that there can be no universal way of defining what behaviours should be considered as 'naughty'. There are considerable variations in how normal and deviant childhoods have been conceptualized not only vertically, that is within the history of any culture, but also horizontally, that is between cultures at any moment in time. These differences are not differences of detail. From individual to family orientation, from prolonged indulgence to early independence, from the predominance of non-verbal to the dominance of the cognitive and verbal, from physical closeness to physical distance, from conformity to freedom of expression, from narrow expectations to complete tolerance, from spiritual centredness to scientific rationality, from ambivalence to conflict, from freedom of movement to close scrutiny, from genderized to non-genderized expectations, from duty and responsibility to play and stimulation – which version is the normal? Which version is the universal healthy and natural childhood from which others have deviated? We cannot define what a naughty boy is (however hard we use a trick of classification) until we have worked out what a normal boy should be like. Worryingly, rather than analysing, embracing and celebrating these diversities, Western high-status professions like medicine and psychology have been imposing their own necessarily culturally conditioned assumptions about what a normal child and naughty boy is. Given the global power hierarchy, these particular modernist Western versions of childhood are being exported worldwide, making other cultures' traditions appear abusive and backward.

The Universalization of Childhood

It is not only modern Western citizens whom Western professionals and governments feel should have a particular sort of childhood, but also worldwide populations who are viewed as in need of civilization and development (according to Western ideals). The export of Western notions of childhood, socialization and education is inextricably connected to the export of modern Western constructions of gender and individuality and family amongst other things (Comaroff and Comaroff, 1991; Stephens, 1995). As particular conceptions of normal childhood are exported so are particular conceptions of deviant childhood. The perception that many third-world children are living deviant childhoods can then be interpreted by Westerners as local peculiarities and instances of backwardness and under-development thus justifying continued efforts to export Western childhood around the world (Stephens, 1995).

The foundations for a global standard of childhood were laid down in 1959, when the UN general assembly adopted the declaration of the rights of the child (United Nations, 1959). The declaration specified a series of rights, which were in effect a collection of moral entitlements, for example, the right to love and understanding. The declaration did not recognize that there might be cultural differences in what constitutes children's best interests or that children themselves might have something important to say about the nature of these interests (Boyden, 1997). In 1989 the UN convention on the rights of the child was adopted by the UN general assembly. The convention was not only a general statement of good intent, but also an instrument that is legally binding to those states that ratified it.

More than previous treaties, the convention recognizes the child's capacity to act independently, bestowing not just protective but also enabling rights such as the right to freedom of expression and association (Cantwell, 1989). The convention also acknowledges that many children live outside families and in situations of war and abandonment and that children need to be protected against abuse and neglect within families (Boyden, 1997). The convention elicited tremendous international interest, being hailed by children's advocacy groups and resulted in UNICEF and other international bodies making explicit policy commitments with numerous conferences dedicated to implementing the convention, being convened (Stephens, 1995). According to Boyden (1997), closer scrutiny of the convention shows that it has a strong interest in spreading to the poor countries of the South, the values and codes of practice devised in the public sector of the medico-psychological-led visions of childhood of the industrialized North. Stephens (1995) asks why there is such intense concern with a legally binding, universal declaration of children's rights in recent times. She suggests that a possible answer is that rights are articulated with risks – as domains of 'nature' previously taken for granted, such as children, animals and the physical environment, come under increasingly visible threats from society, there are corresponding moves to assert their rights. Codified bodies of law must protect spaces threatened with dissolution in everyday life. This is an all too familiar story in relation to 'primitive' societies. The colonial argument can be phrased in the following way, 'we take away and colonize your primordial spaces then give you in return goods and rights including the right to re-make yourselves in our image' (Stephens, 1995: 36).

The view that childhood is a fixed notion, determined by biological and psychological facts rather than culture or society is explicit in international children's rights legislation (Freeman, 1983). This has raised many concerns amongst countries of the South, with the majority of countries there voicing criticisms of the predominantly Western notions of childhood underlying such legislation including the UN convention on the rights of the child (Fyfe, 1989).

The convention argues that the child, first and foremost, has the right to international modernist Western-dominated culture, then to identity (conceived in individual, familial and national terms and in that order of priority) and finally in special cases to minority and indigenous cultures. A few passages make explicit the claim that when conflicts between different constructions of identity arise, the universalized modern form shall prevail. Thus in article 24 it argues that states shall take all effective and appropriate measures with a view to abolishing traditional practices prejudicial to the health of children, presumably as assessed from a Western medico-psychological perspective (Stephens, 1995).

In the name of universal children's rights the UN convention asserts one dominant cultural, historical framework. For example the language of the rights of 'the child' rather than the rights of 'children' suggests a universal free-standing individual child on a particular developmental trajectory. Caution is necessary when transplanting the concept of individual rights to societies where the family, not the individual, is considered the basic social unit. While the industrialized North places a high value on the development of the individual and their individuality, as I have already discussed above, for many societies the desire to maintain group solidarity means that individual aspirations are not given the same level of importance. Therefore, what might be considered an abuse of rights in a Northern context (e.g. not giving children free choice) may in many other countries be perceived as a vital mechanism for maintaining the more highly valued aspiration of group cohesion.

The phrase 'in the best interests of the child', which has become widely used in modern discourse and which developed out of the child's rights movements, has become one of the most unhelpful and abused phrases resorted to in order to justify all kinds of decision-making (Schaffer, 1990). This phrase obscures the fact that interests are not a quality of the child; it is more a matter of cultural interpretation. The challenge is to interpret children's rights and interests in particular economic, political, religious and cultural contexts (Alston, 1994). The rights lobby has thus been in the forefront of the global spread of norms of childhood that derive from the particular historical and cultural particularities of modern Western society.

Although raising children's rights as an international issue is potentially of great importance, greater account has to be taken of regional diversity; one universal standard can only cause further colonial oppression (Newman-Black, 1989). When this occurs important and often-conflicting conceptualizations of children's rights emerge. For example, when the Organization of African Unity (OAU) drew up a charter on the rights and welfare of the child (OAU, 1990), much of the charter was framed in terms of responsibilities and duties of children and families rather than rights and needs of the child. Thus according to the OAU's charter every child should have responsibilities towards their family and society. It is also stated that children have a duty to work for the cohesion of the family, to respect their parents, superiors and elders.

The UN convention on the rights of the child also defines the family in a particular Western-influenced manner. Throughout the convention the child's parents are referred to as the people who have special rights and obligations with regard to children. Yet in many societies custom dictates that children are the responsibility of a community or an extended family rather than the sole responsibility of the typical Western nuclear family. At the same time children are also viewed as having particular responsibilities and duties to fulfil too. Use of this construction of family implies that this is the healthy ideal that we should all aspire to with other family forms thus coming to be seen as in some way inferior.

The UN convention also implicitly calls into question the value of social worlds in which children's lives are not clearly separated from adult spheres of work. An important motivation behind the conventions aim to stop, limit and regulate child labour is the recognition of the exploitative and dangerous nature of some of the work that children end up being forced to do. This exploitation of a voiceless group has much to do with the nature of the global market economy and the powerlessness that comes with economic inequality. However, the convention stops short of locating these problems as being the inevitable result of the encounter between the agents of the world's rich countries and the people of the poorer ones and instead calls attention to the special need for developing countries to put in place child labour laws and national education systems. Such thinking simply perpetuates the problem by penalizing the victim and absolving the perpetrator of any responsibility. Further, it is detached from the realities that many children and their families have to live with. Not all childhood labour is physically taxing or necessarily disliked by the children who perform them. For many a child's work is a vital source of income for families, without which a family may starve (Boyden and Myers, 1995). When such children have been barred from working by law, many have subsequently been found to be worse than when they were in work with few subsequently attending school and their families suffering greater financial hardship (Boyden and Myers, 1995). Consequently, for some parts of the world, implementing this article is tantamount to disenfranchizing children from participating in working lives on which their and their family's very survival may depend.

The UN convention of the Rights of the Child (UN General Assembly, 1989) has sought to codify children's protection and rights. Yet cultural differences in how to interpret these rights have been evident right from the start and reflect the different emphasis given in child rearing beliefs and practices in different cultures (Murphy-Berman *et al.*, 1996). Saks (1996), in a study of differences in the interpretation of the convention, gave delegates from eleven different countries attending a convention meeting, a list of ten different child rearing practices (including such things as corporal punishment and the right of parents to insist on a 14-year old to follow the parent's religious belief). He then asked them whether the convention permitted these ten different practices or not. On all but one of the ten items there was disagreement about whether the convention allowed this practice or not.

Not only is the whole international debate on children's rights moving childhood towards Western standards being imposed globally, but also the Western child psychology and psychiatry have themselves taken part in successful export of their ideology. The deeply embedded nature of the colonial mentality that was behind the whole missionary movement continues spreading its new faiths. For example the *Handbook of Asian Child Development and Child Rearing Practices* (Suvannathat *et al.*, 1985) prepared by Thia child development experts is highly influenced by modernist Western medico-psychological ideology. The book sets out to explicitly assimilate Western child development theory into a third-world context with very little evidence of taking a local perspective into account. This is, in my view, clearly illustrated in the introduction,

In this book the authors suggest that many of the traditional beliefs and practices of Asians prevent them from seeking and using new scientific knowledge in child rearing. It suggests that the handbook of child rearing will require parents to change many of their beliefs, attitudes, values, habits and behaviour as a result of understanding this new scientific knowledge. For example it suggests that children should be given more independence and that children need less use of power and authority during adolescence. (Suvannathat *et al.*, 1985)

Thus childhood and child rearing practices can become the property of Western professional establishments who, often with good intentions, are exporting their particular values and practices worldwide. This has inevitable consequences for how we construct deviance and give it a universal identity that it does not warrant. As well meaning the intentions behind this movement might be, it is a form of colonialism that is deeply rooted in Western mentality and should be resisted.

Conclusion

The biological immaturity of children is the only fact that can with any certainty be said about children's development. The way in which this immaturity is understood and made meaningful is a fact of culture. Technologies of knowledge like psychometric testing, psychological experimentation and psychiatric epidemiology have all been applied to childhood and is influencing and giving structure to modern Western thinking about children, including about how to define a naughty boy. The ideologies that have arisen from this particular way of viewing childhood are being actively exported worldwide.

Modern Western societies have been concerned with and preoccupied with the rights of children following the emergence of the powerful 'children as victims' point of view at the same time as a growing debate has been occurring about children themselves as being dangerous. This has resulted in an increasing preoccupation with childhood deviance and as I shall argue in the next chapter more boys being categorized as naughty, with naughty often being viewed as a medical problem (in other words the naughty child can not help their behaviour because of their illness). This is a neat way of feeling that a child can be a risk (if untreated) and a victim (having a medical problem) at the same time. This is also a convenient way of keeping the explanatory framework in a Western-individualized and 'scientific' framework. As this process continues, new categories of childhood are created, such as, 'the school failure', 'the neglected', 'the special needs', 'the ADHD'.

As I will explore in the next chapter the growth of the perception that we have more and more naughty boys in modern Western culture has been paralleled by a the growth of biomedical explanations for why boys are naughty and a growth of biological treatments being imposed on this ever-expanding group.

Chapter 2

The Genetically Programmed Child

*For almost two decades I have witnessed a dark – I'll be so bold
as to term it evil – trend in psychology and psychiatry. I have
watched, often incredulous, as members of these two respected
professions mass-marketed two nonexistent diseases, Attention
Deficit Disorder (ADD) and Attention Deficit Hyperactivity
Disorder (ADHD), to the American public. The success of this
propaganda effort has resulted in the victimization of millions
of parents and children. Worse has been the elevation of
amphetamines – in street slang, 'speed' – to legitimate status
when used in the so-called treatment of children who have
received this diagnosis. Worse still is the fact that many, if not
most, of these children's parents are actually convinced that the
nature of the 'disease' their children supposedly have necessitates
the use of dangerous drugs, often given in dosage levels that
would satisfy a street addict.*

JOHN ROSEMOND, 2001: ix

James was referred by his general practitioner to our department for a
psychiatric opinion. When I met with James and his mother she
explained to me that she had requested the referral after James's school
had put pressure on her, his year head stating that he believed James was
suffering from ADHD and needed medication. James was in his first
year of secondary school. He had struggled with schooling during his
primary school years and had found the change to secondary school
difficult. James's mother explained that, although he was sometimes
challenging in his behaviour, she did not experience any major difficulties

managing him at home. However, school was now ringing her with increasing frequency stating that James was too disruptive within the classroom and requesting that he be taken home. James's mother had complied with these requests, but had become concerned about the school's response to her son, particularly when she discovered that James did not want to be in school and was happy to be sent home.

James was one of the youngest in his year. His mother felt that he had great difficulty keeping up with the work and as a result he experienced a lot of frustration and demoralization. James confirmed this and stated that he wanted to do well. He singled out particular teachers whom he felt were picking on him and whose lessons he subsequently hated. James's mother was adamant from the first meeting that she did not wish James to be put on any medication. I worked with James and his mother trying to help them build on his motivation to do well. James made good progress over the following few months; however, following an incident at school where James lost his temper, swore at a teacher and stormed out of class crying, a meeting at the school was arranged. School confirmed that James's behaviour was variable with, as he had suggested, particular lessons where he was more likely to behave poorly and achieve poorly and other lessons with other teachers where he was doing well. They also confirmed that he had been making good progress of late.

Nonetheless, during this meeting, the year head and the headmaster kept reiterating that, in their opinion, James was suffering from ADHD and required medication. They did not seem to accept that perhaps I, as a psychiatrist, was in a better position to decide whether this was the most appropriate diagnosis. Neither did it seem to matter that James's mother had repeatedly stated that she did not wish her son to be put on medication. Following this meeting, James's mother informed me that she had received a letter offering her an appointment with a consultant community paediatrician. On discussing this with the community paediatrician (who was well known to be a frequent diagnoser of ADHD and a frequent prescriber of stimulant medication) she told me that the referral had come via James's school. She also told me that there were many other pupils in that school whom she had diagnosed as having ADHD and who were taking stimulant medication.

The above story is not an untypical one. Once the stone is thrown into our social pond, the ripples spread out into the community. The more the schools have experience of docile, conformist children on medication, particularly in this performance league table obsessed and resource-stretched environment for schools, the more the schools are making their own diagnosis and suggesting medication to parents. It takes a very brave parent to follow their gut instinct, not to give their children psychiatric drugs and resist the growing tide of pressure. As for the children themselves they are drowning in the discourse of disability and genetic inadequacy.

When I first started practising child psychiatry in the United Kingdom in the early 1990s, the diagnosis of ADHD was a fairly low profile. In fact in my first year of child psychiatry in a community clinic in central London I am unable to remember having to make this diagnosis once but I do remember the diagnosis of conduct disorder being used frequently. This may have been, in part, a product of the department I was working in, given the popularity of family therapy and psychotherapy in this particular department. Yet, I am pretty sure that if I were to visit that same department now, more than 10 years on, I would discover that the diagnosis of ADHD was being used and stimulant medication being prescribed to children frequently with the diagnosis of conduct disorder having become rare. This is the story of the last decade of child psychiatry in the United Kingdom. More and more children are being labelled as suffering from apparent biomedical disorders, ADHD in particular, but also autism, Asperger's syndrome, childhood depression, obsessive compulsive disorder and so on and are receiving ever greater quantities of medication: psycho stimulants, anti-psychotics, sedatives and anti-depressants. For many of my colleagues the majority of their caseload is now made up of boys carrying these labels and taking powerful psychotropic medications.

Under modernism, our everyday understandings of children have become monopolized by a knowledge industry, manufactured by practitioners and academic entrepreneurs working in the fields of education, sociology, social work, psychology, medicine and psychiatry. They have together invented a particular version of childhood dominated by Western beliefs about children's development. Ingleby (1985) has given the term the 'psy-complex' to these modern, Western experts. The *psy-complex* has spent the last century of scientific research obsessed with a materialist, individualist-centred debate on nature versus nurture. What has emerged as we move into the twenty-first century is a particular story of childhood that revolves around a vision of children having predestined life stories based upon their genetic make-up.

Much of the current popularity of this within-child explanation ideology may well be a reaction to the predominant thrust of the nurture debate within the *psy-complex*, which seems to have targeted mothers for an extraordinary amount of blame. In a culture where there is a strong invitation for mothers to shoulder responsibility for their children's behaviour, the judgement of schools and other parents that a child is beyond control becomes a direct reflection on that mother's parenting. Mothers then experience a profound sense of self-blame, along with a sense of failure, guilt, helplessness and perhaps frustration or anger with their child. Since the growth of the genetic disability story, an apparently better way becomes available. Should such a hypothetical mother accept a new cultural invitation to view the problems she is having with her child as being due to a genetic condition, not only can she have renewed sympathy for her child but she is also freed from mother-blaming, she is no longer a failed mother but a mother battling against the odds with a disabled child (Law, 1997).

As I am suggesting in this book and in my last book (Timimi, 2002) the problem seems to be that while solving one apparent source of suffering, this being essentially a cultural defence mechanism, it stores up a whole new source of suffering at the same time as obliterating less toxic solutions and ways of understanding problems. At the same time this medicalization of social problems to within-child explanations obscures the origins of the difficulties and sets in motion the cultural changes (as in the case example above) that far from helping us solve these social issues end up mirroring the social problem we are trying to deal with.

As we emerge from the so-called decade of the brain and the Human Genome Project the obsession with genetics and in particular behavioural genetics (the idea that certain genes code for certain behaviours) is obsessing psychiatry. Hardly a week seems to go by without some television documentary on British television suggesting that a whole host of social and health problems can best be understood through the lens of a person's DNA. It seems that criminality, obesity, your choice of sexual partner, the number of sexual partners and, of course, naughty children (which often boil down to naughty boys) are the result of bad genes. This is good for drug companies as it continues to give the message that we cannot be held responsible for our behaviour, thoughts and beliefs and are incapable of making choices in life because the power of our genes means that we have little control over these deeper biological impulses (not a new idea of course). It is a short step from there to a society where social control and social harmony is then maintained by medications and eventually new eugenics. This is also good for governments of course, as it renders our social and political circumstances irrelevant to how we then actually behave.

The current vogue within child psychiatry research for this biomedical determinism can be seen in the explosion of papers on behavioural genetics. All this does is construct another story of childhood and its problems because all that DNA can code for is protein. But it seems that impulsivity, hyperactivity and inattentiveness are down to genes (see Chapter 5), social communication and language problems are down to genes, oppositional behaviour and anti-social conduct are down to genes (Connor, 2002), loneliness in children is down to genes (McGuire and Clifford, 2000), verbal skills are genetic (Dale *et al.*, 2000), anxiety and depression in children and adolescents are down to genes (Eley, 1999), aggressive behaviour in children is down to genes (Connor, 2002), perceived competence and self-worth is down to genes (McGuire *et al.*, 1999), and even the way a parent treats their child can be viewed in genetic terms suggesting that by treating children in different ways, different genes are subsequently turned on or off, which thereby influences that child's behaviour (Begley, 2000). In the United States of America (who, given their power and cultural influence are often at the forefront of Western cultural trends) have gone so far as to introduce a national violence initiative within their department of Health and Human Services. The national violence initiative suggests the use of genetic and biochemical markers to identify potentially violent children. The target seems to be, in particular, ethnic minority children where the use of drug therapy and behavioural intervention and possibly even psychosurgery has been proposed to prevent potential adult violence. By implication, violence and crime among certain minorities, for example African Americans, are being attributed to genetic predisposition as opposed to socio-economic circumstances (Breggin and Breggin, 1998; Horne, 2001). Now the drug company funded Bush government plans comprehensive mental health 'screening' for all children including pre-school children, in order to intervene at an early age with kids who are 'aggressive' in a shameless attempt to 'fish for new customers' for the drug companies (Lenzer, 2004). It seems that Western society, in its obsession with biological perfection as the preferred pathway to social harmony, continues to have the worrying spectre of a re-emerging eugenic movement (more about that later).

A Quick Recap

In the last chapter I illustrated how difficult it is to develop a foolproof universal notion of what a normal childhood is and, by implication, of what constitutes problem behaviour. Every culture has its own ideas and beliefs about what a naughty boy is and what meaning should be given to 'naughty' behaviour. Furthermore cultural ideas about what a normal or deviant childhood is change over time within a culture. When we look at the history of how we understand childhood in Western culture, we see that huge changes have taken place over the past few hundred years. Just as modernists today look back at our past as having been a time of backward and ignorant misunderstandings of childhood, there is no reason not to assume that as future understanding of childhood changes, our current conceptions of childhood will also come to be seen as ignorant and backward.

In this chapter, I want to explore the dominance of the biomedical view of what constitutes a normal childhood (and by implication, therefore, a deviant childhood) in current Western cultural ideology. First I look at the notion of development and how this has permeated our culture with talk about development taking place in all sorts of contexts (we talk about childhood development and cultures being developed/underdeveloped in the same way as we talk about technologies developing). The Idea of childhood development has become dominated by biology, reflecting Western cultural hierarchy with doctors having most power to create developmental definitions, then psychologists then others such as educationalists (Timimi, 2002). This Rise in biological thinking has influenced the way Western medicine conceptualizes what it sees as developmental problems with many of the Western-invented diagnoses such as autistic Spectrum Disorder (ASD) and ADHD now being termed 'neuro-developmental disorders' implying an already known medical problem involving dysfunction of the nervous system. Once it has become defined as something 'neuro' the door is open for doctors to take ownership of 'knowledge' in this area.

After examining the impact of developmental thinking, I look at the history of the eugenics movement. Eugenic ideology has a close link with Western attempts to medicalize the problems of living. The more we try to objectify and universalize human experience and ascribe our problems of living onto the de-contextualized individual, the more we are in danger of becoming detached from our humanity. Medicalizing social deviance in children (in Western culture this means mainly boys) leaves our culture wide open to the prospect of repeating in some form the horrors born out of the eugenic philosophy.

Finally I examine the role the Pharmaceutical industry has played in encouraging this medicalized view of childhood problems as it sees opportunities for ever-widening markets opening up.

Developmentalism and Anti-Developmentalism

Much of the energy of the *psy-complex* has gone into a powerful 'story of our time', that of an apparently natural and universal way in which children are supposed to develop from birth through to adulthood. As an inevitable consequence of Western obsession with child development our professional and everyday ways of understanding and making sense of when things go wrong is framed with reference to our Western beliefs about normal child development. My child-and-adolescent psychiatry training consisted of a 4-year course in 'developmental psychopathology', which is the 'science' that studies mental disease processes (psychopathology) with reference to normal development (developmental). In traditional writing on development and developmental psychopathology, a particular approach to knowledge is taken, which for historical and cultural reasons is based on Western beliefs regarding the knowability of the physical world; a form of science that is modelled on the physical sciences. Experimental research is carried out under controlled conditions and where possible statistical analysis of samples is expected. An underlying assumption is that the general laws of developmental change are present in the world and can be discovered by appropriate research (Morss, 1990; Karmiloff-Smith, 1992). Systematic experimentation, observation and appropriate measurement are taken to represent the means to this end. This approach to science is usually termed positivist. When directed towards issues of development, this positivism tends to be accompanied by the belief that developmental change is a natural, biological process (Morss, 1990).

The line of argument is also a functionalist one; that is it treats the activity of children as an adaptation to a relatively stable environment. Developmentalism might therefore be said to be born out of a positivist, naturalist and functionalist view of children (Burman, 1994), a way of viewing that is derived from the success of the physical sciences and application of this philosophy to the study of the inorganic world. These are also the underpinnings that drive developmental psychopathology. Both child development and developmental psychopathology set themselves the tasks of uncovering universal and natural processes by which human infants are transformed into fully adapted adults (or not).

Developmental psychology was one of the first branches of psychology to be established, precisely because childhood was seen as the prime location to investigate how nurture impinged on nature. The assumptions that have developed within developmental psychology and psychopathology are deeply embedded in Western philosophy and thought.

The development of a biosocial science of psychology took place in an atmosphere where the natural sciences had already achieved some very compelling accounts of the inorganic world. It is hardly surprising therefore to find that psychological reasoning drew heavily upon ways of thinking already found fruitful in those contexts. However, unlike the natural scientists, psychologists and psychiatrists have never had any clear idea of how the processes they study actually operate and how the moulding together of nature and nurture actually happens. What we are left with is a metaphor for a process and not the process itself. Psychologists and psychiatrists therefore can only speculate in extremely vague terms about the way their theories actually operate (Stainton-Rogers and Stainton-Rogers, 1992). With the powerful assumption of a natural blueprint for development, genetics came to play an ever-bigger role in developmental theories. Borrowing ideas from the natural sciences meant that genetic material was now held to have the power to specify not only how things are made (e.g. having blue eyes or tall stature) but also behaviour (the so-called behavioural genetics) and a whole host of experiences and beliefs.

One of the strongest stories of modernism is that if we want to know about something all we need to do is measure it. Guided by this recipe, developmental psychologists and psychopathologists have employed those direct means of investigation, for example by using psychometric tests (such as those used to measure a child's intelligence) and diagnostic questionnaires (e.g. to diagnose anxiety or depression). The answers to these questionnaires cannot tell us anything directly about any quality of the child, but only about a hypothetical property of the child (e.g. the child's intelligence) as constructed by the designer of the test (Stainton-Rogers and Stainton-Rogers, 1992). Yet psychological tests are purported to be direct indicators of fixed and stable properties (traits) of a child or to diagnose 'real' medical conditions in a child (such as autism). The use of measurement has beguiled many into assuming that they are finding out some truth about what the child being tested is like. Yet what all such tests achieve is replace one unknown (the child) with another set of unknowns (the traits out of which the child is assumed to be constituted). As soon as we probe further to find out about what these tests and traits mean, we find that they too are subjects about which more tests and debates are written. What often happens is a movement further and further away from the original matter of concern – finding out about the child. Basically, what this means is that there is no device for inquisiting the child which can tell us the 'truth' about what a child is like (Stainton-Rogers and Stainton-Rogers, 1992).

Psychiatry's inability to prove the material reality of the constructs it uses has left it open to justifiable and continued criticism of not only its concepts, but also the way it uses them. In the same way developmentalism also has to face up to some powerful criticism. The Western story of development simply does not stand up to rigorous inspection. Far from offering, as is often assumed, an explanation for the changes that children undergo between birth and adulthood, it merely re-clothes this transition from a ragbag of carelessly borrowed garments and accessories, 'what modern developmentalists measure, investigate, even perceive in their subject-matter is, therefore, still defined by outdated illogical concepts. What developmentalists discover may be determined in advance' (Morss, 1990: xiii).

According to Geertz (1983) all human knowledge is, to some extent, local knowledge relative, in many respects, to the culture in which it makes sense. Thus, Western developmentalism should be seen as one of the 'great stories of our culture' (Morss, 1996: 28). It can be thought of as one of the grand narratives by which modern, industrialized societies regulate themselves. After all, much of the state intervention into its citizens' lives is rationalized in terms of the 'developmental needs' of particular age groups. At the same time, much of the entrepreneurial effort of the private sector is directed at the re-definition of those needs in terms of the products and services it wishes to sell. That children have certain characteristics, that adults have others and that it is natural to grow from one to the other are messages that we receive from all forms of modern communication (Burman, 1994). Morss (1996) points out not only the limits and constraints of child developmental knowledge, but also its cultural specificity, its bio-determinism, the huge impact it has had upon how our culture deals with children (e.g. the impact of developmental theories in education and social work practice) and the constraints it puts upon our ability to develop a broader understanding of children and their problems.

One branch of criticism has come from the so-called social construction of development perspective. Rom Harre has consistently urged that psychologists should take seriously the social processes through which their objects of study are constituted, insisting that human mental life is socially produced through processes such as interaction, language and the sharing of values (Harre, 1983, 1986). Harre argues that stage-based accounts of childhood are, at best, a description of a particular way in which some person is obliged to behave. He knows that there are always alternatives. Instead of the hierarchical account of children's growth as a set of stages, Harre sees them as a set of alternatives, recognizing that traditional developmental psychology failed to positively acknowledge diversity and people's capacities.

Likewise, Shotter (1974) emphasizes the role of interpretation in the study of human development; that is the interpretation of children's actions by adults, by each other and by themselves. Once able to use language, children are described by Shotter as living in a world of shared representations in which they play a part in constructing their own development. Another social constructionist, Gergen (1985, 1991), emphasizes the negotiated, social-collective nature of human knowledge and the historically relative status of childhood and of developmentalism. In a similar vein, Kessen (1979) notes the historical dimension involved in how we situate the knowledge that we use. He notes that if adult treatment and perception of children in the Middle Ages or in the nineteenth century was in any way historically dependent and a product of those times, then it must also be historically dependent today. It is inconsistent, for example, to treat child labour in the nineteenth century as somehow a historically dependent, unnatural state for children while at the same time neglecting the role of present day circumstances in defining childhood. If child labour happened as a consequence of economic conditions, then it follows that present day treatment of children must also be relevant to present day economic and social circumstances. Kessen was, in essence, arguing that modern day perceptions of childhood cannot be the be-all and end-all of a science of human development. In fact, Kessen was also proposing that the scientific study of child development is itself an accident of history in that what we study, how we study and how we formulate our conclusions is relative to our historical circumstances. Kessen also linked those notions by a discussion of the importance of individualism in Western thinking showing that a focus on the individual is central to Western psychology of development.

For Gergen, a valid psychology would accept a plurality of stories whereas modernist psychology has been dominated by the narrative of scientific progress (Gergen, 1992). The assumption of progress in developmentalism is little more than a literary device. Progress is a way of framing a story about psychology, and indeed for Gergen storytelling is an unavoidable aspect of what we might prefer to call science. For those who tell the story, according to Gergen, should never forget the constructed and negotiated character of that story. For Gergen, globalization has meant we are increasingly exposed to diverse alternative lifestyles, and to stories that we can see making sense for other people and that we can less and less easily dismiss as deviance (Gergen, 1991). In Gergen's post-modern world, the post-modern self is thus saturated with possibilities as the number and variety of persons with whom it is in conversation expands, seemingly without limit. Gergen sees these diverse possibilities as being inhibited by professional cultures sticking to a narrow Western 'scientific' view about development.

From a Marxist perspective, what psychologists call development can be thought of as socially produced. 'If people's thinking is, like consciousness in general, the reflection of their social and political status, then changes in that thinking must be thought of in the same way. There is some regularity in the way adults of a certain class think, and if this kind of thinking seems different from the thinking of those people's children, then one might expect the explanation of change to be sought in the social circumstances. If the way the adults think seems desirable from the point of view of the owners of wealth, then it would be misleading to describe it as "mature"...Instead the different kinds of thinking observed, and the fact that individuals tend to move from one state to the other, would be interpreted as a consequence of the social and political situation' (Morss, 1996: 57).

According to the Marxist critic Adorno, conceptual systems always do violence to reality. They aim at completeness, at closure and try to explain everything. At the same time Adorno felt there was no other easy way to grasp reality and that reality cannot be known outside that violent and unending struggle with some conceptual structure (Buck-Morss, 1987). According to Adorno thought is not developing in the individual, the species or the society towards a closer connection with reality. Therefore it cannot be assumed that adult thinking is in any sense more valid or truthful than that of children. Adorno's analysis is connected with the Marxist account of 'commodity fetishism', by which phenomena constituted through social relations come to be treated as real. By implication, development can be looked upon as 'commodification', that is to say changes in people's lives that are entirely social and contingent might come to be looked upon as natural and necessary. The social function of the so-called science of developmentalism is, from a Marxist perspective, viewed as serving the best interests of maintaining the social stability of a particular society, in this case Western capitalist society (Broughton, 1986). The claims and theoretical formulations of developmental psychology are then seen as distortions or incomplete representations of reality. Developmentalism is viewed as typically treating change that is actually produced socially as if it were natural. At the same time, developmental psychology is itself seen as being produced by larger social forces and hence as representing those forces in some way. For example, psychology's claims about the self and the development of the self may be seen as reflecting larger trends of rationalization in society. Thus, developmentalism and the society that produces this knowledge have a close, complex mutual dependence on each other, reinforcing each other's claims about how the natural world is or how it should be. For example, isolation and loneliness, which could be seen as inevitable features of subjective life under capitalism, can be redefined in developmental terms as autonomy and independence (Litchman, 1987). Similarly, the Piagetian glorification of abstract modes of thinking can also be seen as an ideological construct that is more congruent with the intellectual ideals found more readily in industrialized rather than non-industrialized cultures (Buck-Morss, 1987). This is entirely predictable as the ideals towards which developing children should reach in Piagetian theory are those of the favoured modes of interaction of a money-based, capitalist economy.

Not only can we see criticisms of the whole developmental project when we view developmentalism through a cultural or a Marxist lens, but in addition there was a considerable anti-developmental edge to much Freudian psychoanalytic theory. Although Freud is credited with developing the highly influential psychoanalytic theories of emotional and psychosexual development, much of the more systematized way of organizing Freud's theories into a developmental perspective was done by other psychoanalysts interpreting his work. Freud himself appears to have become less and less confident in his developmental analysis the more he developed his theories (Morss, 1996). Thus, much of Freud's writing contains anti-developmental as well as developmental formulations, 'it is often merely a question of our own valuation when we pronounce one stage of development to be higher than another' (Freud, 1922: 51).

Much of Freud's theories developed out of therapeutic work with patients where Freud described the phenomena of transference where the patients' present actions and thoughts appear to be a repetition of actions, thoughts and feelings that occurred in those patients' past, usually their childhood. In this sense the past may exist in the patients' head not as a resource for personal growth but as a tyrannical compulsion where repetition may be the truth behind the illusion of development. In this view of psychological reality humans are condemned to repetition because they are continually trying to do something right that is impossible for them to do right. What might look like progress in a human life is simply the replacement of one doomed strategy with another (Morss, 1996).

But Freud makes an even stronger anti-developmental point in *beyond the pleasure principle* (Freud, 1922). Here, Freud begins to see repetition as an inherent tendency in psychic life and part of all organic life's compulsion to return to the inorganic state from which it once emerged. Freud, thus, introduces his notion of the 'death instinct', a drive that he feels is part of the one goal which all organisms share, 'the goal of all life is death' (Freud, 1922: 47). In this light, development is seen as a distraction, a grand irrelevance and the higher the organism the greater the irrelevance. At the same time, Freud also develops the idea that to balance the death drive there is another general instinctive tendency to build up, combine and reproduce life. This drive he calls 'Eros'. From this perspective, what might appear to be regularity in development is little more than a series of side effects of the conflict of these larger forces that are constantly operating within an organism (Curt, 1994).

From a post-structuralist perspective there is a much deeper loss of faith in any approach that could be described as positivist. Even though there are criticisms of developmental perspectives in both Marxism and psychoanalysis, their analytic claims still have a positivistic element, in other words they are still saying this is how things are. In the post-structuralist (often called post-modern) approach, science is no longer treated as relevant to the search for answers to problems that arise outside science. Nor can science be seen as generating objective forms of knowledge that can be used to inform practice. Instead, scientific procedures are seen as playing a part in producing the objects that they study and the interventions that they sanction. Thus, although Foucault suggests that governmental and scientific scrutiny has come to focus on matters of population surveillance and population control (Rose, 1990) he is careful to avoid the suggestion that all these state systems work together in a smoothly functioning way, as a Marxist analysis might assume. Foucault suggests that scientific and medical studies of populations are closely related to changes in the regulatory role of the state, for example in education, welfare and health provision, but not in an obvious way of wielding power through deliberate manipulation of population. Foucault sees the way power typically functions in modern, Western society as having more subtle elements that interact with the way people define themselves and thus it is hard for most professionals and the populations they serve to recognize the subtle ways in which power and control operate within everyday discourse (Foucault, 1981; Parker, 1992).

This is the same in Foucault's discussions of the family and childhood in that he sees them as also constituted through interactions with social processes. Thus the same person who is treated as a child in some circumstances may be treated as an adult in others. It becomes difficult to pin down what childhood is or what childhood should be in any definitive sense. Such matters seem to be consequential on cultural values, beliefs and practices, and people's behaviour tends to be a reflection of that activity. Thus human subjectivity is seen as socially produced, with individuals retaining some personal agency and choice but whose beliefs, choices and practices tend to be highly influenced by the prevailing cultural discourses of the time (Foucault, 1981; Curt, 1994). In this way of looking at things universal stages of development can be thought of as no more than bodies of knowledge, forms of scientific, professional and lay discourse of a particular culture.

Walkerdine similarly insists that what we call development, which parents and teachers for example may treat as inherently, naturally regulated change, can only be an effect of normalizing and regularizing practices (Walkerdine, 1993). She sees, for example, teachers' recognition of developmental achievements of the individual child as a subtle kind of regulation. Although this regulation may be less obvious than the more formal old-fashioned classrooms with rigid rows of desks, control is still being exercised. She notes how schooling practices rely on certain kinds of the so-called expert knowledge about children in general on which the curriculum is based. Furthermore, within the classroom, teachers' observations and the types of behaviours and achievements that they privilege contribute to making up this expert knowledge defined as it tends to be in terms of developmental achievements (Walkerdine, 1984).

Bradley (1989) meanwhile concentrating on theories about infant development describes how the general discourse of our time tends to blame and devalue women in their role as mothers. As with psychiatric and psychological literatures pathologizing of mothers, developmental theories are set up for blame in that there is an expectation that mothers should be capable of providing a hypersensitive, interactive partner for the young baby, a partner who is at the same time meant to be natural, educational and constructive (but non-directive), and who must at all costs enjoy what she is doing. He illustrates how theories of infant development assume quite specific caretaking conditions and functions that it treats as natural in the same way that development itself is seen as natural.

In this brief summary of some of the criticisms of the naturalistic, predetermined theories of development, I have tried to illustrate why developmental ideology and developmental psychopathology are simply this culture's way of interpreting how children should be rather than a scientific endeavour that is leading us ever closer to the 'truth' about the nature of childhood. In discussing how, he believes, Foucault would have questioned these practices, John Morss reflects, 'what, he asks us, is actually going on? What are people doing to other people when that word development is used? What happens as a result of its invocation? How is developmental knowledge spawned? Foucault urges us to maintain the questionings of the discipline' (Morss, 1996: 150). For within the developmental discourse there is a constant subtext that is saying there is a superior and inferior position. Development says to the child, the parent and the teacher this is your future and if you do not reach it you are, in some senses, inferior (Morss, 1995). It is not just children who are said to develop but also peoples and economies (Sachs, 1992; Rahman, 1993). Development is about modern hierarchies of superiority and inferiority, it is about dismissing diversity. Developmental explanations instil the notion of individual competitiveness; from the moment you are born you will have developmental milestones thrust upon you. As parents we are desperate to see our children achieve these age-bound expectations. Development of our children is under constant professional surveillance starting with health visitors and community paediatricians and moving on to general practitioners, nursery nurses, teachers and a whole range of specialists. We are concerned when our children seem to be falling behind and we are constantly encouraging them to achieve these expectations. If we are not concerned and not encouraging, presumably we are neglecting.

And what of the children themselves? If there is a belief that these are natural, unfolding processes for which professionals must be involved in helping children achieve, does this not encourage competitiveness from a very early age? How much do the children get caught in these parental and professional anxieties? How relaxed can children, from the moment they are born to just be, as opposed to having to do something to ease these cultural anxieties. When these anxieties cannot be comforted and there is a perception that a child has strayed from their predestined development path, who is to blame? In this blame-ridden culture that needs an explanation for everything much of the developmental psycho-pathology literature has generally pointed towards the mother for blame and more recently towards the child's genes. In a culture where families have shrunk and fathers seem to disappear and relinquish duty and responsibility in ever-increasing numbers, mothers have to shoulder not only the responsibility for caring for their family (a role given much lower status in Western culture than many non-Western cultures), but also the responsibility for things going wrong. In a final stab from the developmental discourse mothers are then denied credit for their work when things do go well as children are then simply seen as achieving their biological destiny.

Within this context the more bio-deterministic aspects of the developmental and developmental psychopathology culture has, at least, appeared to provide a get-out clause for the beleaguered mother. Now problems can be viewed as being the result of a fault in the genetic programme for development and thus intrinsic to the child. But this approach to understanding the problems of children is equally guilty in its simplistic theoretical assumptions (masquerading as truth) in denying alternative possibilities and it never solves the nagging doubt in the back of a parent's mind that it is their fault.

Nor does it even begin to tackle the question of what impact such a system has on children themselves. Why is it boys who consistently outnumber girls by somewhere between two to one and ten to one in most of these apparently developmental disorders. Why does our view of development appear to discover such massive genetic fault in boys as opposed to girls? It would seem that modern, Western society has developed a set of beliefs and expectations about development (and its problems) that girls find easier to achieve than boys. Perhaps part of the modern 'naughty boy' problem is the inevitable outcome of a developmental story that our culture insists on, which marginalizes many aspects of 'boyhood'.

These beliefs heavily influence the education system our children grow up in. For example, special needs resources in schools go to a much higher proportion of boys than girls (Daniels *et al.*, 1998). Furthermore, the defining of a disability requiring special needs help at school is shaped by the disciplines of medicine and psychology (Hey *et al.*, 1998). The adherence of these two fields to measuring physical and mental competence in order to determine normality inevitably conveys assumptions about deviance and failure and these labels then become attached to both individuals and groups which have failed to measure up/conform. Special needs practice within schools rests on within-child explanations (Ainscow and Tweddle, 1988) and on the whole are focused upon reading ability or acting-out behaviour (or naughtiness) (Daniels *et al.*, 1998). There are also obvious differences in special needs provision within schools by race, with black pupils appearing to be systematically diverted from the category of specific reading difficulties and allocated to mild to moderate learning difficulties and black boys in particular to emotional and behavioural difficulties, while white boys tend to dominate the reading support resources (Hey *et al.*, 1998). Like the professions of psychology and psychiatry, teaching has fallen victim of rationalist, scientific, market values and has moved towards a more 'technicist' approach, with greater emphasis on specialization and less acknowledgement of the human social exchange nature of a teacher's activity, leading to deskilling, greater emotional detachment from their work (Skelton, 2001) and the return of more didactic beliefs and practices in school that revolve around concepts derived from a child development perspective. The language of development has far-reaching consequences on how we deal with children in our culture, on how we define naughty boys and how we then interpret the meaning of their perceived problems.

The Spectre of Eugenics

Towards the end of the nineteenth century and the beginning of the twentieth century a new sinister movement appeared in Western psychiatry. A belief, touted as being grounded in science, was emerging that the 'mentally ill' were carriers of defective 'germplasm' (in other words bad genes), and as such posed a serious threat to the future health of Western societies. In a stream of scientific articles, newspaper editorials and popular books the mentally ill were described as a degenerate strain of humanity that bred at alarming rates and burdened the 'normal' population with the great expense of paying for their upkeep. In North America this led to a wholesale societal assault on those deemed mentally ill. They were prohibited from marrying in many states, forcibly committed to state hospitals in great numbers, and many were sterilized against their will (Whittaker, 2002).

Much of this thinking began with studies conducted by Sir Francis Galton (cousin of Charles Darwin). In 1869, Galton published a scientific work, *Hereditary Genius*, in which he concluded that it was nature, rather than nurture, which made the superior man. Galton had tracked familial relations among nearly one thousand prominent English leaders and found that this top class came from a small, select group of people. Although this was probably stating the obvious that in a class-conscious England privilege led to success, to Galton the data provided proof that intelligence was inherited and that a small group of successful English families enjoyed the benefits of superior 'germplasm' (Kelves, 1985). In 1883, Galton coined the term 'eugenics' derived from the Greek word 'well-born' as a name for the science that would improve the human stock by giving more 'suitable' races a better chance of prevailing speedily over the less suitable stock. It was to be a science devoted to dividing the human race into two classes, the eugenic and the cacogenic (or poorly born). The latter group would be seen as having inherited bad 'germplasm' and thus, as a group, should, at the very least, be not allowed to breed. In this new eugenic view of humankind the mentally ill were seen as among the most unfit, with insanity seen as the final stage of a progressive deterioration in a family's 'germplasm' (Kelves, 1985).

The eugenic ideology found a receptive audience in the United States where many prominent authors and scientists began arguing that the mentally unfit should not be allowed to breed. At the turn of the century, private funding to Harvard-educated biologist, Charles Davenport, began the trend into the so-called scientific study of the genetics of human inheritance with the underlying agenda of proving the 'scientific' validity of the eugenic proposal. Davenport applied a genetic model to studying complex behavioural traits in humans, proposing that a single gene controlled each trait. He was soon suggesting that immigrants, the mentally ill and all sorts of societal misfits were genetically inferior and confidently writing that people could inherit genes for shiftlessness, thieving, prostitution and insincerity (Whittaker, 2002).

The selling of eugenics in North America began in earnest in 1921, when the American museum of natural history hosted the second international congress on eugenics, a meeting financed in a large part by the Carnegie institution and the Rockefeller foundation. At this conference, papers on the financial cost incurred to society by caring for defectives, the inheritability of insanity and other disorders, and the low birth rates of the elite in America were presented. Talks were given on topics such as the Jewish problem, the dangers of Negro and white intermixture and the pedigrees of pauper stocks. At the close of the conference a national eugenics society was established, sending out a message that warned of racial deterioration and the need for societal leaders to resist the complete destruction of the white race. The congress was covered in the leading national newspapers that reported on the eugenic ideals in a sympathetic manner (Chase, 1980; Whittaker, 2002).

At the close of this international conference Davenport together with other prominent eugenicists formed a committee which led to the establishment of a national eugenics society. The American Eugenics Society (AES) focused on promoting eugenics to the American public through textbooks, pamphlets and information campaigns, aimed at building support for sterilization laws. By the 1930s, eugenicists had the public ear. Franz Kallman, Chief of research at the New York State Psychiatric Institute, claimed that even lovers of individual liberty had to agree that mankind would be much happier if societies could get rid of their schizophrenics and other mentally ill individuals who were not biologically satisfactory (Kallman, 1938). Earnest Hooton, Harvard professor of anthropology, in his 1937 book *Apes, Men and Morons*, compared the insane to malignant biological growths whose 'germplasm' should be considered poisonous slime, suggesting that the situation in America was now so critical that it demanded an urgent surgical operation (Hooten, 1937).

From the late nineteenth century, American eugenicists had been arguing that the mentally ill should be prevented from having children. This propaganda began to influence state legislators in the United States from 1896 when Connecticut became the first state to prohibit the 'insane' from the right to marry. By 1914, more than twenty states had passed such laws and by 1933 all states in the United States had passed laws effectively prohibiting marriage for those deemed to be mentally ill. Yet few eugenicists believed such laws did much good, most considering this to be a grossly inadequate response to the perceived problem. Eugenicists were instead arguing that the insane should firstly be segregated in asylums and then sterilized to prevent further multiplication of the bad genes.

In 1907, Indiana became the first state in the United States to pass a compulsory sterilization law. It did so in the name of science, the bill stating that heredity had been shown to play a dominant role in the transmission of crime, idiocy and imbecility. Over the next two decades thirty state legislatures approved sterilization bills and repeatedly they did so based on an argument that science had proven that defectives bred defectives (Whittaker, 2002). Opponents, who included Catholics and non-English immigrant groups, argued that these laws violated constitutional safeguards against cruel and unusual punishments, leading some states to be challenged on their sterilization laws. However, in 1927 the US Supreme Court, by an eight-to-one majority in the case of Buck V. Bell, ruled that sterilization laws were constitutional, noting that experience had shown that heredity played an important part in the transmission of insanity and imbecility (Chase, 1980). Soon institutions such as the California department of mental hygiene began listing sterilization as a medical treatment that could be provided to 'mentally ill' patients in its state hospitals (Popenoe, 1935). The laws tended to discriminate against poorer people and minority groups. In California, for example, the sterilization rates of blacks and foreign immigrants were twice as high as would be expected from their representation in the general population (Kelves, 1999).

Two years after the US Supreme Court deemed it constitutional, Denmark passed a sterilization law. Over the next few years Norway, Sweden, Finland and Iceland did too. America's influence on Nazi Germany was particularly pronounced and it was, of course, in that country that eugenics ran its full course.

Much as US geneticists had, German eugenicists sought to develop scientific evidence that mental illnesses were inherited and that such genetic disease was spreading through its population. In 1925, the Rockefeller foundation gave two-and-a-half million dollars to the psychiatric institute in Munich, which quickly became Germany's leading centre for eugenic research. The Rockefeller foundation also gave money to the institute for anthropology, human genetics and eugenics in Berlin, which used this money to pay for a national survey of 'degenerative traits' in the German population (Whittaker, 2002).

After Hitler came to power in 1933, Germany passed a comprehensive sterilization bill. The German eugenicists who drew up that legislation had gone to school on the US experience, which many American eugenicists noted with some pride. Many in Germany and in the United States saw the Nazi bill as morally superior to any US state law, praising Germany's sterilization programme as an example of a desirable modern health programme. Praise for German eugenics found particular favour amongst American psychiatrists. For example, the American neurological association published an official report on eugenic sterilization, praising Hitler's sterilization programme. Two senior authors in this report were psychiatrists, Leo Alexander (who was to become the chief medical investigator at Nuremberg) and the world famous Abraham Myerson (Breggin and Breggin, 1998). A year before war broke out with Germany, American psychiatrist Aaron Rosanhoff, in his textbook *Manual of Psychiatry and Mental Hygiene*, favourably compared the German sterilization programme to the American sterilization programme, concluding that eugenics is a scientific rather than political exercise (Rosanhoff, 1938).

With eugenic discourse talking about the 'mentally ill' as social wastage, malignant biological growths and so on, it was only a short step to move from sterilization to getting rid of them altogether. In 1935, Alexis Carrel, a Nobel Prize winning physician at the Rockefeller institute for medical research in New York, made the point explicit in his book *Man, the Unknown*. In this book Carrel questioned why societies preserve useless and potentially harmful beings by suggesting that society should dispose of criminals and the insane in a humane and economical manner in small euthanastic institutions supplied with proper gasses (Carrel, 1935).

Learning from American rhetoric, Nazi Germany began killing their mentally ill with these 'proper' gasses in January 1940. Over the course of the next 18 months the Nazis gassed more than seventy thousand mental patients. Euthanasia forms were filled in on thousands of patients by hospital doctors throughout Germany and these forms were then sent to Berlin for the final life-and-death determination by a team of 50 psychiatrists, including ten professors of psychiatry. Unlike the subsequent mass enslavement and murder of the Jews, the killing of mental patients drew heated criticism from the public and some religious leaders and in August 1941, Hitler withdrew his approval. However, acting without official sanction doctors continued killing on their own in local mental hospitals, a practice that spread to occupied countries, for example in France where without an official order, psychiatrists killed an estimated forty thousand of their patients (Breggin and Breggin, 1998). A path that had begun 75 years earlier with Galton's study of superior traits of the ruling English elite had wound its way through the corridors of American science finally reaching its stated goal in the hands of German psychiatrists who took the lead in developing Germany's murderous euthanasia programme.

To help us understand how doctors in general, and psychiatrists in particular, have played such a leading role in developing first the ideology and then the technology, which led initially to the extermination of thousands of psychiatric patients and then millions of Jews, we need to examine the dynamics of medicalization. Human experience deprived of context and examined through the prism of apparent scientific objectivity lends itself perfectly to be used by the political system of the day (Timimi, 2002). Medical concepts of mental illness naturally focus on individuals' differences and perceived inadequacies when compared to the cultural norm. The absence of 'treatments' that return a deviant group back into the desired cultural norm, together with the embedded idea that these deviants are corrupted with poor genes, makes it a short step to proposing eugenic solutions for this perceived 'medical' problem. Medical practitioners can then excuse their actions by believing that they are participating in a 'treatment' that is for the good of the future medical well-being of society. Thus psychiatrists involved in exterminating inpatients did not merely supervise, but it was often the duty of a psychiatrist to open the valve of the cylinder containing the carbon monoxide as if they were supervising a treatment (Muller-Hill, 1991). If doctors legitimize and carry out murders then others can more easily rationalize their own participation in this endeavour. Following the euthanasia programme on psychiatric inpatients, the equipment used in these euthanasia centres was dismantled and then used to construct the holocaust extermination camps. Not only was the equipment that psychiatrists had helped develop used but also in addition psychiatrists went to the camps and conducted the first official, systematic murders of Jews. These teams diagnosed and then selected victims using the euthanasia forms and then had the inmates sent to their deaths at the psychiatric extermination centres during the early stages of the holocaust. Furthermore, historians agree that the psychiatrists were in no way coerced, indeed they were empowered to do so, fulfilling their task without protest and often on their own initiative (Proctor, 1988).

With this grizzly episode in the history of medicine and psychiatry behind us one would have thought that the eugenic ideals would be firmly confined to the pages of history. Not so, as the central ideological force that made the eugenic ideal possible and then turned it into a reality is still not only alive but thriving – that of medicalizing the social complexities of the human experience. As can be seen from the neuro-developmental model of childhood discussed above, doctors have a huge influence and power to turn our social and cultural expectations for children's behaviour into medical definitions of physical health with those who do not conform to our social and cultural expectations being labelled as medically dysfunctional in some manner. Furthermore, in a culture with dubious ideals and values that shows an increasing intolerance and lack of time for children (see Chapter 4) the numbers receiving these invented medical labels and accompanying drug treatments continues to rise alarmingly in the Western world. Eugenics is slipping in through the back door. Once we have defined our perception of what we consider to be socially deviant as being caused by a medical disorder, it is only a short step towards the idea of preventing these behaviours from happening in the first place by use of medical means (Harper and Clarke, 1997).

The field of behavioural genetics (the linking of behaviours to particular genes in a way not dissimilar to what Davenport, discussed above, was doing at the turn of the twentieth century) has been discussing with great optimism the findings of the Human Genome Project, suggesting that in the not too distant future we will be able to test children's genes before they are born and provide the so-called gene therapy to correct any genes that are considered undesirable (Farmer and Owen, 1996; Corvin and Gill, 2003). Do not we offer abortions for children with known genetic abnormalities? If we discover genes or perhaps a group of genes that contribute towards let us say hyperactivity, which is now defined as a medical disorder, is it beyond the realms of possibility in our current culture that we would then start offering abortions on medical grounds for children found to be carrying these genes? And what of the children already born with those genes. If we have already medicalized this problem to what extent would we go to in order to 'treat' these children?

A telling example comes from the government-funded violence initiative in the United States. Back in the seventies Mednick and Christiansen (1977) proposed a bio-medical screening programme, including screening approaches based on teacher ratings, to take place at elementary (primary) school for early detection of future criminals. This book came out at a time when government agencies were indeed funding psychiatrists and neuro-surgeons who claimed that the urban uprisings that had occurred were caused by genetic defects and brain disease in individual African Americans. Some of these doctors were advocating psychiatric brain surgery for selected rioters and even their leaders. One independent project in Mississippi was actually performing psycho-surgical operations on the brains of African American children deemed to be hyperactive and aggressive (Breggin and Breggin, 1998). Fortunately, critics at the time compared these so-called treatment programmes to measures used in Nazi Germany and many of the programmes were abandoned under pressure, or took on other guises. For a time bio-psychiatrists were then discouraged from publicizing their efforts towards finding biological forms of control for urban violence.

Then, at the beginning of the 1990s, Dr Goodwin, who was chief scientist at the National Institute of Mental Health in the United States and one of the Government's top research psychiatrists, feeling that public attitudes were more favourable again, re-publicized the idea that the violence-prone individual was suffering from a physical brain ailment that could be diagnosed and treated. Indeed, in one of his speeches Goodwin went on to compare inner city youth to monkeys who live in the jungle, who just want to kill each other and have sex (Breggin and Breggin, 1998). Goodwin not only re-proposed the idea of developing screening programmes to be administered to school children to discover potential violent offenders, but in addition proposed that many might then be treated from an early age with psychotropic medication.

Goodwin's ideas soon found favour in Government circles leading the national research council in the United States to publish the report *Understanding and Preventing Violence* (Reiss and Roth, 1993), which provided a blueprint for a national violence initiative sympathetic to Goodwin's ideas and suggesting an important role for finding bio-medical causes and treating them. During the same year a review of violence research taking place at the National Institute of Health in the United States found that violence research was very much alive in the United States with over 300 research projects, totalling US$42 million being funded in 1993 and with the bulk of the work taking place at the National Institute of Mental Health. Many projects were funded by Government agencies as well as private foundations and included many prominent psychiatrists, including a professor of child psychiatry at Harvard Medical School (Felton Earls). Earls' vision, like Goodwin's, was based on disease prevention with the aim of screening and identifying individual children as potential offenders in need of preventative treatment or control. As with many in similar projects, Earls hoped the research he was involved in will link key biological, as well as environmental factors that play a role in the development of criminal behaviour with a particular emphasis on searching for bio-medical markers such as neurotransmitter problems and genetic abnormalities that can then be targeted for preventative treatment (Earls, 1991).

Nobel Prize winner and driving force behind the Human Genome Project, James Watson, clearly feels that science in the shape of manipulating genes should be left to get on with it and should ignore any of the moral or ethical implications,

> My view is that despite the risks, we should give serious consideration to germ-line therapy. I only hope that the many biologists who share my opinion will stand tall in the debates to come and not be intimidated by the inevitable criticism. Some of us already know the pain of being tarred with the brush once reserved for eugenicists. But that is ultimately a small price to pay to redress genetic injustice. If such work be called eugenics, then I am a eugenicist. (Watson, 2003: 401)

In his book *DNA: The Secret of Life*, Watson (2003) completely ignores any discussion about what makes one person somehow more valuable or important than another and is eager that we start exploring how biotechnology could eliminate 'mental illness', 'violence' and 'learning difficulties'. All the same fundamental philosophical mistakes that inspired the original eugenicists to try and biologically engineer a society free of genetic 'misfits' and that led eventually to such unimaginable human tragedy, are made. Watson's main criticism of the eugenics movement is that they were poor scientists (not that their goals were so abhorrent)

> There is no legitimate rationale for modern genetics to avoid certain questions simply because they were of interest to the discredited eugenics movement.

The critical difference is this: Davenport and his like simply had no scientific tools with which to uncover the genetic basis for any behavioural trait they studied. Their science was not equipped to reveal any material realities that would have confirmed or refuted their speculations. (Watson, 2003: 365)

Will we ever learn?

The revival of the impulse to medicalize social issues has led to a revival of interest in dangerous and brain-damaging so-called treatments, with children increasingly seen as a primary target for such 'preventative' interventions. Methods such as lobotomy (in other words deliberately damaging brain tissue), electroconvulsive therapy as well as using high doses of toxic, unlicensed psychotropic drugs normally used in adults with severe and chronic so-called mental illnesses are increasingly advocated for 'treating' young children with a variety of problems including aggression (see for example Chapter 5). The world's second largest industry – the pharmaceutical industry – are seizing their opportunity to contribute to the development of this worrying trend.

The Culture of Medicalization and the Pharmaceutical Industry

In addition to the influence of the culture of developmentalism and the medicalization of social life, another important factor pushing forward the genetic deficiency view of naughty boys is that of the second most powerful industry in the world, the pharmaceutical industry. Just as advances in genetics have been opening up the possibility of defining almost all of us as sick, by diagnosing deficient genes that predispose us to disease (Melzer and Zimmern, 2002), so the global pharmaceutical industry have found a clear interest and strategy to help them medicalize life's problems (Freemantle, 2002; Moynihan *et al.*, 2002). It seems there is now an ill for every pill (Mintzes, 2002).

Genes that play a part in the pathogenesis of most common disorders are, for the most part, as yet unidentified and their role poorly understood. Their predicted value is low and at present there is little to suggest they will have any greater clinical value than more conventional physiological risk markers (such as blood pressure) in the future (Melzer and Zimmern, 2002). This is the case for known physical pathology. When it comes to the behavioural genetics that is running rampant in developmental psychopathology the usefulness of genes and genetics becomes even more questionable. However, there is a continuous tendency within medicine generally and psychiatry in particular to expand diagnostic and treatment boundaries. Indeed by showing that everyone's genome is different, genetic science is, in a sense, suggesting that we are all in some sense biologically abnormal. However, the possibility of great commercial rewards for new medical tests and treatments has driven all sorts of new claims about the potential revolution that genetics will bring to our everyday understanding of disease and its treatment.

Genetics is only one of the forces helping the pharmaceutical industry widen the boundaries of treatable illness as a way of expanding markets for their products (Illich, 1990; Payer, 1992). The market forces of a capitalist economy has been a helpful vehicle for drug companies to build informal alliances with doctors and various consumer pressure groups whose special interests are engaged in apparently raising public awareness about under-diagnosed and under-treated problems. By promoting the view that a particular condition (for example, ADHD) is widespread, serious and treatable (in the case of ADHD by the drug Ritalin) drug companies are expanding markets for their products (Moynihan *et al.*, 2002).

It is also in the interests of certain groups of professionals to promote this discourse of medicalization. For example, the number of consultant psychiatrists in the United Kingdom has more than doubled over the past 22 years with a parallel increase in the number of prescriptions being given, for example anti-depressant prescriptions have more than doubled over the past decade (Double, 2002). Rates of diagnosis of psychiatric disorders in children and prescription of psychotropic medication to children have also increased dramatically over the past decade (Zito *et al.*, 2002). This trend goes hand in glove with the pharmaceutical industry's marketing strategy where, for example, the anti-depressant Paroxetine is now licensed for the treatment of depression, generalized anxiety disorder, social anxiety disorder, panic disorder, obsessive compulsive disorder and post traumatic stress disorder (Charlton, 2002). It is also worth mentioning that the numbers of disorders psychiatrists diagnose have continued to increase. The numbers of diagnostic categories have increased in the diagnostic and statistical manual of mental disorders (DSM) from 106 disorders in DSM-I in 1952 (American Psychiatric Association, 1952) to 357 in DSM-IV in 1994 (American Psychiatric Association, 1994).

The profit motive means that we are now as a culture gripped by the story of the genetically programmed child. We are as a culture writing scripts of disability, dysfunction and life-long illness into the lives of essentially biologically healthy boys. Our professional wilful ignorance

Chapter 3

Carrot, Stick and Other Popular Ways of Dealing with Naughtiness

> *One of the first Western practitioners to examine Eastern tech-*
> *niques, the Swiss existential psychiatrist Medard Boss, declared*
> *that in comparison to Asian approaches, even the best Western*
> *training is not much more than an introductory course.*
>
> GOONATILAKE, 1998: 174

I grew up in a family-orientated culture. My childhood in Iraq revolved around extended family. There were a group of women who looked after the needs of all their children collectively. When I needed a tonsillectomy when I was 10 years old it was arranged that my cousin (of a similar age and who also needed a tonsillectomy) would have the operation on the same day. My mother, her mother and an older cousin slept on mattresses on the hospital floor next to our beds while we recovered. Adults did not play with us, we had a constant supply of other children to do that, instead they showered us with affection and called me 'champion of the world' when I insisted. There were no rewards for good behaviour. If I were 'naughty' my father would smack me or affection would be withdrawn. At primary school every teacher had a ruler at the front of their class, which would be used at the slightest sign of disobedience or disrespect. At playtime the deputy head 'policed' the playground by walking around, holding a thick ruler in her hand and making it clear that minor indiscretions were not tolerated. I learned a clear hierarchy that kindness and help should always be given to those younger than you and respect and obedience to those older.

I have had many interesting conversations about dealing with naughty boys with colleagues of mine who grew up in non-Western cultures.

A colleague of mine who grew up in Pakistan explained to me how in his country, boys have a lot of freedom to be physically active and play with their peers throughout most of their childhood. At the same time, obedience to parents and elders was expected and demanded, particularly once you come to school age. Expectations were frequently enforced through physical punishment both at home and at school. He remembered that within his extended family there was an aunt who was well known for being good at controlling children through a mixture of understanding and discipline. If he or one of his siblings were being persistently 'naughty', then they would be threatened with being sent to this aunt, or actually sent there if the threat did not work. Very occasionally some families would use opiates to sedate an unruly child. Having worked as a family doctor in Pakistan for a number of years this colleague said he saw a variety of children within his medical practice for a variety of problems, but could not recall any occasion when a parent brought him a child to ask for his advice as a doctor on how to manage their child's unruly behaviour. Neither could he recall any occasion when a parent brought a child because they were concerned that the child's unruly behaviour was due to a medical condition. When he came to work with me for a six-month placement in child-and-adolescent psychiatry he was shocked and surprised at the number of naughty boys being referred to our service for assessment and treatment of ADHD. He could see very few differences between the children he was assessing for this condition and the children he grew up with or his own children. He sat in one of the local paediatrician's ADHD clinics and could not believe how quickly the diagnosis of ADHD was given and how many children this paediatrician was prescribing stimulant medication to. The extent to which naughty boys has become a medical problem requiring medical solutions in this culture came home to him when he discovered that one of the neighbour's children, with whom his own children played, had a diagnosis of ADHD and was taking stimulants. He discovered this when, one day, this child was playing with his children in their home and one of the child's parents came around in an apologetic frame of mind stating he was sorry if his child had been misbehaving or was a handful in any way as they had forgotten to give him his stimulant medication. As far as my colleague was concerned, even at this point when the medication would have worn off, his own children were more hyperactive than this neighbour's child!

Another colleague of mine who grew up in Ghana told me about the way misbehaving children are dealt with in Ghana. He explained to me that within Ghanaian society there is a strong affiliation to your tribal background. According to this colleague different tribes are known to have different temperaments and therefore have different attitudes and practices towards misbehaving children. For example, the Ashanti tribe, who tend to be better off and are more of a warrior tribe, have higher expectations of their children's social behaviour and would use a lot more physical methods, such as the cane, in their punishments. My colleague's own tribe, the Fante tribe, is temperamentally more sedate, their background being in fishing, and tend to use less physical methods and more verbal ones in dealing with misbehaviour. He told me that in Ghana once children are ready for school (about 6 years old) they start to be taught about responsibility and it is at this stage that discipline becomes more of an issue. In his own tribe if a child breaks or loses something valuable or is disobedient to parents, for example refusing to wash or refusing to help with chores such as fetching water or firewood, then they are likely to be punished. If there is such misbehaviour, first the mother or father will take the child aside, talk to them about their behaviour and give them a warning. If repeated warnings are ignored then the child is punished with the cane on the hands, the legs or the backside. In his recollection it is mostly boys who tend to reach this stage of punishment. As far as behaviour outside the house, such as being rude or disrespectful to elders, is concerned, within the community this is usually reported back to the parents who are then expected to deal with this as they see fit. In school most of the punishment tends to occur in primary school with discipline problems much less common in secondary schools. Typical punishments given in schools include doing work in school, such as gardening, being given lines to write, for example being asked to copy lines from the bible (usually a passage chosen for its particular relevance to the misbehaviour being punished) and lashing with the cane by the class teacher in front of the class, usually on the hands or the backs of the legs. In his recollection, 'naughtiness' was never considered a medical problem and generally considered to be a normal part of family life that parents were expected to accept and deal with within the family. The general approach seemed to be that of punishment for unwanted behaviour with good behaviour being expected rather than something that is rewarded in any overt way.

Another colleague who is a paediatrician from Iraqi Kurdistan said something to me that I think summarizes the basic thesis of this book beautifully. This colleague had been practising in the United Kingdom for about four years at the time we had this conversation. As part of her responsibilities she was running a 'behaviour clinic' in which she was expected to assess children for ADHD and prescribe stimulant medication once the diagnosis was made. She told me 'I was working as a paediatrician for 18 years in the north of Iraq and despite all that we have been through, the wars, the gassing, the oppression by Saddam's regime, I swear to you the children I used to see in my clinics in Iraq were so much happier than the children I see here (in the UK). I've always known about ADHD but I only ever made the diagnosis once in those 18 years even though I saw far more children on a daily basis than I do here. We really felt like we belonged to our families. I remember often having to look after younger children or help my mum with housework. But I wanted to, I liked doing it, it made me feel useful and wanted.'

The Influence of Culture When Dealing with Naughty Boys

Once behaviour has been interpreted as being a problem, in the same way that there is great diversity in what is considered to be a problem, there is also great cultural diversity in how you deal with this problem. Much of this diversity comes from what meaning is given to the behaviours that are now viewed as a problem. For example, if the problem behaviours of a misbehaving boy are believed to be result of unhappy ancestral spirits then a visit to the local healer for advice would seem to be the natural first port of call. On the other hand if it were believed that the problem behaviours could be due to a medical condition then a visit to the appropriate specialist doctor would be the natural first port of call.

In this chapter, I wish to examine the variety of approaches that are used to try and deal with 'naughty' behaviour, both between different cultures and within any given culture.

Carrot and Stick

Modernist, Western culture has been and continues to move in a general direction away from the use of physical punishment as part of the strategies available for parents and others to discipline children. The debate on the use of physical force with children is not a new one nor is it confined to Western culture. However, it would be fair to conclude that modern, Western culture has gone further than any other culture in viewing physical punishment as unacceptable once physical punishment became a possible criminal act on the part of a parent in the eyes of the law (where it can now be termed physical abuse). In some Western countries such as Sweden any physical punishment of children is against the law. In the United Kingdom the situation is less clear as, despite physical punishment of children not being outlawed, some agencies such as social services sometimes give the impression that they are operating as if physical punishment is against the law in the United Kingdom. At least that is the impression many parents have. Physical punishment in United Kingdom schools has been outlawed and, at the time of writing, consideration is being given in the UK to banning certain types of physical punishment that occur elsewhere, for example to children under three years of age.

One factor that has had a big influence on the development of the Western anti-physical punishment trend has been the influence of the 'psy-med' complex with parenting coming to be viewed as the remit of professionals and scientific experts. These expert opinions have influenced government legislation, which in turn further strengthens the anti-physical punishment climate.

The history of Western childhood (see Chapter 1) shows that the debate about the appropriateness and usefulness of corporal punishment for children is not a new one for Western society. Over the past few hundred years the argument has yoyo-ed between calls for greater use of physical punishment and calls for liberating children from this. At the same time, reflecting changing social emphasis, the task of discipline and who has the central role in child rearing has changed from being the mother, then the father and then back to mother. In the latter half of the twentieth century, the debate in Western society (which as I have shown is attempting to universalize its beliefs) has moved back towards an anti-physical punishment stance. It is often incorrectly assumed that historically we have progressed (in the West) from abusive attitudes and child rearing practices to more enlightened attitudes and practices. However, evidence from a variety of sources show that Western parents over the last 500 years have shown affection for their children, recognized various stages of their children's development (according to the common expectations of the day), disciplined their children and worried about their offspring's present and future well-being (Pollock, 1983; Calvert, 1992). The course of change is not so much a progression from bad to good as a succession of alternative approaches.

Modern, Western, professional advice on providing children with discipline was recently summarized by the American Academy of Pediatrics (1998), as being composed of three essential elements: (1) a learning environment characterized by supportive parent–child relationships; (2) a strategy for systematic teaching and strengthening of desired behaviours; and (3) a strategy for decreasing or eliminating undesired or ineffective behaviours. These three elements are derived from what the professionals would consider sound scientific principles. As I have shown in my last book (Timimi, 2002), science, in the context of human behaviour, operates in the same way as religion in requiring a great deal of faith on the part of the believer as opposed to having concrete material evidence to back up the claims. The first of the three elements emphasizing a positive parent–child relationship is related to attachment theory (Bowlby, 1969, 1973) with its emphasis on the parent (usually meaning the mother) having strong, constant and consistent positive feelings for the child. The language relates to a small individualized unit of parent–child. The other two elements identified are derived from social learning theory (Patterson, 1975). Social learning theory basically emphasizes rewarding the good or desired behaviours and ignoring the bad or undesired behaviours. In this version of discipline the emphasis is on paying positive attention to children when they are behaving well, and little or no attention when children are misbehaving. In this method of providing discipline there is, theoretically, no such thing as punishment. In fact, many punishments such as smacking or telling off are seen as potential causes of further bad behaviour on the basis that they provide the child with further attention following unwanted behaviour. Instead, what is recommended is removing as many sources of attention as possible for unwanted or bad behaviour. The most familiar technique for doing this is that of 'time out'. 'Time out' is viewed by social learning theory as a form of ignoring when the behaviour has got to a point where you need to intervene to manage the situation. The idea is that the parent takes the child away from the situation to sit them on a chair or in another room for a period of time, leaving the child on their own thereby removing all attention from them. To me this is just punishment by another name, and my own experience both as a parent and as a professional working with parents and children is that children become just as distressed, in fact more so sometimes, by being given 'time out' rather than a smack. In fact, my suspicion is that 'time out' is only effective when the child becomes distressed enough to want to avoid a similar consequence the next time.

Having emerged from the culture of the 'stiff upper lip' where physical punishment was used widely within schools as well as homes, British culture has seen a re-emergence of considerable tension between those who wish to combat the perceived unruliness of modern youth by a return to more 'old fashioned' discipline and those who continue to blame forms of harsher discipline for the unruliness of boys. Thus, much of the 'psy-med' complex continues to promote non-physical forms of discipline to emphasize encouraging goodness as opposed to punishing badness. For example, in their influential book *Raising Cain*; Kindlon and Thompson (1999) state, 'we believe that boys need discipline that is clear, consistent and not harsh. The best discipline is built on the child's love for adults and his wish to please. If that impulse is respected and cultivated, children will continue to be psychologically accessible through their love and respect. If they are unduly shamed, harshly punished, or encounter excessive adult anger, they will soon react to authority with resistance rather than with a desire to do better.' (Kindlon and Thompson, 1999: 266). They go on to argue that harsh discipline, in which they include excessive telling off as well as physical discipline, leaves lasting emotional scars and causes impulsive and disturbed behaviour as opposed to being a cure for it.

It appears to me that, guided by their own faith in the language of science, professionals have simply rediscovered the well-known carrot-and-stick method, couched it in scientific language to provide them with ownership of these techniques and imposed their own particular moral values (e.g. abhorrence of physical punishment). This has resulted in a vibrant parenting industry with books on how to parent, parenting groups and even legislation forcing certain parents to attend parenting classes.

The debate on how to balance the carrot and the stick is of course not confined to Western culture. Debates about the use of punishment with children can been seen stretching back thousands of years in a variety of cultures (see for example Kakar, 1978).

In medieval Muslim society during the heyday of the Muslim empire many religious writers gave instruction on how to rear children effectively. The issue of discipline featured highly in these writings with a variety of opinions expressed on what to do and what was effective. Islamic essays of the middle ages show several different attitudes towards corporal punishment from approval, with certain qualifications, to proposals for alternatives to physical punishment and its integration into more sophisticated methods of dealing with children's behaviour. Many essays criticize the use of corporal punishment (Gil'adi, 1992). Al-Qabisi (quoted in Gil'adi, 1992) wrote a treatise on the rules of conduct of schoolmasters encouraging them to use a more controlled method of applying force to children in consultation with the children's father. He recommended that before inflicting any corporal punishment, the number of lashes should be decided based upon what the child could tolerate. He also wrote about parts of the body that should not be struck, such as head and face, and stressed that corporal punishment was intended to further the education of the lax pupil, not to provide the teacher with an outlet for his rage.

Al-Ghazali (quoted in Gil'adi, 1992) although expressing approval of traditional methods of bodily chastisement, combined this with a recommendation for its reasonable and balanced use. He suggested that a balance needs to be found between the two extremes of using too little or excessive force, arguing that excessive force could act not to spur the student on but to suppress him. He also wrote about the importance of balancing corporal punishment with gentleness and compassion towards children, including in his writings examples of the kindly attitude of the prophet Mohammed towards children. Al-Ghazali and Ibn Miskawayh (quoted in Gil'adi, 1992) also proposed alternative means of rousing the child's fear of his father and god (which are the main aims of corporal punishment in Islamic society). These alternatives included warnings and rebukes as well as ways of trying to reinforce good qualities through rewards and positive public responses to the child on the part of the father. They also warned that belittling a child in public may ultimately dull the child's fear of his teacher and his father and exacerbate their impudence.

Ibn-Khaldun (quoted in Gil'adi, 1992) is also critical of undue bodily punishment, not only with regard to its immediate effectiveness but also to warn of the possible long-term damage he believes is caused by this method. He warned that excessive bodily punishment can cause the child to feel too pressured making the child passive, dispirited and lethargic in the long term. This he felt could induce the child to cheating, lying and dishonesty in their relations with their elders in order to avoid punishment. Ibn-Khaldun believed that in the long term these traits become ingrained in the child and then incorporated into their adult character. He believed that children who had been excessively punished lose the quality to protect and defend themselves and their homes, and become too dependent on others once they are adults. He felt that as adults they fall short of their potential and do not reach the limit of their humanity, becoming too passive to acquire virtues and good character qualities.

Discipline continues to play a central role in child rearing in Muslim-influenced countries. Many Muslim parents see disciplining a child as a Muslim duty, particularly for the child's father and believe that children require discipline until they have reached an age when they can show *aql* (literally translated means brain or mind, but more generally it is used to mean the capacity to reason independently) (Davis and Davis, 1989; Timimi, 1995). Fathers, it is believed, are better equipped than mothers to control boys' behaviour. Shame is often used by fathers as a powerful psychological tool to influence and control their offspring's behaviour (Davis and Davis, 1989). In many Middle-Eastern societies fatherless boys are considered to be at risk to becoming overly wilful and unruly and to have a delayed acquisition of a sense of responsibility (Dorsky and Stevenson, 1995). The majority of the time it is boys who get punished physically, with physical punishment still used widely in schools (Davis and Davis, 1989; Brink, 1995; Dorsky and Stevenson, 1995).

Despite the prevalence and advocacy for physical punishment in much of the developing world and the apparent intolerance towards this in Western society, it would be wrong to jump to simplistic conclusions about the nature and frequency of use of physical punishment amongst ethnic minority communities in Western culture. Many studies have shown that the vast majority of parents in Western societies where smacking is not outlawed still use physical punishment as a form of discipline. Conversely, a number of studies among second-generation parents from South Asia who have settled in the United Kingdom show that around a half to two-thirds of mothers do not believe that physical punishment is effective and rarely, or even never, use this form of punishment (Dosanji and Ghuman, 1996).

On the other hand, growing up in a culture where restrictive parental discipline, including the use of force, is used commonly will also lead to different meanings being attached to this form of discipline by the child concerned. In a social context where the common pattern of family control is characterized by permissiveness, such as in many European societies children may perceive restrictive parental discipline as a form of rejection. However, in a society where restrictive discipline is common, children may well perceive such discipline as normal or even a sign of parental caring and warmth (Pettengill and Rohner, 1985; Trommsdorff, 1985; Kagitcibasi, 1989).

Whilst praise and encouragement has been a central preoccupation in modern Western approaches to child rearing in general, as well as in dealing with difficult children in particular, this contrasts sharply with the central preoccupations of other contemporary cultures. For example in their study, LeVine and colleagues (1994) found that whereas praise is an important part of maternal speech to her children amongst American mothers, amongst the Gusii people of Kenya praise towards children is very rarely found. In fact, praise is explicitly rejected by Gusii mothers as a verbal device because of their belief that it encourages conceit and would make even a good child rude and disobedient. The majority of Gusii mothers' speech to children comprised of commands intended partly to prevent or stop their children getting into danger. Gusii mothers considered it useful for their child to acquire fear, not only of actual hazards such as fire but also of domestic animals and imaginary creatures which can then be used to frighten a child into compliance. By this method Gusii parents hope that the child develops respect and obedience towards the parents with the goal of having a compliant child who comprehends maternal commands, obeys them and makes as few demands on her limited time as possible.

In summary then it can be seen that the use of carrot-and-stick (reward and punishment) methods have been known about for centuries. Different cultures' philosophies have some similar and some differing opinions on what the balance between carrot and stick should be and what are acceptable and non-acceptable methods of providing carrot or stick. In Western culture the debate has become owned by professionals who believe that their methods are scientifically grounded. With the advent of globalization these professionalized notions are exported and indigenous, arguably far more effective methods are criticized as being harmful to children (with the inference that this professional Western ideology is morally superior – see Chapter 1). This colonialism is wrong and damaging, given the poor state of children's behaviour in Western society we must ask ourselves what right we have to moralize about which method is correct.

Acceptance and Encouraging Emotional Expression

Another familiar way of dealing with naughty behaviour is to do nothing. In this version of problem-solving, there is acceptance that a problem exists and the solution is perceived to be that of expecting the behaviour problem to disappear on its own accord as in the familiar cultural expression, 'it's just a phase he's passing through'. This implies that the best way to deal with unruly behaviour when it surfaces is to tolerate it and sooner or later it will subside again. The more permissive end of the *psy-med* complex sees unruly behaviour as a form of communication that should not only be accepted but also understood, and the emotional needs behind this communication should then be worked with and emotional expression of suppressed feelings encouraged. In this version of solution to unruly behaviour the theory is that the child is behaving in this manner due to unmet or unexpressed emotional needs and the goal of any intervention would be to allow that child the opportunity to express their emotional needs in a more constructive way.

In many non-Western cultures the acceptance of unruly behaviour as a solution is particularly evident with younger children. In Chapter 1, I illustrated how in many non-Western cultures the period of total dependence of infancy is longer when compared to Western culture. In Western culture, expectations of self-directed, independent functioning on the part of the child are expected from a very early age resulting in much less tolerance of anti-social behaviour amongst the young (e.g. in nurseries and pre-school play groups).

This attitude towards younger children which seems to be deeply ingrained in Middle-Eastern, south Asian and Mediterranean cultures can be seen in some of the teachings from medieval Muslim scholars. According to the practical and moral guidance given to parents by Muslim scholars a thousand or so years ago, parents were encouraged to accept and soothe children and limit their expectations up to the age of about seven years. It was believed that any attempt to force children to deal with a subject they are neither able nor ready to cope with would necessarily end in failure (Gil'adi, 1992). The recommendation of sensitivity to young children included discussions of the proper treatment of a shock caused by frightening sights or sounds. There was concern that these shocks could cause damage to the intellectual capacities of the child that may affect him into adulthood. It was recommended that should an infant be shocked in such a way the mother should do her best to calm the infant by amusing him, by breastfeeding him, by rocking him and helping him to sleep thus diverting the child's attention from the traumatic event to erase it from their memory (Ibn Qayyim al-Jawziyya quoted in Gil'adi, 1992). Although a more accepting attitude is obvious in these writings with young children, with older children a debate seems to have taken place between a more restrictive attitude and a more permissive one. Nonetheless, it is recommended that individual differences are taken into account and children's differing abilities are accepted. Thus a child who is found to be more able and interested in an intellectual vocation should receive a different education from that of children who are inclined to be horsemen or craftsmen.

Compared to traditional Muslim attitudes, Aboriginal parents seem to continue the use of acceptance as a method of dealing with unruly children for much longer. It seems few demands are made, which result in externally regulated development; in other words adults expect little of children, while children can demand all from adults. Fathers do not seem to get involved in much chastizing or demanding, in fact they are more likely to protect an unruly child from a mother's anger and exasperation. One of the few pressures that are brought to bear on Aboriginal children is the requirement that they share food. This is done mainly by adults modelling rather than by direct training of the children. When young children display aggressive feelings they are not restrained and often their mothers will react passively towards their child's aggression when it is directed to them. Adults who are being attacked by a child will either ignore it or at worse will swear at the child. Sometimes laughter may also greet aggressive behaviour by children towards adults. As they grow older what might be considered major behaviour problem in many other cultures, such as stealing, will usually be dealt with in a fairly low-key manner, for example by the parent returning the stolen article to the rightful owner. Again, the principle seems to be to educate the children in the moral values of the tribe by modelling rather than active training. When children are more than five years of age and up to early puberty the main agent for conformity is the peer group and within their peer group children work out the appropriate behaviour patterns for the role that they have been cast in (Hamilton, 1980).

The idea that unruly behaviour is a symptom of a different problem that is occurring at an emotional level has been popularized through the influence psychoanalysis has had on Western culture. Freud's theories on the emotional development of children and the idea that symptoms represent unresolved internal and often-unconscious conflicts have seeped into the collective unconscious of the West. Although there are a great variety of views on the nature of these internal conflicts, popularized versions of this basic idea appears in many media. Kindlon and Thompson (1999) state, concerning their work with unruly boys, 'a large part of our work with boys and men is to help them understand their emotional life and develop an emotional vocabulary... We try to teach them emotional literacy – the ability to read and understand our emotions and those of others' (Kindlon and Thompson, 1999: 4).

Developing a Value System

Fables, parables and folk tales have been used in every society to educate and impart values. Christ's parables in the Bible, just like Mohammed's in the Koran, or Buddha's in the Jātaka, convey powerful teaching messages on what values to adopt and how to conduct yourself accordingly. Similarly, fairy stories and folk tales have been a popular way of imparting to the young of any culture the value system of that culture.

Stories have been used universally, not only to impart the values of a particular culture, but also to provide hope, meaning and purpose. Stories perpetuate the knowledge, heritage and traditions of a culture, linking successive generations to their past. In some sense it could be argued that stories provide a map for the soul – a body of knowledge capable of providing shelter, healing, instruction and inspiration (Gersie and King, 1990).

Using stories to help solve 'the problems of living' by imparting moral messages has been practised for centuries. Many see India as the original home of storytelling (Shamasundar, 1997). From India, Persians learnt the art and passed it on to the Arabians. From the Middle East, the tales found their way to Constantinople, Venice and eventually to all Europe. Incidents in stories well known to European children had already existed in India thousands of years ago (Penzer, 1968). Erna Hoch summarizes the richness of Indian mythology in her statement, 'There is hardly any discovery of modern Western psychotherapy that cannot quite easily be confirmed by some precept, parable or proverb from the writings of Indian religion' (Hoch, 1960: 87). Thus in Hindu culture, the use of stories for their educative and problem-solving properties has been a constant for a long time. Stories are chosen for their particular relevance to a given problem and the individual or family are left to meditate upon its meaning after the story is told or read (Harper and Gray, 1997).

Much of the teachings of Eastern cultures place an emphasis on learning to go beyond egocentric outlooks in life. These teachings reflect a cultural orientation towards family, rather than the individual, and are reflected in the cultural practices associated with bringing up children in Eastern cultures (Dwivedi, 1993, 1996, 1997). In Buddhism, the 'sense of self' is viewed as a product of an illusory process with an attachment to our self, ideas, theories and relationships similarly being seen as illusory processes. Viewed from this perspective, the ultimate reason for anger is the sense of self that we all habitually carry. Buddhist teaching is thus devoted to cutting through these illusory processes although this is seen as a task that often requires many lifetimes (Dwivedi, 1997).

Developing Self-esteem, Independence and Mastering Emotions

When I was growing up in Iraq there was no such thing as self-esteem or self-confidence as an issue to be tackled with growing children. I expect it is a more noticeable issue within individualist, Western culture where each person has to stand out in some way as an individual and whose sense of self-worth thus becomes an individual matter as opposed to something that is tied to the primary importance of the family and community. Western psychology, embedded as it is in Western cultural tradition, is typically individualist and popularizes individualist solutions. From the starting point of the need to look after your own interests as a cultural priority has developed the notion of the importance of loving one's self and self-esteem (Dwivedi, 1996). One way of conceptualizing unruly behaviour amongst boys is that it stems from low self-esteem and that the solution lies in developing the self-esteem of the youngster, typically by providing them with praise and positive remarks about themselves and their abilities.

When examining non-Western cultures it is possible to find similar approaches to dealing with unruly behaviour, approaches that involve encouragement and positive feedback to the child but often with crucial differences in the eventual goal of the intervention. Whereas in Western culture building up the child's strengths and abilities may have the goal of developing their self belief and self confidence in traditional Muslim culture for example, the goal and main purpose of this sort of education is to ensure the future of the believer in the next world and to help the child's developing soul be as pure and as open to God as possible (Gil'adi, 1992). In his advice to fathers, the medieval scholar El-Ghasali (quoted in Gil'adi, 1992) draws the father's attention to the onset of the facility for discernment (Tamyiz). According to El-Ghasali, this begins to appear at about the age of seven and is to be encouraged in the child by further helping the child make the distinction between good and evil. El-Ghasali recommends that encouraging a child to perform a certain act by the promise of a sweet or to discourage the child from an act by being beaten can do this. He also mentions that it is possible to address the child's logic and direct his actions through words of encouragement and praise and stresses the need to increase the supervision of the child once the appearance of *tamyiz* (the facility for discernment) becomes manifest. It is also at these ages that it is recommended that the child has the intellectual capacity to begin to understand religious commandments and to be introduced to them. Al-Ghasali also encourages introducing relaxing rather than boisterous games to allow the child to rest and to learn the value of a calm, reflective mind that will be useful in adult life. At the same time Al-Ghasali also encourages parents to make use of the tendency to play, so characteristic of children, to motivate them to what he perceives as activities on a higher plane. He recommends that children can be diverted from unproductive, anti-social behaviour, first through supervised games to attract the child to study and then gradually through the use of other temptations, such as clothes, positions of leadership and honour, and finally the reward of the world to come. This attitude towards encouraging children to develop their minds but with a very different goal continues within many Muslim and Middle-Eastern cultures and is backed by a hierarchically organized culture that puts a strong emphasis on the importance of respecting the advice of parents and elders. For example, it is said that the prophet Mohammed said (you are) 'close to God if you are kind to your parents you are a Hajj (Pilgrim), you are a Mu'tamer (Minor pilgrim) and a you are a Mujahed (fighter)'

(Yamani, 1995: 121) and 'you fight by being kind to your parents' (Yamani, 1995: 121).

Although the encouragement of the development of the self but with a different ultimate goal can be seen in many non-Western cultures, the stress laid on emotional and social independence and training of the young child is viewed differently. As a Punjabi grandmother living in Britain remarked 'we are not like the Goras (whites) who after feeding the baby leave her in the upstairs bedroom – cry or no cry...in my family if a baby is slightly ill the whole family is awake to comfort and support the young mother. A completely different tarika (way of doing things)' (Dosanji and Ghuman, 1996: 51). Thus training the child to be more independent emotionally and socially is not usually seen as a solution to problems with unruly behaviour amongst south Asian and Middle-Eastern and probably many other non-Western cultures. Instead, from the age of five or so onwards children are encouraged to be obedient and to honour their elders (Segal, 1991; Dosanji and Ghuman, 1996). However, physical independence is encouraged from a much earlier age than in most Western cultures, thus young children are expected to take on what may be considered to be adult chores in Western cultures, including caring for younger siblings, cooking, fetching, running errands and wage earning.

Indian culture has a long tradition of encouraging emotional expression and refining a person's understanding and use of emotions. The ancient Indian theory of emotions known as the *Rasa* (extract, flavour, essence, juice) encourages the activation and then refinement of different emotional states. Through the use of drama, dance, ritual and poetry, the audience has to cultivate their own aesthetic sensibility so that they begin to respond (Lynch, 1990; Dwivedi and Gardner, 1997). This view of and attitude to emotional life contrasts greatly with many Western concepts that view emotions as passive (things that happen to us) and irrational. In the Indian concept, emotions are grounded not only in the self but also in play, food, music, scent and so on. The mind and body are viewed and experienced as continuous not only with each other but also with the world outside the person. Thus for Indian culture, emotions like food are experienced as necessary for a reasonable life and, like taste, cultivable for the fullest understanding of life's meaning and purpose (Lynch, 1990).

The familiar methods of the 'psy-med' complex to encourage self-esteem is that of building more positive feedback and praise into behavioural programmes with disobedient children as well as trying to build on children's strengths. In addition the 'new age' influence on certain sections of Western culture has meant that some sections of the West have imported their own version of traditional non-Western approaches. Thus, encouraging children to build confidence and self-discipline through training in martial arts, the use of relaxation methods and meditation are being used more commonly as part of building inner strength and as another technique for combating unruly behaviour.

A deeper question that Western culture appears to be struggling to solve is the state of gender relations amongst growing children and how to deal with boys' anxieties about their masculinity. According to some (e.g. Kaufman, 1994; Jackson, 1998), many men and boys actively buy into patriarchal power systems as a way of trying to deal with their anxieties and fears about their masculinity. According to these authors men's assertion of power is a response to the terrors they feel of self-annihilation and alienation from their feelings, their longings and their need for closeness. These boys then divide the world into masculine and feminine and carry on with behaviour that they identify as masculine (including unruly behaviour, anti-academic and anti-school attitudes). For these authors there is a great need for us to raise our awareness of this issue and for more active debate and discussion of these dynamics to take place (e.g. in schools).

The Role of Religion and the Supernatural

When people live in the world differently it is as if they are living in different worlds (Shweder, 1991). This is particularly true in relation to people's spiritual orientation. For the majority of the world's population, supernatural forces as opposed to predictable material ones drive the world. This orientation to understanding events in the world has a massive impact on how individuals from many cultures interpret the significance and meaning of events that happen in their lives and how they then subsequently deal with them. Thus, in many non-Western cultures, religion and traditional healing methods that rely on interventions aimed at influencing supernatural events are used as part of that cultures intervention for many problems, including those of naughty and unruly boys.

Passing on religiosity to the next generation is an important task for Muslim parents. Traditionally, within Islam the age at which training and education begins is at around six or seven. Thus, it is advised that when a child reaches the age of *tamyiz* at about six or seven, then he can begin to learn purification rituals and prayer and should be told to fast for several days during Ramadan. The quality of religious education that the child receives is then believed to influence whether a child will gain reward or suffer punishment in the world to come. Once the age of *tamyiz* has been reached correct conduct on the part of the child, in accordance with the expectations of Muslim parents, is emphasized. Should the growing child's conduct show deterioration then further education in understanding and complying with the Islamic path is often recommended for that unruly child. Islam remains a very strong religion in the world with many of the younger generation in the Muslim Middle East identifying with a more radical version of Islam, seeing in Islam an identity based on strength and the capacity to stand up to the influence of the powerful West (Fernea, 1995). At a time when Christianity seems to be on the decline within Western countries, Muslim parents who have immigrated to the West are noted to have a strong desire to pass Islam on to their children (Dosanji and Ghuman, 1996).

In many parts of the world traditional healers draw on a local culture's beliefs with regard to supernatural forces' capacity to disrupt a person's life for a variety of reasons (Timimi, 1995). In many parts of Central and Southern Africa daily life is felt to be influenced by ancestral spirits and/or the work of magic. Dreams (both of the healer and the patient) are often used to diagnose problems, to foretell the future, to redress an issue that has been neglected, to caution against immoral behaviour and to make connections between the past and present (Reynolds, 1996). When a child who may be presenting with difficult behaviour that is not responding to other measures is brought to a healer, once the root cause of the behaviour has been identified (e.g. an unhappy ancestral spirit who is punishing a family), then an intervention will be suggested. Many of the interventions are in the form of rituals, some to be performed by the individual alone, some within a family context and some within a community context. For example, cleansing rituals can be used to help a person be cleansed of evil airs, the evil imprint from contact with a corpse, evil spirits and evil actions that result from another's envy, jealousy or ill will. Cleansing rituals may also be accompanied by actions on part of the individual or the family to redress a situation, for example, compensation being paid for any harm caused to others as a result of their actions or that led to the affliction in the first place. A wide range of plants, especially aromatic herbs, and animal parts are used as emetics and purgatives, through incision in the skin, or in bathing or drinking water. These cleansing rituals are seen to strengthen the mind to help it chase evil and secure protection (Reynolds, 1996). It is also seen as a way of clearing the heart from anger (Harris, 1978).

Similarly traditional Arab beliefs about the origin of many emotional and behavioural problems relate them to supernatural causes, although there is usually an interpersonal context (e.g. the phenomenon of the 'evil eye' is thought to operate directly through a wish. Thus those who envy prosperity, health or beauty of others are believed to be able to harm them just by their gaze). Indeed the most popular word used by Arabs to indicate 'madness' is the word *djinoon*, which derives from the word *djin* meaning spirit. Also, the word *wiswas* can refer to both the devil and the worrying thoughts (Timimi, 1995). Consequently, the first port of call for many if not most Arabs who are concerned to find a solution to their child's behavioural difficulty is the traditional healer or the mosque imam. Treatments include forms of exorcism to expel the spirit, prayers, rituals performed by members of the extended family/community and amulets (a piece with specially chosen extracts from the Koran designed to ward off the devil and which is put in carefully chosen places).

In Western culture, formal rituals have all but disappeared apart from amongst those groups with religious affiliations. Although formal rites of passage have largely disappeared from Western culture there remain some aspects of shared communal experience that are age-related and that can help that sense of common purpose amongst developing youngsters. For example, the first day of school and other communal events around the school community such as the parents' evening and the sports day can be viewed as part of existing Western rituals that help children and their families' sense of belonging to a community. Another 'belonging' ritual that still exists in some Western countries is the requirement for young men to do a period of service in the army or in non-profit volunteer work if there are moral objections to serving in the army.

Medication

As I argue in Chapters 2, 5 our vision of children's development in Western culture has been heavily influenced by the *psy-med* complex to the point where the 'natural' inclinations of parents are no longer assumed to be sufficient for them to become good-enough mothers or fathers. Thus, childcare has been taken over as the remit of professional experts, making women subordinate to a new kind of male authority, the authority of scientific knowledge. According to some this new male authority has had the effect of challenging the traditional role of the father's/husband's authority within their immediate family (Donzelot, 1979). Thus, the professional institutions that now advise on childcare and children's problems (such as schools, general practitioners, paediatricians, child psychiatrists, psychologists and counsellors) can be experienced as alternatives to the authority of the father within the family and sometimes as a direct threat to male power within the family. Whether this is a good or bad thing depends on your perspective and on how this particular form of male power is being wielded. On the one hand it could encourage fathers to further disengage from the task of looking after their children, feeling that they have no role, on the other hand it could be used to empower a more female or feminine approach to childcare and child rearing.

With ever-greater levels of medicalizing childhood in Western society (Timimi, 2002), ever-increasing amounts of medication are being used to try and control unruly behaviour amongst children, which mainly means boys. The spiralling rates of prescription of psychoactive drugs to children and adolescents is most graphically illustrated by what is happening to children in the world's most powerful country, the United States of America. Recent data has shown that the overall annual rate of psychotropic medication used by children under 18 years of age increased nearly threefold between 1987 and 1996 with about 4 per cent of children taking a form of psychotropic medication in 1996 (Olfson *et al.*, 2002). The most significant increase was in the use of stimulants, the drug most frequently linked with use as a solution for unruly behaviour, with rates going up fourfold between 1987 and 1996, with an estimated 6.2 per cent of boys in the United States between the ages of 6 and 14 years using a stimulant in 1996 (Olfson *et al.*, 2002), a figure that is likely to be much higher now (see Chapter 5).

No other culture has used the medical model as extensively and aggressively as Western culture for understanding and subsequently dealing with unruly behaviour. The use of medication for combating unruly behaviour has never been witnessed in the same scale in any other culture. However, it is possible to see examples of what is, in effect, the use of sedating medication to sedate an unruly or otherwise agitated child for a limited period of time. For example, within traditional Western culture you often hear stories about giving children a small amount of whiskey to help them sleep if they have been too disturbed or disturbing. Similarly, opiates have been used in the same way in many societies, for example within Muslim society opiates were sometimes used to sedate overactive children (Gil'adi, 1992). In Ayurvedic medicine common in South Asia, an essential oil plant extract *Vacha* is also sometimes used for its sedative properties (Ayensu, 1983).

Traditional medicine in many parts of the world (e.g. Ayurvedic, Unani, and Chinese) does not operate the mind/body dualism found in Western medicine. Thus the approach to behaviour problems is unlikely to be as rigid and concrete as in the West, with the traditional practitioner being more likely to search for other elements in the system, which are perceived to be out of balance or needing strengthening. Dietary interventions, supplements and plant extracts often feature in the intervention. Ayurvedic medicines that have been used in relation to improving children's performance and/or behaviour include *Bangiya Brahmi* and *Centella Asiatica* (Goonatilake, 1998).

The Role of Schools and Education

In Chapter 1, I explained how the idea of mass education came into being partly in response to the ruling class's anxiety about street children and delinquents from working-class families. In this sense mass education first became a popular social development as part of a strategy that was aimed at controlling children from the 'dangerous classes'. Thus, formal education is itself part of a set of social and cultural strategies aimed at controlling children's behaviour, a strategy that is exported worldwide with mass education desires of many third-world countries often becoming part of population control strategies of that country (Stephens, 1995). Furthermore most Western countries have in recent years been restructuring their education with technical rationality becoming the dominant epistemology of practice. The preference for technological views of teaching is creating conditions under which a reflective approach to professional development becomes impossible and underplays the fact that teaching is basically a human social activity in which what we feel is as important as what we know (Mac An Ghaill, 1994).

Within mainstream schools in the United Kingdom the main pathway for dealing with behavioural problems amongst pupils is that of 'special needs' provision. Every school in the United Kingdom should have a special needs provision or department or teacher (responsible for special needs). Children can get extra input from the special needs section of a school for either learning difficulties or behavioural difficulties. If a special need in either of these areas is identified then children are put on a stage of the code of practice for special educational needs. The stages go from one to five with five being for those who are deemed most in need of extra input. Once you reach stage five of the code of practice a statement of special educational needs is applied for and if this is obtained it implies extra resources (such as a classroom assistant for a certain number of hours a week) for the child concerned.

Special educational needs (SEN) practice in the United Kingdom has been historically shaped by the disciplines of medicine and psychology

(Hey *et al.*, 1998). The practice of measuring physical and mental competence in order to determine normality and deviance means that SEN practice rests on within-child explanations for any difficulties a school perceives with a child (Ainscow and Tweddle, 1988). In junior schools, SEN practice focuses primarily upon reading ability and acting-out behaviour (Daniels *et al.*, 1998). With reading and behavioural problems being a primarily boy-related difficulty, most SEN provision is for boys (Delamont, 1989; Riddell, 1996). Since corporal punishment is now outlawed in British schools, within-school solutions tend to focus on giving extra resources and extra attention to the child with behavioural problems. As I have argued elsewhere in this book and previously (Timimi, 2002) this has also led to many schools looking for solutions from outside the school, mainly through the *psy-med* complex on which its theories so depend with the consequent rise in the number of children who are being labelled with medical conditions and prescribed medication for primarily school-based difficulties.

British schools are increasingly resorting to excluding children from school as a solution. With an increase in pressure on schools and teachers to show that the academic performance of their school has been improving, more and more schools have resorted to exclusion in order to deal with those troublesome pupils whom they feel will effect their performance in the national league tables. Since the introduction of the national curriculum, league tables and routine testing of children in British schools, the rate of exclusion has raised sixfold (*Guardian Society*, 19 September, 2001, *Asian Times Public Sector*, 21 September, 2001).

Within any individual school, big differences can be found with the philosophy and practice involved in implementing SEN practice. Hey *et al.* (1998) in their study of SEN practice in a number of schools described different philosophies that underpinned the SEN approach within the schools they studied. For example, in some schools the head teacher was trying to shift the school's SEN practice away from a reactive model that responded to 'boys behaving badly', towards the creation of more systematic special needs procedures. Whereas in the majority of schools the SEN practice was heavily geared towards boys, shortcomings this was not the case in all schools. In one of the schools studied the head teacher had decided not to classify boys who had behavioural problems as having special educational needs. Instead the school had developed policies and procedures for the management of behaviour. The resolution of incidents was central to this behavioural policy and the existence of this proactive, inclusive regime meant that children did not need to stand out to obtain (learning or other) support.

In Jamaica recently the government has taken a more explicit approach to trying to tackle under-achievement and behavioural difficulties amongst boys in the school setting. From the starting point of recognizing that boys are different from girls and so need to be taught differently, they have been promoting a number of strategies within the school community. This has included involving fathers, making the curriculum more boy-friendly and other strategies to keep boys interested in education and in the education system. Special fathers' days when sons bring their fathers to school, a mentoring programme involving fathers, giving boys more practical problems to solve, getting them to use computers if they are reluctant to read books, encouraging stricter discipline and keeping lower streamed classes (which usually have mainly boys) are smaller part of the strategies being used (*BBC news*, Monday, 11 March, 2002).

Hartman (1996) encourages Western schools to develop better strategies to accommodate the more active males into the school culture. He notes that children in Hong Kong's schools, who have a shorter school year, regularly outperform Japanese students in many subjects. In Sweden, one of the countries with the highest literacy rates in the world, children do not start school until they are 7-year olds with Swedish high-school children then graduating after 9 instead of 12 years of schooling (as in the United States). Hartman also reflects on a visit he made to Taiwan where young children are not required to sit quietly; instead they are allowed to jump up from their seats, to write on the board, to speak up, to shout out answers, all without waiting for permission from their teachers. Despite this, Taiwanese pupils are generally ahead of most of their Western counterparts in terms of academic achievement. Hartman (1996) suggests that to make progress with how boys present in mainstream schooling we need to look at smaller classes, more stimulating tasks for those brighter students and giving less new material to learn for those who have more difficulty absorbing new material, to make schools more hands-on as boys generally enjoy more practical approaches and to give boys more positive messages about their abilities. Kindlon and Thompson (1999) make similar suggestions feeling that school culture that allows boys to be more physically active is less condemning of boys' shortcomings and allows boys more room for emotional expression and understanding.

Whilst these more contemporary commentators suggest that school cultures need to change to become more boy-friendly as part of the strategy involved in combating the excess of challenging behaviour amongst boys within the school setting, the majority of ethnic minority parents, certainly in the United Kingdom, feel that one of the main problems with British schools is the lack of discipline. Whereas, an education in British schools was once sought after the world over, the perception amongst many ethnic minority communities within the UK is that standards of discipline in UK schools are now so poor that they are better sending their children back to their countries of origin for their education (Dosanji and Ghuman, 1996). This reflects some complex and often contradictory political dynamics. Whilst white liberal discourse of the seventies and eighties spoke about the desire to expand freedom and equality in an effort to combat racism and sexism in schools, what was harder to examine were the historical contexts that shaped the classroom itself. Thus teaching methods that were informed by non-Western thinking and which were more popular with many ethnic minority parents (such as a more 'traditional' approach to discipline) were dismissed as oppressive (Goldin, 1998).

The Role of Government

According to Foucault's formulation, governments and their countries' institutions interact in complex way. He suggests that scientific and medical studies of populations are closely related to changes in the regulatory role of the state, for example in education, welfare and health provision, but not in an obvious way of yielding power through deliberate manipulation of population. Foucault sees the way power typically functions in modern, Western society as having more subtle elements that interact with the way people define themselves and thus it is hard for most professionals and the populations they serve to recognize the subtle ways in which power and control operate within everyday life (Foucault, 1981; Parker, 1992).

In agreeing with this it is possible to see how government policies reflect mainstream practice within each discipline as well as influencing it. More powerful institutions will have a bigger impact on policy than less powerful ones as can be seen with the way Eli Lilly developed a close association with George Bush senior's government, thereby paving the way for Prozac's quick approval by the Food and Drug Agency in the United States and its subsequent 'blockbuster' status as a best-selling drug (Breggin and Breggin, 1994). The National Institute of Clinical Excellence (NICE) in the United Kingdom (a body set-up by the government to develop practice guidelines for the National Health Service) recently produced guidelines for the use of Methylphenidate (Ritalin) in children which has resulted in the diagnosis of ADHD becoming an officially recognized diagnosis and the use of prescribed amphetamines to children being officially sanctioned albeit with some controls.

As I illustrate in Chapter 4, Western free market capitalist ideology is essentially bad for children and their family's mental health. As a result, government policy is unlikely to be able to reverse the current crises of unruly behaviour amongst our boys without influential professional bodies developing a more sophisticated value system and understanding of the nature of the current problem facing us (see Chapter 8). All too often policy develops as a result of knee-jerk reactions in an attempt to capture votes. Recent examples in the United Kingdom include compulsory parenting classes and 'zero tolerance' policies such as curfews. Whilst in principle these may seem like good ideas, in practice they are unlikely to have a meaningful effect on the problem. Parenting classes are only going to be as good as the philosophy underlying the approach being taught, which currently lacks any multi-cultural awareness and will often result in failed attempts to impose an unacknowledged white middle-class Western value system onto alienated sections of the community. Similarly curfews and other high-level policing initiatives are unlikely to affect some of the fundamental socio-cultural problems such as absent fathers.

Chapter 4

How Western Culture Encourages Anti-Social Behaviour

We should do well to remember that in terms of loving care and family support, their children may be receiving far more than our children; our material conditions of living are so transformed that we might be living on another planet, but that does not mean that we do not have to learn much about child rearing from developing countries.

BRIMBLECOMBE, 1980: 6

I grew up in a different world. In Iraq the extended family ties were deep. I had a constant peer group and rarely needed to play with adults. As I entered adolescence, conversations with cousins and peers revolved around a search for meaning. We talked about life, religion and politics as well as football and sports. I came to England as a 14-year-old dazzled and impressed by the advanced technology, cleanliness of the streets and abundance of goods. My new peer group had very different interests. They talked back to teachers and passed round porn magazines. Conversations revolved around girls, parties, music and films as well as football and sports. New gender relations, the expectation of romance, having a girl friend, manhood being defined by sex, drink and rebelliousness all confronted me. Drugs soon reached me along with bullying, subtle and not so subtle racism. When later I did my psychiatry and psychotherapy training, I learned that compared to the West my Arab culture of origin was psychologically primitive and less sophisticated!

Culture functions to provide a set of values, beliefs and practices to guide a group of people in how to deal with the difficult business of social relationships (Timimi, 2002). Cultural values and beliefs provide mechanisms for social cohesion and reduction of perceived interpersonal suffering as well as a set of constraints to keep a lid on certain human impulses. Different cultures and different traditions develop different ways of providing this function. The result is that different cultures produce different experiences of childhood (as a general trend) and therefore encourage and discourage different types of beliefs and behaviours in children, their parents, their families and their communities. In this sense different cultural practices produce different childhoods, each of which are real within their own context and often look unusual or abnormal to outsiders to that context (Prout and James, 1997).

Let us take the issue of gender as an example. In some cultures boys are more highly prized than girls for a variety of reasons. Boys then grow up in a more privileged position and often with a view of themselves that reflects the preferential treatment they have received. They are much freer to conduct themselves as they wish compared to girls and have fewer expectations and pressures on them to behave in a particular manner. Parents report few experiences of what we, in the West, would consider rebellious or aggressive behaviour towards them. In some cultures there is a big concern about emergent female sexuality and these cultures develop a set of practices which are aimed at controlling any propensity to sexual behaviour by the female adolescent, with the main concern being young women's behaviour at this time, young men being spared the brunt of socio-cultural pressures to conform.

This, of course, is a simple stereotype that I have used to illustrate a general trend rather than a concrete and necessary outcome of the different preoccupations different cultures have. Culturally institutionalized sexism that favours boys is evident in many cultures around the world and will obviously have an impact on the way boys and men view themselves. My experience of working for many years in East London where there was a large ethnic minority population mainly of South Asian origin was that, compared to the white, working-class population (where behavioural problems amongst boys was the most common reason for referral to our department), problems such as attempted suicide, eating disorders and other self-harm behaviour in adolescent girls were the most common reasons for referral of children from these Asian/British Asian families, with relatively few boys being referred for behavioural problems. But before we in the West get smug about Western culture being more advanced and liberated in its sexual politics, read on that, as I suggest (later in this chapter), our whole culture in the West is being driven by masculine 'macho' ideals that are providing an even worse image of what it is to be a man than that of many more overtly patriarchal cultures.

In addition to exploring different cultures' preoccupations and the impact these may have on actual behaviours, I will also examine the impact of the broader political climate. As Coles (1986) has argued, a nation's politics becomes a child's everyday psychology. This goes from basic needs, such as food and shelter, through to the influence political decisions have on the structures within which children live, such as their family and school and right through to the big picture of how political developments influence beliefs and practices through the local discourse (including the powerful influence of media) that children are then exposed to as they grow. With free market capitalism now dominating the world economy it is worth examining how the value system that underpins this worldview affects the beliefs, values and consequently behaviour of children and adolescents.

Lessons from India and South Asia

In traditional Indian thinking the human life cycle is conceptualized as unfolding in a series of stages each having unique tasks. Although most of the writing and thinking focuses on youth and adulthood, traditional Indian medicine and philosophy in the form of *Ayurveda* describes childhood *Samskaras* (which are expressive and symbolic performances) including rites and ceremonies that are held over the child to mark her/ his transition from one stage to another. The contribution of *Ayurveda* to the Indian image of childhood lies in its formal recognition of different periods of childhood and its assignment of appropriate ages to each period. Each period is then reflected and affirmed by rituals with the major rituals of childhood taking place at ages that mark the transition from one period to another (Kakar, 1978). The purpose of the demarcation which occur around six months, two to three years, five to seven years, and eight to twelve years is, through the use of rituals, the gradual integration of the child into the wider society. These *Samskaras* seek to counteract the child's regressive longings and primal fears of abandonment and separation, which are invariably activated in the transition from one stage of life to another (Kakar, 1978). For example, at somewhere approaching the child's third year, the important rites of *Chudakarana* mark the child's 'psychological birth'. In this ritual the child is taken to the temple of a mother Goddess and his baby hair shaved and offered to the Goddess. He is then dressed up in new clothes, which are a miniature replica of the clothes worn by adult members of his community. The symbolism of death and rebirth is at the heart of many of such rituals. In popular tradition it is only after this particular ritual that the child is deemed ready for the process of discipline and any of the family's socialization efforts.

Within these stages of development in traditional Indian society, the general attitude can be summarized through proverbs such as 'treat a son like a king for the first five years, like a slave for the next ten and like a friend thereafter' (Kakar, 1978: 205). *Ayurvedic* texts contain copious details and instructions on the care of young children and constantly emphasize the importance of compassion and tenderness for the young. *Ayurveda* strives to develop the adult caretaker's capacity to comprehend the needs and emotions of the child, insisting that children should not be irritated and should be kept happy at all costs as this is crucial for their psychological development and future well-being (Kakar, 1978). When you add to this the importance of sons in traditional society, not only because sons are seen as instrumental in the fulfilment of sacred duties but also because they are portrayed as a source of emotional and sensual gratification (Kakar, 1978), you can begin to appreciate the sense of love and security young boys in this culture grow up with.

Thus boys grow up in a system where they are the favoured sex, where a nurturing and, to many Westerners, an indulgent attitude is encouraged and where integration into wider society takes place in recognized stages with concrete rituals to mark the move from one stage to the next. In addition, these boys are growing up in a system that emphasizes a family orientation to their personal identity as opposed to an individual orientation. This reflects not only on their view of themselves as individuals and their aspirations, but also on the behaviour of those around them and towards them. In 'collectivist' cultures (i.e. cultures whose value systems are orientated towards the importance of the group as opposed to the individual) like this, people are, from birth onwards, integrated into strong, cohesive groups that continue to offer them protection in exchange for loyalty throughout that person's life (Hofstede, 1994). The sense of 'we' dominates over the sense of 'I' with obligations and duties often overriding personal preference in importance (Triandis, 1995).

Traditional Indian culture is also rich in mythology that comes to life in their experience of childhood through the oral tradition of storytelling (Penzer, 1968; Shamasundar, 1997). Not only does this help enrich the young imagination but it also provides a means for passing on certain wisdoms about life that is based on appreciating the sequential rhythms of life moving through 'darkness and light' (Harper and Gray, 1997). In the West, instead of introducing our young to this understanding, we are guilty of promoting a view emphasizing the avoidance of 'hurt and pain' as a pre-requisite for contentment in life, a short-term approach that cannot help our children develop the strong sense of resilience that is often needed to survive the harsh realities of life.

When functioning well and without outside interference, this way of life, provides sufficient emotional security, guidance and a view of life that makes, for most boys, displays of defiant and aggressive behaviour less likely. With a greater number of adults available for care, nurturing, friendship and physical affection and a greater number of peers readily available to entertain you, we have a good model of a system that is much better for the emotional nurturing of children than the individualist nuclear family orientated models of the West.

The role of authority within this system, particularly that of fathers, is interesting. South Asian value systems place greater worth on responsibility and duty than freedom and liberty (in the individual sense). In this respect fathers play a pivotal and clearly proscribed role in family life. Indian family life demands that a father be restrained in the presence of his own son, as he has to divide his interest and support equally among his own and his brothers' sons. This culturally prescribed pattern of restraint between fathers and sons remains widespread in India and whether a father is strict or indulgent, cold or affectionate, they are most usually distant (Mandelbaum, 1970; Kakar, 1978). The presence of a father who is involved but psychologically at a removed distance (certainly compared to the mother) may well enhance the authoritative nature of any instructions he gives. Thus in situations where the voice of authority is needed for discipline, a father whose role with his younger children is clearly not that of friend and confidante is likely to carry more weight and provoke more fear and shame, allowing him to carry out that role more effectively. As a result, it is possible that a system that encourages distant but responsible fathering (as opposed to the Western distant but ambivalent) maybe more effective in enforcing discipline when needed.

When comparing traditional Indian ideology towards children with Western ideology, the conflict between rejecting and fostering attitudes towards a child, so marked in Western culture, is simply not a feature found in the Indian tradition (Kakar, 1978). The child in Indian tradition is ideologically considered a valuable and welcome human being to whom adults are expected to give their fullest protection, affection and indulgence. Interaction between adults and children are not conceived of in terms of socialization as in Western tradition, but in terms of interplay. This inter-play emphasizes the adult/child unit where mutual learning and mutual pleasure in each other occurs and differs sharply from the socialization model that concentrates solely on the child and his movement towards adulthood. This ideology is particularly noticeable in its impact on boys.

Boys grow up in an atmosphere where they are accepted for just being rather than for achieving certain 'developmental milestones'. This high acceptance, low pressure, low competitiveness approach fosters children's desire to show respect and obedience as opposed to becoming preoccupied with self-esteem as is so often the case with children growing up in the Western tradition.

As Brimblecombe (1980: 6) has noted:

> We should do well to remember that in terms of loving care and family support, their children may be receiving far more than our children; our material conditions of living are so transformed that we might be living on another planet, but that does not mean that we do not have to learn much about child rearing from developing countries.

And Holme (1984: 117):

> A child in India is hardly ever alone. Babies are carried around by their mothers, and it is a common sight to see a girl, even as young as six with a younger brother . . . Children play with other children much more than they do with objects . . . A regular bed time is virtually unknown. They tend to play or listen to the older members of the family until they drop off to sleep, the younger ones probably in their mother's lap . . . Children learn to respect their parents because they see them showing respect to their parents.

And in Dosanji and Ghuman (1996: 67) a Sikh shop owner talking about differences between her way of life in the Punjab and in England says,

> Here we are in Western culture. In India there is respect for elders and family relationships are honoured . . . So you call somebody your brother in India they would look after you. But over here, no. They would turn around and say I don't think of you that way at all. Meaning, who wants to be your brother? I miss those relationships and respect .

And in Hackett and Hackett (1994: 199): 'This communal ethic could promote psychiatric wellbeing by ensuring a degree of joint responsibility for children'.

Lessons from Arab and Middle-Eastern Countries

There are a number of similarities between Arab and Middle-Eastern cultures and Indian culture. For example, in both cultures children are welcomed without ambivalence and the early years tend to be marked by physical and emotional indulgence (when compared to Western child-hood). As with Indian families boys are favoured over girls (Dorsky and Stevenson, 1995; Fernea, 1995). In both Arab and Indian cultures the orientation is towards the community rather than the needs of the individual, and family structure is clearly demarcated with seniority being afforded to those who are older and male.

The dominant religion in Arab and Middle-Eastern countries is Islam. Islam has arguably become even more important to the indigenous populations in post-colonial times as a powerful source of emotional strength, pride and identity amongst a population who feel they have a proud history (the Islamic empire was once the leading 'civilization' in the world and the centre of literature, culture and science). Having been dominated and colonized by Western powers with their insulting hypocrisy in the way they deal with Israel as compared to other nations in the region, Islam has become a vehicle for expressing defiance. Events such as the Iranian revolution of 1979 demonstrated a newfound political strength in Muslim ideology, something that has affected the consciousness of many young people growing up in Arab and other Middle-Eastern countries. This new strengthening of the young's religious identity has represented not a return to tradition, but a radically different and more modern form of Islam. With many Arab leaders becoming aware of the central importance that the Muslim identity holds for their population, the place of Islam in education has become more central with the teaching of the importance of the knowledge of God as being the basis of all other kinds of knowledge becoming a standard ideological starting point of many Arab countries' education systems (Yamani, 1995). Teaching of the Koran often starts from the first year of school with children having to memorize short chapters from the holy Koran, learn about religious duties and learn about the social values of Islam such as co-operation, truthfulness, helping the elderly, obeying parents and the importance of cleanliness of the body (Hasan and Al-Qattami, 1995).

Thus, within the security of a culture that emphasizes the importance of family, of welcoming children into their fold and of teaching a value system based on Muslim ideology, children have every chance of growing up with a sense of basic emotional security and a clear purpose to their lives, particularly if they are from the favoured gender – boys.

In adolescence, instead of the conflict often encountered in Western culture (which is associated with the idea of developing autonomy and independence from the family), in Arab and Middle-Eastern society ado-lescents do not expect the degree of autonomy many Western adolescents feel is their due. Arabs are aware that they are part of a larger kin network and that the individual's desires are seldom the first and almost never the only consideration. Rather, the mature adult is the one who can balance responsible social behaviour with the maintenance of individual honour and the satisfaction of basic needs. Adolescence is thus viewed as a time in which the adolescent is learning to establish this balance and develop their social conscience. This limited expectation of autonomy, a value system that includes a great respect for age, kindness and sharing to those younger and where religion is of great importance, less open conflict between parents and adolescents is encountered than in Western societies (Davis and Davis, 1989; Timimi, 1995).

Within the code of Islam, not only are you taught to show obedience to your parents, it is also an expectation and duty for parents to discipline their children. The role of father as disciplinarian is very strongly ingrained in most traditional Arab and Middle-Eastern families. Unlike their Indian counterparts, most Arab fathers are very tactile, loving and affectionate with infants and young children. However, as children grow older and are expected to show more pro-social behaviour, fathers then assume a more distant, stern and authoritative relationship with their children. A man's power and authority over his children is meant to be a sign of love and responsibility and is unquestioned at home, with fear of punishment often being used as a deterrent to control unruly behaviour (Brink, 1995). The beginning of discipline coincides with the age at which children, both girls and boys, are first given responsibilities. This occurs at a much younger age – at the age of four or five – than would be the case in Western culture, with girls expected to perhaps share responsibility for a younger sibling, or in the case of a boy to care for an animal or run errands for the family (Fernea, 1995). As the child grows older they are taught societal norms of behaviour, including the importance of religion, respect for food, respect for those who are older, kindness to those who are younger, hospitality to guests and, above all, respect for and obedience to the authority of the father (Fernea, 1965, 1995).

Arab and Middle-Eastern society is family- and community-orientated. Consequently, it is not only the child's parents who are involved in instilling good habits and discipline. Grandparents, aunts, uncles and cousins are also expected to participate in a child's rearing and usually do so by acting as disciplinarians if the parents are perceived to be neglecting the child's progress towards becoming *mu'addab* (polite and disciplined) or by acting as affectionate, supportive figures if it was felt that the child's parents were being too harsh or were not sufficiently available. Neighbours, too, often become involved in the child's socialization as does school and

Koranic school teachers. Thus, many adults are participants in the task of nurturing and disciplining a child, reinforcing each other and providing alternate role models and sources of support for the child as she/he grows to maturity.

Arab and Middle-Eastern society are the so-called 'honour and shame' societies that stress responsibility and the reputation of the group. Traditionally, the moment of testing the honour of a man would be at the climax of the marriage ceremony, the consummation. A man's honour and that of his family require him to be virile enough to consummate the marriage. A blood-stained sheet, which family members would traditionally display publicly, would be offered as tangible proof that the groom's honour and the bride's honour were intact. Children would be present at weddings from their earliest years so these tests of honour would be made clear through observation and example and presumably through the discussions of those at the ceremony. Thus, honourable as opposed to what is considered shameful behaviour is part of a strong cohesive value system, which gives the message that an individual's behaviour reflects in the reputation of the group and is passed on to children from an early age. Indeed parents often categorize much of their children's behaviour as either honourable or dishonourable (Peristiany, 1965; Fernea and Fernea, 1981; Abu-Lughod, 1986; Fernea, 1995).

Although this is a cultural system that favours males and, like Western society, is unacceptably sexist in its power structures, it does nonetheless possess a clear coherent value system, a set of mechanisms and an ideology that has been developed over centuries. Boys who grow up within this system grow up emotionally secure and with fewer behaviour problems.

Lessons from Central and Southern Africa

As with Indian and Arab cultures, traditional African ideology emphasizes a communal orientation, which is reflected in its child rearing beliefs and practices. Take for example the Efe forager tribe of Zaire. Efe infants and toddlers experience a diverse array of social contact with many individuals, beginning shortly after birth when there is extensive handling and passing around of the baby (Tronick *et al.*, 1992). These contacts continue during the first three years of life with *Efe* toddlers spending almost all of their time in social contact with other individuals with between half and three quarters of this time in social contact with individuals who are not their mothers (Tronick *et al.*, 1992). Efe infants and toddlers are almost never alone in the sense of being out of sight or hearing of other people. The social and work relationships that Efe community members have with one another are publicly enacted both in and out of the camp setting and these people are often the same individuals with whom the Efe infants and toddlers participate in activities. Thus, the people that infants and toddlers regularly interact with are also the people who regularly surround them (Tronick *et al.*, 1992). This early social experience of Efe infants and toddlers is in marked contrast to that commonly found in Western society. Clarke-Stewart's (1973) work on the early social experience of US infants show that infants between 9 and 13 months spend about 84 per cent of their time in the same room as their mother with this figure dropping to 77 per cent by 17 months of age. Only 1.7 per cent of 9–13-month olds' time and 2.2 per cent of 16–17-month olds' time was spent in social activity with individuals other than their mothers (Clarke-Stewart, 1973).

Although the model in the Efe community is a familiar one to much of traditional Africa, as with South Asian and Middle-Eastern child rearing methods, there are important differences between tribes, regions and classes. For example, research carried out on the !Kung, a Savannah-dwelling, gathering and hunting community, showed that !Kung infants were in physical contact with their mothers for about 70–80 per cent of their time over the first year of life, although by the second year the !Kung children's social network had expanded to include mixed aged peers in greater number and variety than would commonly be seen in Western society (Konner, 1972).

It is likely that growing up in such a pro-social environment, experiencing many caretakers and easy and continuous access to other children contributes to the development of pro-social attitudes and orientation amongst the children of such communities. From an early age these children are learning to negotiate interactions with other family/tribe/community members and to deal psychologically with the often-unpredictable material resources that affect the community's daily life.

Not only are there important and major differences in the amount of exposure to social experiences with non-immediate family members but many differences can be seen between Western and traditional African child rearing practices in relation to parent–child relationships. LeVine *et al.*'s (1994), Study comparing infant life amongst the Gusii tribe of North Eastern Africa and their middle-class counterparts in Boston in the North East of the United States illustrates this (see Chapter 1). Bronfenbrenner (1994) in the foreword to LeVine *et al.*'s (1994) book, notes that in many respects the two cultures studied produced rather different kinds of human beings. For example, by contrast with Americans, the Gusii are much less expressive of their feelings. They avoid disclosing information, particularly pleasurable facts about themselves, which Americans routinely share. In addition, both children and adults are more compliant to authority and ask fewer questions. These patterns seem to begin early in life with Gusii babies of three to four months of age crying less than half the time than their American counterparts did.

Major differences in child rearing methods can be seen from the very first year of life. For the Gusii, holding and physical contact are frequent throughout the early years whereas for Bostonians, looking and talking to the infant are the dominant interaction throughout the early years. In the American model, having fostered the infant's capacity for verbal communication and active engagement, the mother finds herself engaged in an expanding relationship with the toddler who sleeps less, talks more and takes initiative in the interaction. American mothers frequently use questions to promote the infant's excited participation in a social exchange creating a proto-conversation with repeated questioning and lavish praise on the infant for each vocal or motor response which is taken as if it were an answer to a question. In contrast, Gusii mothers are less likely than their American counterparts to respond with speech to their baby's vocalization or to return eye contact. Gusii mothers try instead to keep their babies calm, avoiding positive or negative arousal states by preventing or dampening down excitement. As the child grows older, in the American model, praise continues to be an important part of the parental speech with the parent thinking of him or herself as building self-confidence by rewarding the toddler with their verbal approval for each new sign of mastery. In contrast, the Gusii script indicates a rarity of praise and questions in speech directed to Gusii infants and the predominance of commands intended partly to prevent the infant getting into danger, particularly as they grow older. Gusii mothers in fact considered it useful in terms of control for a baby to acquire fear, not only of actual hazards such as fire, but also of domestic animals, especially dogs and imaginary creatures, which are used by the mother or siblings to frighten the child into compliance. From around two years of age, the Gusii child is integrated into the sibling network with the expectation that the rest of the child's socialization, including play, speech and social interaction, will occur within the sibling group. In the Gusii model, praise is explicitly rejected as a verbal device and strategy with the accompanying belief that praise would make even a good child rude and disobedient (LeVine *et al.*, 1994).

Reflecting on the differences between the Gusii and Bostonian models of child rearing, Bronfenbrenner (1992, 1994) suggests that a key requirement for the American model to remain effective is that it must take place on a fairly regular basis and over extended periods of time. In other words, if you set up a model of child rearing based on an intensive mother–child relationship where the mother is the pivotal and only pivotal person responsible for developing the socialization of that infant and where this is done through the more labour-intensive use of questions, praise and stimulation of vocal interactions, then to be effective these methods must continue to be applied regularly, consistently and continuously throughout the child's growing years.

Unfortunately, in much of Western society today we have a hectic pace of life where communities tend to be unstable with regular, consistent and predictable support for families unavailable, making it physically and mentally more difficult to apply the praise and intense parent–child relationship model continuously throughout that growing child's life. In contrast, the degree of stability found in more traditional cultures, such as that of the Gusii, makes their model a practical and pragmatic model of child rearing that seems to work to the extent that unruly behaviour is less commonly encountered amongst Gusii children (LeVine *et al.*, 1994). It is likely that the child rearing model of progressively more complex reciprocal interactions between mother and infant (and more generally between adults and children) in American society is becoming harder to sustain and is therefore increasingly less powerful in its impact due to the modern life pressures on parents. The difficulty of culturally maintaining this Western model of child rearing may well be contributing to levels of unhappiness and stress amongst families and their children and to greater occurrences of unruly, oppositional and rebellious behaviour amongst children and adolescents in Western society (Bronfenbrenner, 1992, 1993).

It should not be forgotten that Africa is a vast continent and moral and social rules can vary considerably from one ethnic group to another. There are great differences of opinion that can be found with regard to attitudes towards the expression of aggression amongst children and the use of corporal punishment by adults. Thus, the Rwandese and the Nuer tribes encourage their children to fight amongst themselves, whilst the Gusii ask them to take their quarrels to an adult and then to fight in front of him or her (Erny, 1981). The Pedi and the Loaedu tribes have profoundly different attitudes to aggression and corporal punishment. The former aim at subjecting the child to the authority of the group and inflict frequent and often severe corporal punishments on mainly boys and seek to make their boys aggressive and quarrelsome. Meanwhile, the latter believe that corporal punishment does serious injury to the personality and aim to make their children basically peaceful (Erny, 1981). Amongst the Mossi tribe, punishment is rarely given with parents allowing their children to act as they like, even letting them hurl the grossest insults at their mother and make a fist at her, contenting themselves by saying that the child will one day be a great fighter (Erny, 1981).

Traditional African cosmology leans heavily towards a supernatural explanation of the world and events within it and it is to this supernatural world that most African children arrive. Even before a child is born, premonitions and dreams in which the mother might have seen ancestors following or touching her or asking her to drink are brought to bear. The Soothsayer is consulted, dreams as well as any other significant coincidences are interpreted and as a result a suitable name is picked for the child. From the moment a child enters the world the inheritance which it is believed to receive transcends the purely biological order, touching on the spiritual being and most intimate aspects of the personality. Being born itself is often thought of in terms of the category of passage. To come into this world is to leave the world beyond, it is to be in transit, to change one's state. Being born into this world means dying in the other world and at the end of life, the opposite is true; to die in this world is to be born back in the other world.

In this conception of the world, childhood, like old age, constitutes an intermediary or transitional stage where the child tries to free himself from the control of the other world and the old man prepares himself to return there. This spiritual dimension to a child's life is further reinforced in their view of themselves and the world they live in by a series of important rituals that represent the passage from one stage to another. The child learns of their importance through the importance afforded to the child as being somebody who is attached to the ancestral state, in other words the link between the dead ancestors who are believed to reside in the spirit world and the current generation. The child is also the connecting link between the wife's family and that of the husband and given the importance of children to successful marriage, children are proof that the matrimonial exchange has been successful (Erny, 1981).

Thus in traditional Africa, children grow up in a system where the child is viewed as a vital part of the glue that links members of the community together, as well as linking the past to the present. Children are also vital members of the workforce needed to contribute to the survival of the tribe. They are raised according to child rearing models that have been developed over hundreds of generations and through highly complex systems of local knowledge. The accumulated wisdom reflects in models that are in tune with the local ecology and that ensure survival of a socially cohesive tribe. Children are born into a world governed by unseen supernatural forces in stable communities that offer copious opportunities for socialization and multiple attachments. Boys develop respect, self discipline and rarely display unruly behaviour despite what, to Western eyes, would seem like harmful practices such as corporal punishment and lack of praise being central to many tribes' child rearing philosophy.

The economy and politics of empire and globalization have had a devastating and disrupting effect on these functional local, indigenous ecologies. From the slave trade through apartheid to post-colonial global markets whose exploitation of Africa has resulted in widespread famine and disease in certain parts of the continent, these politics have a lasting effect on the lives of many of the continent's children. For example in apartheid South Africa the poverty and powerlessness of black boys and men gave their masculinity a dangerous edge. The struggle against apartheid was often violent and for black South Africans being given honour and respect was rare during the apartheid years. Post-apartheid the continued poverty together with high expectations and the ending of the shared meaning that the struggle against apartheid provided has fostered a growth in violence amongst boys and men (Morrell, 2001).

The Effect of Contemporary Western Culture on Children's Behaviour

So far in this chapter, I have attempted to show that as children are socialized by belonging to a particular culture at a certain stage in that culture's history, so certain differences in children's behaviour can be seen as a result of different child rearing philosophies and socialization processes. In other words the different social practices of different cultures produce different childhoods each of which are 'real' within their local regime of truth (Prout and James, 1990; Stephens, 1995). In modern Western capitalist culture, children and then adults come to acquire their subjective selves through incorporation of values, beliefs and practices that sustain the desired social relationships of this culture (Althusser, 1969). People, Althusser argues, can only know themselves through the mediation of ideological institutions and some of the most important of these institutions, such as schools, focus their attention on children (Althusser, 1969). So how does the ideology of modern capitalism influence the way children and their parents see themselves, their roles and subsequently the way they behave?

One of the dominant themes used by advocates of capitalist market economy ideology is that of 'freedom'. At an emotional level the appeal to freedom can be understood as an appeal to rid us of the restrictions imposed by authority (such as parents, communities and governments) (Richards, 1989). By implication this value system is built around the idea of looking after the wants of the individual, who should despise any form of dependency. This is reflected in the language used, for example welfare-orientated, interventionist governments may be described as the 'nanny state'. The image of the nanny state is of a fussy, restrictive, asexual female, imposing her own idea of what she believes is good for her charges and thereby keeping them emotionally at least in the nursery (Richards, 1989).

Taking this a step further, once the individual is freed from the 'nanny' they are (in fantasy at least) free to pursue their own individual self-gratification desires, free from the impingements, infringements and limitations that other people represent. Thus at the heart of this modern freedom-loving, free market, capitalist value system is an individual freed from the need to think about others in order to pursue self gratification. The effect of this on society is to atomize the individual and insulate their private spaces to the degree where obligations to others and harmony with the wider community become obstacles rather than objectives. In this 'look after number one' value system, other individuals are there to be competed against as they too chase after their personal desires. This post-Second-World-War shift to a more 'fun-based morality' was already being noted by commentators in the United States in the mid-1950s, who saw that with Western culture now privileging fun over responsibility; having fun was becoming obligatory (the cultural message becoming that you should be ashamed if you were not having fun) and with the increase in new possibilities for excitement being presented, experiencing intense excitement was becoming more difficult (Wolfenstein, 1955), thus opening the doors to the mass use of drugs (legal and illegal) in pursuit of the ultimate 'high'.

In this value system, others become objects to be used and manipulated wherever possible for personal goals, and social exchanges become difficult to trust as the better you are at manipulating others the more financial rewards you will get. Dependence still occurs but is more likely to happen with professionals thereby reinforcing the idea and status of the expert. As Amin (1988) points out, Western capitalist ideology has necessarily led to the domination of market values, which penetrates all aspects of social life and subjects them to their logic. This philosophy pushes to the limit of absurdity an opposition between humankind and nature. The goal of finding an ecological harmony with nature disappears as nature comes to be viewed as a thing to be similarly manipulated for selfish ends.

In a capitalist, market-driven economy, mass consumption is vital to the maintenance of the system and therefore becomes an important part of our self and consciousness. In Western society even personal relations and the self become objects of consumption (Broughton, 1986); like the stereotype consumer wife comparing the whiteness of her sheets with those of her neighbours, the subjects of consumer societies constantly compare their own inadequacies with those of others. This practice of self-examination causes a cult of self-awareness. In doing so it actually creates inner qualities, including whatever passes for personal growth with every day one seeking to make oneself a better product – new, improved, best and brightest yet. Reliance on consumerism has also led to a kind of growth fetish, whereby Western culture and politics are obsessed with an ideology that demands never-ending growth and expansion (Hamilton, 2003). Yet, despite several decades of sustained economic growth, we are no happier. Growth not only fails to make people contented; it destroys many of the things that do through weakening social cohesion (Hamilton, 2003). Like the rest of our culture psychiatry too is gripped by an ideology of growth, as we are encouraged to produce more and more 'knowledge' through wisdom-less research.

As Richards (1989) pointed out, such a value system, which ultimately seeks to eradicate social conscience (or the superego if you prefer the language of psychoanalysis) as a regulator of behaviour, cannot sustain itself without our moral conscience beginning to feel guilty. Thus it is no coincidence that those right-wing politicians who are the most vociferous advocates of free market ideology tend also to advocate the most aggressive and punitive forms of social control. Whereas some of these guilt-induced policy proposals are aimed at putting some restraint on unfettered competitiveness, greed and self seeking (most notably in more centre and left-wing capitalist governments) amongst those more fanatical believers in the sacredness of market ideology, the most common defence used to try and deal with the anxiety produced by this guilt is through finding target scapegoats for this anxiety (or by projection if you prefer the language of psychoanalysis). Like a child who does not want to feel guilty at having done something they know is 'naughty', they try to blame someone else for the damage that has happened as a result of their naughtiness. This is the basis of the knee-jerk 'something must be done about it' ethos that leads to ill-conceived policies in response to media hysteria following high-profile incidents. This is what a kleinian psychoanalyst might call a 'paranoid–schizoid' reaction as it reflects the inability of our culture to tolerate risk and anxiety and the constant need to find target groups to carry our collective burden of guilt (Haigh, 2003). As a result the institutions which deal with our children from education, health through to social services are ruled by faceless, emotionless technical procedures and policies designed to maintain distance, boundaries and regulate levels of human contact between these agencies and the people they are meant to serve.

In order to keep this self-seeking individualistic value system intact, capitalism thus needs 'baddies' to blame for the personal suffering that is occurring as a result of its encouragement of selfishness. In other words instead of facing up to the suffering the encouragement of manipulation of people that greed brings to the world, our leaders need to convince us that our problems are due to other evils (like fundamentalist Islam, communism, asylum seekers, homosexuals, single parents, bad genes, etc.). As a result another hallmark of Western culture's psychological basis in immature (or primitive if you prefer psychoanalytic language) impulses, which encourages it to avoid taking responsibility for its beliefs and practices, is the so-called 'blame culture', which fills the media and contemporary discourse more generally.

The attention given to individual cases of child abusers whom society can disown as not belonging to or being (at least in part) the product of our culture masks Western governments' implementation of national and international policies that place children at great risk and the extent to which we are an abusive culture. Right-wing policies of the 1980s and 1990s cut health, social, welfare and education programmes as well as enforcing similar austerity measures on developing countries, policies that had a particularly adverse effect on children and families (De Mause, 1984; Scheper-Hughes and Stein, 1987; Kincheloe, 1998). This also has a class-specific character with the plight of poor children being viewed as self-inflicted and the more insidious problem of neglect of their children by middle-class parents passing unnoticed (Rabin, 1994). With the increase in the number of divorces and two working parents, fathers and mothers are around their children for less of the day. A generation of 'home aloners' are growing up; kids who have to by and large raise themselves. Since the late 1960s the amount of time children in the United States have with their parents has dropped, from an average of 30 hours per week to 17 hours per week by the early 1990s (Lipsky and Abrams, 1994). As kids are forced to withdraw into their own culture, the free market exploits this, praying on their boredom and desire for stimulation (Kincheloe, 1998). In this environment poor children are constantly confronted with their shortcomings by media that tells them they are deficient without this or that accessory. In this unhappy isolation Western children respond to the market's push to 'adultify' them (at the same time as the culture of self-gratification 'childifies' adults) by entering into the world of adult entertainments earlier and without adult supervision. Thus the post-modern Western child is sexually knowledgeable and has early experience of drugs and alcohol (Aronowtiz and Giroux, 1991). Adultifying children may also be exposing them to greater risk of sexual abuse through consumer culture's eroticization of the young as seen in popular images (e.g. in advertising) presenting highly eroticized, alluring little girls with make-up (Walkerdine, 1996) and beauty pageants who no longer look like little girls but coquettish young women who are encouraged to walk suggestively across the stage (Giroux, 1998).

With the goal of self-fulfilment, gratification and competitive manipulation of relationships to suit the individual's own selfish ends (or narcissism if you prefer psychoanalytic language), together with the discouragement of the development of deep interpersonal attachments, it is not difficult to see why the so-called narcissistic (or self-centred) disorders (such as anti-social behaviour) are on the increase (Lasch, 1980; Dwivedi, 1996).

Children are cultured into this value system by virtue of living within its institutions and being exposed daily to its discourse (most notably through television). Through this they are socialized into a system that embraces a capitalist idea of freedom through promoting individualism and competitiveness. They are expected to renounce dependence and show independence from an early age. Ultimately this is a system of winners and losers, a kind of survival of the fittest where compassion and concern for social harmony contradicts the basic goal of the value system. As this system is showing itself to be bad for children's happiness, a similar process as above works to try and distance us from the anxiety arising from the guilt thus produced. Instead of asking ourselves painful questions about the role we may be playing in producing this unhappiness, we can view our children's difficulties as being the result of biological diseases that require medical treatment (we can blame their genes).

These social dynamics also get projected directly onto children. Children come to be viewed as both victims (through adults using and manipulating them for their own gratification) and potentially 'evil' scapegoats (as if it is these nasty children's bad behaviour that is causing so many of our social problems). This reflects a profound ambivalence that exists towards children in the West. With adults busily pursuing the goals of self-realization and self-expression (these being the polite middle-class versions of self-gratification), having unconsciously absorbed the free-market ethic, children when they come along 'get in the way'. A human being, who is so utterly dependent on others, will inevitably cause a huge rupture in the Western value system goals of self-seeking that individuals who have grown up in this society will hold to a greater or lesser degree. Children cannot be welcomed into the world in an ordinary and seamless way. They will make the dominant goals of modern life more difficult. They will to some degree be a burden.

This essentially narcissistic value system has led to a 'masculinization' of culture. Major worldviews are usually reflections of the interests and experiences of the most powerful social groups (Foucault, 1977; Connell, 1995). In gender terms this is undoubtedly man. Men in the West are the main beneficiaries of the contemporary world order that has delivered great wealth to them; with the world's richest fifth in 1990 receiving 83 per cent of the world's income compared to the 1.4 per cent that the world's poorest fifth received (United Nations Development Programme, 1992). Western history of empire, conquest and – in its most nakedly and violently masculine form – fascism was made by men. Classical Western philosophy of reason and science through oppositions with the natural world and emotions led to Western science and technology becoming culturally masculinized and dominated by 'masculine' metaphors, particularly in comparison with Eastern philosophies and guiding metaphors (Seidler, 1989). Connell (1995) coined the term 'hegemonic masculinity' to describe the dominant form of masculinity found within a social group. In the West, hegemonic masculinity emphasizes physical strength, adventurousness, emotional neutrality, certainty, control, assertiveness, self-reliance, individuality, competitiveness, skills, public knowledge, discipline, reason, objectivity and rationality (Kenway and Fitzclarence, 1997). These attributes then become important aspects of growing boys developing gender identities. With a narrowing of the emotional range allowed of our masculine heroes and a distancing from displays of tenderness, compassion and dependence being culturally prescribed for boys, it is no surprise that many boys grow up feeling isolated, and misunderstood, from fathers with whom they wish to have closer relationships (Frosh *et al.*, 2002).

As growing boys absorb these masculine values, the absence of responsibility and the pursuit of self-gratification are then often bragged about in the adolescent playground. (Where boys compete to drink the most pints and sleep with the most women, etc.) The impact this masculine value system has on family and community life is profound. The system seems to have been designed for men. Men can follow the central premise of this value system to its logical conclusion. Having brought children into the world, responsibility for child rearing and for maintaining family life usually falls on the mother. If the going gets too tough then many fathers in the West choose to leave the family in order to chase freedom and self-gratification, their sense of duty, responsibility and personal attachment disappearing with them. Guilt is often dealt with by displacing this through blaming the child's mother. (She tried to control me, would not let me have my freedom) or their child (he has chosen not to see me.) The price boys are paying for this rampant masculinization of our culture is incalculable. Not only are boys denied secure, stable and nurturing homes to whom they can feel the sense of loyalty that comes through belonging, but in addition they are given a model of masculinity to aspire towards, which devalues notions of responsibility, duty, love and emotionally intimate relationships based on mutual dependency.

The process of having a child can also be viewed through the prism of a consumer value system. Thus the desire to have a child can be seen as linked to a perceived selfish need, many feeling that they are only 'complete' once they have had a child(ren). In this way of viewing the nature of childhood in Western culture, adults have children for their own emotional gratification (Stephens, 1995). This causes a cultural shift in relation to gender, with girls being more highly prized for this purpose than boys, as girls are more likely to reciprocate and provide these emotional 'presents' to their parents. For some boys these dynamics leave them in a lonely place, where they feel unwelcome, unvalued and caught in cycles of progressive alienation, jealousy and guilt with few male role models to turn to and find a healthy way out of their situation.

The institutions that work with children and parents reflect various aspects of this masculinized freedom/guilt dynamic. Schools in the United Kingdom have been colonized by free market managerial style, with the encouragement of greater competitiveness between schools and with each school's success being measured by the exam grades of their pupils. We see more and more winners and losers both for schools as a whole and for the individuals within them. You have to be pretty thick-skinned to survive as a loser in this system without this affecting your view of yourself and your behaviour in some way. Particular groups end up at particular risk. Thus many black and ethnic minority pupils in Western schools, feeling like humiliated 'loser' outsiders, turn to a macho subculture that shows both defiance towards the authority of the system that is hurting them as well as embracing a culturally congruent solution that is 'hyper-masculine' (Mac An Ghaill, 1994; Sewell, 1995). For many working-class boys the change in educational demands, which has shifted the expectation for qualifications upwards (reflecting the decline in manufacturing and a rise in demand for a more skilled labour force), has made experience of educational failure even more problematic (Frosh *et al.*, 2002).

Within a value system that promotes freedom to pursue your wishes/ instincts a number of common escape routes are available to those who feel like they are the losers/failures/rejects of this culture. Within adolescent and increasingly younger childhood subculture there is a powerful culture of cruelty in existence (Kindlon and Thompson, 1999). If you perceive yourself to be a failure within the school system then there are other ways to rebuild your sense of self-worth and personal power such as a hyper-masculine subculture of cruelty that encourages you to seek gratification through alternative routes, including theft, drugs, alcohol and violence. This is often done through gangs (which operate like mini capitalist cultures where those who can be the most self-serving are to be most admired). These dynamics start in school where it has been found that those students who are most likely to develop an anti-school value system that includes asserting their masculinity through physical strength are boys who are failing academically (Mac An Ghaill, 1994).

Since the introduction of the national curriculum into UK schools the rate of children being excluded from schools has been raised sixfold (Guardian Society, 19 September, 2001). The national curriculum introduced routine testing of children at various ages and the production of national league tables, which rate school performance as assessed by the academic performance in these tests of the children in their schools. The vast majority of children excluded are boys. Consequently, in this education market, where school examination performance is increasingly tied to reputation and recruitment, girls become a valuable and sought-after resource (Ball and Gewirtz, 1997). The permeation of this perspective that girls are successful and boys are failing is reinforced by statistics on girls' achievement in all girl settings, across school type and across social class (Arnot *et al.*, 1996; Benn and Chitty, 1996). As well as their lesser contribution to performance league tables, boys in general absorb the larger proportion of resources for additional support and special needs (Daniels *et al.*, 1996; Riddell, 1996).

Boys have become the gender that schools experience the most problems with. Some of the behavioural problems they display may reflect the type of labels they attract (such as problem, failure, disabled, naughty and stupid) and their subsequent reaction to these. Some critics (e.g. Brod, 1987) have argued that traditional masculinity exists in a state of contra-diction and crisis in which every new generation rediscovers the problem of young men. Others have argued that although models of masculinity are always changing there are specific historical junctures when gender certainties are particularly threatened (e.g. Kimmel, 1987). In this respect, it could be argued that modern, Western society is experiencing one of these disorientating, historical junctures and what many boys are left feeling is a bitter sense of the pointlessness of their labour. Culturally congruent alternative of an aggressive culture of heterosexual masculinity can be seen as a strategy some boys use to fill in these despairing gaps.

Within male students, a sorting and sifting into an academic hierarchy increases the gap between 'failed' students and 'successful' students (Connell, 1989). Successful students construct their masculinity through an emphasis on rationality and are rewarded by social power giving them access to higher education and entry into higher-status occupations. Failed students look to other sources of power and other definitions of their masculinity. Thus, sporting prowess, physical aggression and sexual conquest may become the avenues by which failed schoolboys find their self-worth. A subculture can develop where rejection of academic success is supported by a view of school and learning as an effeminate activity to be rejected. An image of reluctant involvement is cultivated among many boys, resulting in many boys managing their academic careers carefully by avoiding an open commitment to work. In schools where an anti-school masculinity has become hegemonic, boys who are openly committed to academic success, or who are poor at 'cussing' or who show their emotions easily, become targets for ridicule and bullying (Bleach, 1996; Frosh *et al.*, 2002). Within these subcultures boys are often very aware of their vulnerability, strive to display hyper-masculine performance and are often caught in a conflict between defending themselves from their perceived failure in school at the same time as trying to gain the approval of the anti-school peer group (characterized by Mac An Ghaill (1994) as the fighting, fucking and football culture). Similarly, certain minority groups have developed their own macho subcultures that ironically, sometimes incorporate elements from institutionalized stereotypes, such that many young black Afro-Caribbean boys use an idealized phallo-centric masculinity to contest institutional conditions of dependency, racism and powerlessness. Some of these pupils actively brought about their own academic failures by being indifferent to school work, labelling black boys who work hard at school as 'batty men' (gay) or 'pussies' (effeminate) (Sewell, 1995).

Although this system may be a good training ground for many of the future participants in the capitalist, market economy, where it is desirable for individuals to be competitive, self-seeking and able to use relationships for the purpose of manipulating others to serve their own needs, this leaves the problem of how to deal with the failures that this system inevitably produces.

Ingleby (1985) makes the claim that as groups of children become the new dangerous classes then governments perceive that the socialization process for children can no longer be trusted to families but has to be taken over by the state and its agencies. According to Ingleby, there is 'a growing army of professionals operating in the psychological sphere' (Ingleby, 1985: 79) whom Ingleby dubs the *psy-complex*. The *psy-complex* aims to apply psychological technology to the task of socializing children. Professionals who are essentially acting on behalf of the state maintain power through the parent, by educating the parent about the professional's worldview and are ultimately aiming to produce ways of living and thinking consistent with the dominant social order. Professionals themselves are duped into thinking that the ends are benevolent and the means of achieving them are rational.

Thus, on the one hand, children and their families are cultured through institutions such as media and education into high competitiveness, individualistic and low-dependency beliefs and practices, which produces winners and losers, and on the other hand the system deals with its guilt and anxiety through the development of cultural defence mechanisms (Timimi, 2002) such as social services, child-and-adolescent mental health services and compulsory parenting classes which targets blame for failure and its consequences on individual children (who are then deemed disabled and suffering from a medical condition) or their parents (who are then deemed incompetent). The cost to children's mental health of this value system has been and continues to be immense.

Globalization and Universalizing

With capitalism achieving unchallenged dominance of the world economy, the ideology and value system that underpins it, aided by global communications and mass media, has been infiltrating consciousness the world over. With a system that is based on self-interest, the powerful capitalist nations, most notably the United States, consolidate their position as winners at the expense of the economic interests of those countries that become losers. The implications of this global system for children all over the world are huge. For many third-world countries this means widespread economic uncertainty, unemployment and powerful pressure for conformity to the market economy that is serving the West. This usually means cutbacks in public services such as healthcare, childcare and social benefits, all of which drastically affect the lives of children. In debt-ridden third-world countries austerity measures imposed by institutions such as the World Bank and the International Monetary Fund mean cuts in social welfare programmes and disruptions in local support networks. For many living in these countries they mean increasing numbers of children who are living and working in conditions of poverty while the global media provides them with representations of ideal childhoods which surely sharpen the experience of material poverty as some sort of inner deprivation (Stephens, 1995).

Far from providing greater global stability the demise of the Eastern Block socialist countries and the end of the cold war has sunk the world further into winners and losers, us-and-them mentality, fuelled by the sense of omnipotence that winning the cold war has given countries such as the United States. Ethnic, religious and racial conflicts have been set free, causing massive destruction in social networks and escalating numbers of refugees and migrants, with resulting dissolution of the protective effect traditional extended family systems gave to many of the children of the poor. Western culture's ideas about organizing society then come to dominate and with it the West's highly masculinized ideals are imposed. For example, in post-cold-war Eastern Europe, Western gender ideologies have been installed together with a free market system, and the old state guarantees of equality for women were lost.

The free individual – you can become whatever you want to be – philosophy of Western capitalism hides the fact that in capitalist cultures, because of their economic differences, equality and freedom are both delusions. If people could control their own lives, how many would choose the lives that they have? The greater the awareness of the gap between the idealized images Western culture sells of free choice and self-realization and the reality of economic and cultural oppression infiltrates globally, the greater the likelihood for frustration and dissatisfaction, particularly within indigenous peoples.

However, no process is only one-way. Arguably as a result of globalization those who inhabit the industrialized north of the globe are also exposed to diverse, alternative lifestyles. This makes it less easy to dismiss as deviance values, beliefs and practices that we can see make sense for other people. It is becoming more difficult to seek the comfort of ignorance concerning different possibilities, for no culture is now truly foreign any more, with the whole social world of human kind opening up to us. In this post-modern reality how we view our world and how we live in it is saturated with possibilities as the number and variety of persons with whom we have contact expands, seemingly without limit (Gergen, 1992).

Chapter 5

Attention Deficit Hyperactivity Disorder: A Cultural–Political Perspective

> *The assertion that ADHD is neither viral nor bacterial is not supported by an everyday experience of this phenomenon. ADHD seeps its way through a classroom like the latest strain of flu and there are certain risk factors that make children vulnerable to infection. For instance, having an older sibling with ADHD appears to dramatically increase a child's risk of diagnosis, by the same doctor or psychologist, by the time the child has reached the older sibling's age. However, close proximity to a classmate with ADHD seems only to be a risk when the caregivers of the respective children are good friends.*
>
> IAN LAW, 1997: 284

Something strange has been happening to children in Western society in the past couple of decades. The diagnosis of ADHD has reached epidemic proportions, particularly amongst boys in North America. National surveys conducted in 1997 and 1998 found that about 1.6 million cases of ADHD had been diagnosed in American elementary school children (about 7 per cent of 6–11-year olds, and given that three to four times more boys diagnosed were around 11 per cent of 6–11-year-old boys) (Gottlieb, 2002). The diagnosis is usually made by a child psychiatrist or paediatrician with advocates of the diagnosis claiming that children who present with what the diagnoser considers to be over-activity, poor concentration and impulsivity are suffering from a medical condition which needs treatment with medication. The main medications used for children with a diagnosis of ADHD are stimulants such as Ritalin, whose chemical properties are virtually indistinguishable from the street drugs speed and cocaine. Boys are three to ten times more likely to receive the diagnosis and stimulants than girls with children as young as two being diagnosed and prescribed stimulants in increasing numbers (Zito *et al.*, 2000). By 1996 over 6 per cent of school-aged boys in America were taking stimulant medication (Olfson *et al.*, 2002) with more recent surveys showing that in some schools in the United States over 17 per cent of boys have the diagnosis and are taking stimulant medication (Le Fever *et al.*, 1999).

In the United Kingdom prescriptions for stimulants have increased from 6000 in 1994 to over 150,000 by 1999 (Department of Health, 1999), over a quarter of a million by 2002 (BBC news, 24 July, 2003), with the most recent figures showing that about 345,000 children in the United Kingdom are taking prescribed stimulants in the latter half of 2003 (about 2–2.5 per cent of schoolchildren) (Wright, 2003), suggesting that we in the United Kingdom are rapidly catching up with the United States. Early in the twenty-first century we in the West are living in the bizarre paradox of Western governments spending billions every year to fight a war on drugs with the right hand whilst the left hand hands out millions of prescriptions for cocaine-like stimulants to its children. Concerned professionals and parents are increasingly vocal in their criticism of the excessive use of stimulants.

The multi-billion dollar psycho-stimulant industry has well and truly arrived in the United Kingdom. I have been paid to go to advisory bodies (with no mention of drug industry sponsorship in the letter of invitation) as a consultant only to discover that the discussion was a 'cover' for an ensuing presentation concerning a new slow-release form of stimulant. I have received mailings of glossy 'educational' material to give to parents and teachers, from drug companies in which they talk about ADHD as a genetically inherited condition caused by an imbalance of chemicals in the brain. They have pretty pictures of nerve cell synapses 'showing' the problem with these cells and how their drug 'corrects' the deficiency. I get calls from drug company representatives wanting to present to the staff group I work with in return for a free lunch. I get questionnaires sent to me asking me about my prescribing habits with regard to stimulants and offering me a fee if I agree to complete the form and return it.

And what are doctors in the United Kingdom doing about this? Falling wittingly or unwittingly into the arms of the drug companies to the point where the entanglement is so great that evidence-based practice is socially conditioned by the drug companies' profit motive (see the 31 May, 2003 (Volume 236) edition of the *British Medical Journal*, an edition specifically devoted to exploring the links between doctors and drug companies). Of course it is in the drug companies' interests to highlight studies and conclusions that are likely to enhance their product's sales, after all who knows how many negative trials whose results do not please the drug companies have been discarded by them (Ruesch, 1992). Where there is a conflict between giving accurate information and making sales it is not always the worthier motive that carries the day.

I have heard an American professor talk about his 'success' stories in treating adults with Ritalin. He spoke of high-flying lawyers who complained that they could not concentrate in meetings. He diagnosed ADHD and prescribed Ritalin and the lawyers were delighted with their improved ability to concentrate. I have heard a prominent paediatrician tell us that most problems of childhood, adolescence and young adulthood (such as substance misuse, behavioural problems, delinquency, depression, learning difficulties, bullying, poor peer relationships, poor academic achievement and so on) are caused by untreated ADHD. I have heard doctors talk about stimulants in terms of miracles. I have seen patients who have been prescribed three times the maximum licensed daily dose of Ritalin and I have seen families whose 3-year-old child has been put on Ritalin and an anti-psychotic drug for behavioural problems I managed to help the parents resolve in one session without medication. At meetings and conferences with other child psychiatrists I am often a lone voice when I raise questions with regard to the validity of ADHD as a medical diagnosis; or the risks and controversies associated with prescribing stimulants. All too often I leave these mainstream events feeling like I had attended a cult convention, not a scientific conference, so bad has the lack of democratic debate or interest in non-drug-industry-driven perspectives become.

In a failed attempt to silence its critics, ADHD advocates published an extraordinary consensus statement (Barkley and 78 co-endorsers, 2002) in which the most prominent professionals in this field accuse those who raise questions about the science and ethics of ADHD diagnosis and medication use, of being unscientific. In fact they say 'To publish stories that ADHD is a fictitious disorder or merely a conflict between today's Huckleberry Finns and their caregivers is tantamount to declaring the earth is flat, the laws of gravity debatable, and the periodic table in chemistry a fraud' (Barkley and 78 co-endorsers, 2002: 90). Most of authors of the statement are well known to have financial links with the pharmaceutical industry (which they do not declare in their statement) and it is no surprise that they conclude (despite the above studies that show an alarming rise in the amounts of stimulants being prescribed) that 'studies indicate that less than half of those with the disorder are receiving treatment' (Barkley and 78 co-endorsers 2002: 90). The evidence is becoming clearer all the time and it does not make comfortable reading for the ADHD advocates. If the evidence in favour of conceptualizing ADHD as a neurological or neuro-developmental condition were already that good, then no statement would be needed (Timimi and 33 co-endorsers, 2004). The ghost of nine eleven hides behind the tone adopted by their statement. Although the advocates have long dismissed their critics, nine eleven has seeped into Western collective cultural unconscious and given licence to those who wish to kill proper enquiry and debate through use of power and the 'You're either with us or against us' mindset.

I bought Dr Green and Dr Chee's (1997) book *Understanding ADHD: A Parent's Guide to Attention Deficit Hyperactivity Disorder in Children*, this being the book parents are most often encouraged to get by pro-medication support groups. I read that parent's with children who have ADHD say things like: 'What I tell him goes in one ear and out of the other'; 'With homework I get nowhere unless I stand over him'; 'He's impossible in the morning'; 'He can remember details of what happened to him last year but forgets what I said two minutes ago'; 'He doesn't seem to learn from experience'; 'He has no road sense'; 'He's got such a short fuse'; 'She was such a demanding baby she took up every minute of my life'; 'This toddler is constantly on the move'; 'She hates to be restricted, she loves to be outside' and so on. I could not understand this. The book was describing mine and I reckon most parents' children. Why were these extremely common behaviours (particularly amongst boys) being listed as if they were signs of what the book refers to as a 'biological, brain-based condition' (Green and Chee, 1997:2)? It felt like I was reading an astrological prediction, the descriptions were so general that after reading it my wife and I were both convinced that we as well as our children must be suffering from ADHD! I wondered what I would have thought on reading this, if I were a parent who was worried about my child's behaviour or development?

I began to think about the 'big picture'. What was this all about? It dawned on me that the concept of ADHD was intimately tied up with our modern Western beliefs about childhood and child rearing. Social pressures build up certain expectations for children to live up to. Parents (and other guardians such as teachers) feel blamed when their children cannot be squeezed into a socially desirable shape. Doctors as powerful priests of knowledge then define this problem medically and hey presto – a gravy train for the multi-million dollar pharmaceutical industry.

But is all this medicalization good for children and their families? I guess it has helped some. But then I see boy after boy who has been diagnosed and medicated for years coming to my clinics. I see boy after boy who hates taking these medicines. I discuss the controversies with the parents and nearly all want to subsequently reduce the dose or bring their children off their tablets. I have seen boy after boy come off stimulants. Parents tell me children started eating normally again, put on weight, came out of their shell and began to express themselves again. They were transformed (as a pro-Ritalin advocate might say). I wondered what all those years on these tablets were doing to their brains and bodies for such dramatic changes to be noticed. I wondered if this is another Valium story in the making. I wondered how many of my colleagues discuss the controversies and air both sides of the story with their clients. I wondered how many parents are routinely denied the information about risks they need to make a properly informed choice. I wondered if this individualized medicalization of a child is a sign that many doctors have completely forgotten what a community is. I wondered if the problem is this apparent enormous rise in the number of boys suffering from a medical condition or is it a growing problem in the system/society that manages them.

A New Category of Childhood – the ADHD Child

In Chapter 2 I illustrated how childhood in Western society is increasingly viewed through a biological 'genetic' framework and the dangers for children this holds. Schools are struggling with being under-resourced, using labour-intensive 'modern' educational methods in highly stimulating colourful classes, under pressure to demonstrate ever-improving academic achievement in their pupils, with ever less methods for behavioural control of children at their disposal. John, One of their more distractible and boisterous children gets a diagnosis of ADHD and starts taking Ritalin. He is no longer a big problem; he does as he is told. The school has saved money, instead of having to provide extra input for his 'special' needs, the teachers realize that John had a medical disorder and now that it is being treated he is fine. John's teacher realizes that John's friend Paul seems to be similarly distractible and boisterous. She meets with Paul's parents and tells them that she wonders if Paul too has this ADHD and advises them to see their general practitioner. Paul gets a diagnosis and starts taking Ritalin too. Soon other teachers have started identifying children in their classes like John and Paul. A process has been set rolling. A year down the line John's old pattern of behaviour seems to be returning.

Teachers agree that there could be many reasons for this (His parents have split up and he has started with a new teacher) but wonder if it could be due to the treatment for his medical condition (ADHD) not being adequate. The school writes a letter that John's mum takes to his consultant and John's dose of Ritalin is increased. Soon Paul's dose also goes up. Other teachers talk about this and become aware that some of the children in their class may not be getting adequate medication. Another process is set in motion.

Meanwhile John's consultant has attended a couple of drug company–sponsored seminars, has been contacted by a drug company representative and has been given parent and teacher information booklets by this representative (which describes ADHD as being caused by an inherited chemical imbalance in the brain and has pretty pictures of nerve cell synapses to 'show' exactly what is going on in ADHD brains). This literature now goes into local circulation and other parents start contacting their doctor expressing concern that their child may have ADHD. A local parents' support group is set up and they join a national consumer pressure group (who organize yearly conferences with drug company's financial help). The local paper interviews the parents' group who talk about 'hidden disabilities' and how for years they struggled but no one recognized the psychiatric problem their children had. By now ADHD is firmly established in local culture with economically and politically powerful groups (drug companies, doctors, teachers) having had a major, but often unacknowledged impact on local communities' conception concerning the nature of childhood. A new category of childhood has emerged – that of the ADHD child.

In the last three years I have inherited many children who were diagnosed with ADHD and prescribed a stimulant at the time I took over their care. One of the most obvious impacts of the ADHD diagnosis on the previous professional's views about these children was the almost complete lack of attention to context. Thus I saw children who were missing their absent father, I saw parental discord, I saw children from failing schools that were under special measures, I saw depressed mums who were not coping, I saw families with poor support networks, I saw children with attachment issues, I saw adopted/fostered children who were used to rejection, I saw children who could not grieve a lost relative, I saw very bright children who used their intelligence to get round a system, I saw frightened parents whose children knew what buttons push, I saw busy parents who didn't have the time to get to know their children, I saw frightened teachers who were unsure how to handle the boys in their class, I saw tired and worn-out teachers who had had enough of teaching and so on. I looked in vain to see if the previous doctors had noticed the strengths and abilities of these children and their families.

I seriously wondered why we doctors get paid so much. For what? If we have lost the ability to work with and take account of even the most basic 'barn door' obvious psychosocial issues, how, as consultants, could we be expected to deal competently with complexity and the common but subtle problems that arise in interpersonal family life? These children were now on toxic addictive drugs, whilst the problems in their psychosocial context had yet to be tackled. What sort of medicine is this?

I started as a consultant child-and-adolescent psychiatrist in Lincolnshire some three plus years ago. In my first two years I was working in a community patch that was part rural and part inner city urban. I inherited 26 children who, at the time of my starting in this patch, were taking stimulants. Many of the clients I inherited had been seen by a consultant child-and-adolescent psychiatrist (who still had a local community patch that overlapped mine) and who was a strong believer in the ADHD diagnosis and the use of psychopharmacology (often multiple prescriptions and in high doses) in children. The local community paediatrician was also a firm believer in the diagnosis and use of stimulants in children. Consequently, the local community had already been 'cultured' into believing in ADHD and the merits of drugging children to control their behaviour. Amongst the 26 children on stimulants I inherited at the time I took over, the average age was 12.7 years, the average daily dose these children were taking was 41 mg of Ritalin (or Ritalin equivalent, the maximum licensed dose for Ritalin is 60 mg per day, the maximum I inherited was a child on 100 mg a day) and the average number of years the children had been taking a stimulant was 3.5 years. By the time I moved jobs after two years, only 6 of the 26 I inherited remained on a stimulant, 16 children had come off the stimulant through a co-operative effort with the child's parents, two children had their prescription discontinued through persistent non-attendance (in the United Kingdom Ritalin prescription requires that the child is followed up by a specialist) and two children were lost to follow up by me after I raised child protection concerns. Of the six who remained on stimulant medication at the time of my departure, the average daily dose was about half the dose they were taking when I inherited them. During the time that I was working in this community patch I commenced medication for five children on a low dose of stimulants, two of which had discontinued by the time I left. Many families expressed dissatisfaction at previous interventions feeling that the medication-centred approach was too narrow and did not take into account their history and particular situation. I continue to discover that many families have a far more sophisticated understanding of psychosocial causes of behavioural problems than most psychiatrists and paediatricians I meet these days.

I then moved to a smaller community patch that is predominantly rural and had been working there for just over a year when I audited the number of children under my care who were or had been taking a stimulant. Prior to my starting in this patch, this area had not had a permanent consultant child-and-adolescent psychiatrist for the two years prior to my arrival. Instead a succession of locum consultants had been covering the vacancy including several stints from a consultant whose main practice was in Canada. Despite my new patch having a much smaller population than my previous one (this being only part of my current responsibilities, the other being the Lincolnshire in-patient adolescent unit), I inherited 28 children on stimulants. At the time I started seeing these children the average age of the children on stimulants I inherited was 10.2 years, the average daily dose of Ritalin (or Ritalin equivalent) was 18.9 mg and the average number of years the children had been taking a stimulant was 1.7 years. Just over a year on only four children remained on stimulants. Two children (siblings) are now seeing another doctor (after I raised child protection concerns). I have not needed to start medication for a single child on a stimulant and am hopeful that the remaining four will be able to come off their medication within a year. The local community paediatric service are much more cautious prescribers than that in my previous patch and having met with them I am aware that they are prescribing stimulants to no more than eight other children in my area.

A Brief History of ADHD

Over-activity, poor concentration and impulsivity in children were first conceptualized as medical phenomena earlier this century. The first recorded interest in children with poor attention and hyperactivity dates back to the turn of the century when a paediatrician, Frederick Still, described a group of children who showed an abnormal incapacity for sustained attention, restlessness and fidgetiness, and went on to argue that these children had deficiencies in volitional inhibition, but offered no treatment other than good discipline (Still, 1902).

Hyperactivity and poor attention in children then came to be viewed as linked when the diagnosis of minimal brain damage (MBD) was coined. The idea of MBD had originally gained favour following epidemics of encephalitis in the first decades of the twentieth century. Post-encephalitic children often presented with restlessness, personality changes and learning difficulties. Then, in the 1930s, came a chance discovery that psycho-stimulant medication could reduce the restlessness, hyperactivity and behavioural problems that these children presented with (Bradley, 1937). Bradley believed that this calming effect he observed is likely to apply to anyone who took low dose of stimulants, not just the hyperactive kids he was treating.

Not long after this episode, a number of doctors began to speculate that children who presented as hyperactive might have organic lesions in the brain, which was causing their hyperactivity. Strauss's writings in the 1940s (e.g. Strauss and Lehtinen, 1947) strengthened this idea further by his suggestion that hyperactivity, in the absence of a family history of subnormality, should be considered as sufficient evidence for a diagnosis of brain damage, believing that the damage was too minimal to be easily found.

By the 1960s, however, the term MBD was losing favour as evidence for underlying organic lesions in children who displayed poor attention and over-activity was not being found. Instead, with the growing interest in behaviourally defined syndromes, the goal posts were moved and a behaviourally defined syndrome was first articulated at that time. Despite the abandonment of the minimal brain damage hypothesis the assumption that this syndrome does indeed have a specific and discoverable physical cause, related to some sort of brain dysfunction, survived in the new definition. Yet, studies have shown that demonstrable minimal brain damage due to a variety of causes predisposes the child to the development of a wide range of psychiatric diagnosis as opposed to a particular type, such as ADHD (Schmidt *et al.*, 1987). Rutter (1982) concluded that the available evidence shows that over-activity is usually not a sign of brain damage and that brain damage does not usually lead to over-activity. I am not aware of any research that contradicts that conclusion.

So it was that in the mid-1960s the North American-based Diagnostic Statistical Manual (DSM), second edition (DSM-II), coined the label 'Hyperkinetic reaction of childhood' to replace the diagnosis of MBD (American Psychiatric Association, 1966; Sandberg, 1996). Over the follow-ing three decades this new behaviourally defined condition rose from a matter of peripheral interest in child psychiatric practice and research in North America to a place of central prominence.

In the early 1980s, DSM II was replaced by the third edition (DSM-III, American Psychiatric Association, 1980). The disorder was now termed Attention Deficit Disorder (ADD). This could be diagnosed with or without hyperactivity and was defined using three dimensions (three separate lists of symptoms): one for attention deficits, one for impulsivity and one for hyperactivity. The three-dimensional approach was abandoned in the late eighties when DSM III was revised (and became DSM-III-R, American Psychiatric Association, 1987), in favour of combining all the symptoms into one list (one dimension). The new term for the disorder was 'Attention Deficit Hyperactivity Disorder', with attention, hyperactivity and impulsiveness now assumed to be part of one disorder with no distinctions. When the fourth edition of DSM (DSM-IV, American Psychiatric Association, 1994) reconsidered the diagnosis the criteria were again changed, this time in favour of a two-dimensional model with attention deficit being one sub-category and hyperactivity-impulsivity the other. With each revision, a larger cohort of children is found to be above the threshold for diagnosis. For example, changing from DSM-III to DSM-III-R more than doubled the number of children, from the same population diagnosed with the disorder (Lindgren *et al.*, 1994). Changing from DSM-III-R to DSM-IV increased the prevalence by a further two-thirds, with the criteria now having the potential to diagnose the vast majority of children with academic or behavioural problems in a school setting (Baumgaertel *et al.*, 1995). Indeed according to DSM-IV, the diagnosis 'ADHD not otherwise specified' should be made if there are prominent symptoms of inattention or hyperactivity-impulsivity that do not meet the full ADHD criteria (DSM-IV, American Psychiatric Association, 1994). If we were to interpret this concretely (as doctors often do) it suggests that nearly all children (particularly boys) at some time in their lives could meet one of the definitions and warrant a diagnosis of ADHD.

In the United Kingdom, child psychiatrists, in the past, have generally followed the diagnostic guidelines of the International Classification of Diseases (ICD) in preference to DSM. The latest edition of ICD (ICD-10, World Health Organization, 1990) has a more explicit definition of hyperkinetic disorder than its predecessor, ICD-9. In common with the trend in DSM revisions, centres that changed from using ICD-9 to ICD-10 criteria also noticed that the diagnosis was being made more frequently (Steinhausen and Erdin, 1991). However, practice in the United Kingdom has moved towards using ADHD as the diagnosis of choice in preference to hyperkinetic syndrome thereby following the terminology used in American practice (Britain after-all has a reputation of being America's poodle).

Just to muddy the waters further, there is another related diagnosis – that of DAMP (pun intended, as these diagnosis just get more ridiculous by the day). DAMP refers to 'Deficits in Attention, Motor control and

Perception', and is a term developed and commonly used in Nordic countries to cover most of the children previously referred to as having MBD and which can also be applied to many children with a diagnosis of ADHD (Gilberg, 1987; Gilberg *et al.*, 1989). In the rest of this chapter and for the sake of convenience I will mainly refer to the diagnosis that is the driving force behind the current epidemic of prescriptions of stimulants to children – ADHD.

The modern champion of the ADHD diagnosis and one of the strongest advocates for a brain dysfunction model and the use of drugs to 'treat' these children is Prof. Russell Barkley. Barkley's (1981) book *Hyperactive Children: A Handbook for Diagnosis and Treatment*, received widespread attention from both the public and the professional community. From there Barkley's campaign quickly caught the interest of the pharmaceutical industry and soon an avalanche of research to find more support for the disease theory and drug treatment ensued. Despite the volume of research and publications there is still no good evidence that supports the conclusion that ADHD is a medical disorder or that drug treatment is safe and effective (pp. 119–139). DeGrandpre (1999) has aptly summarized the research that is being produced by the ADHD industry as 'junk science'.

The Genetically Programmed Child and ADHD, is the Scientific Evidence Good Enough?

Domination of the world's markets allows American culture to be successfully exported. Along with Coca-Cola, McDonalds and Hollywood, pseudo-medical constructs such as ADHD are becoming a part of everyday culture in other Western countries and slowly creeping into the collective consciousness of many non-industrialized countries too. An enthusiastic drug industry and drug-industry-funded pro-medication parent groups, using the tools given to them by prominent bio-psychiatrists helped establish ADHD as the main diagnostic label to use. This is evident by clinics that have been set up in this country (the United Kingdom), both private and National Health Service (NHS), being called ADHD clinics as opposed to 'Hyperkinetic disorder' clinics (the term used in ICD 10). Titles used in publications, media reports and academic conferences now refer to ADHD, with it the less money-spinning term 'Hyperkinetic syndrome' seems disappearing into the pages of history.

So what is the evidence for the existence of this disorder? Is there a medical test that will diagnose it? No. Are there any specific cognitive, metabolic or neurological markers for ADHD? No. ADHD is a cultural construct diagnosed on the basis of clinical opinion and faithful belief of the practitioner and often presented as if it were a biological fact. Those who have argued that ADHD does not exist as a real disorder start by pointing to the obvious uncertainty about its definition (McGuiness, 1989). Indeed, despite years and billions of dollars spent on research, the validity of ADHD or hyperkinetic disorder as a disorder distinct from other types of behavioural disturbances in childhood, particularly those involving aggressive and defiant behaviours, has not been established (Prior *et al.*, 1986; Werry *et al.*, 1987a, b). Because of the uncertainty about definition, it is hardly surprising that epidemiological studies have produced very different prevalence rates for ADHD or hyperkinetic disorders, ranging from about 0.5 per cent of school-aged children to 26 per cent of school-aged children (Taylor and Hemsley, 1995; Green *et al.*, 1999).

Epidemiological studies have found a preponderance of boys over girls in ADHD symptomatology in the region of four (or more) to one (McGee *et al.*, 1992). This is very similar to the gender distribution found in conduct disorder and other so-called externalizing behavioural disorders in children. The meaning of this gender distribution never seems to be questioned. What sort of biological variable are we attempting to categorize here if this is a biological abnormality? Is it that boys generally have bad genes compared to girls? Is it something to do with the normal biological differences between male and female genes? Is there an interaction between boy's behaviour and changes in social expectations regarding children's behaviour generally? Do social changes in family structure, lifestyles, teaching methods, classroom sizes, rates of violence, rates of substance misuse and so on have an effect on perceptions and beliefs about boy's and girl's behaviour, or even on their behaviour directly? Has life got harder for boys in some way? Has life got harder for parents trying to control normal boy behaviour? Are we still compelled to pay more attention to the externalized behaviour of boys than the internalized behaviour of girls, only now we medicalize this (after all adults in Western societies are usually more tolerant of hyperactivity in girls than in boys (Battle and Lacey, 1972)? Do changes in teaching methods and a pre-dominance of female teachers have an effect on how we understand and deal with boys' behaviour? These and other social/cultural questions relating to ADHD are never discussed in the medical literature in general and child psychiatric literature in particular, where there is a shocking lack of engagement with perspectives from other disciplines. The gender distribution problem, has led some researchers to try and bypass this cultural construct issue by rather creatively suggesting that biologically the same disorder may present as attention deficit without hyperactivity in girls, thereby evening out the gender ratio (Lahey *et al.*, 1994).

Despite attempts at standardizing criteria and assessment tools in cross-cultural studies, major and significant differences between raters from different countries continue to be apparent (Mann *et al.*, 1992). For example, a cross-cultural study examining clinicians' ratings of the same video tapes of hyperactive and anti-social children (Prendergast *et al.*, 1988) showed that at the time the study was done, British child-and-adolescent psychiatrists in the study tended to give more weight to anti-social features and select a diagnosis of conduct disorder, whereas their American colleagues paid attention to hyperactivity signs and identified a primary hyperactivity disorder more readily. It was suggested in this paper that the difference in prevalence between the two countries was an issue of diagnostic practice, training and attitude, not a true epidemiological difference and as a result that British child psychiatrists should diagnose a 'primary hyperactivity disorder' more often. Not only does this illustrate the political direction favoured when clinicians disagree but also that these categories are cultural constructs in the first instance and therefore whatever constructs you have grown to believe in will naturally lead you to focus in that direction. This example of two groups of psychiatrists is quite interesting, as it would seem to show that the different belief systems that the psychiatrists held led to a different focus when it came to observing the same sets of behaviours and therefore a different diagnostic conclusion. I am not here suggesting that one is better than the other, but I am making the point that both are culturally constructed belief systems.

This is further confirmed when you look at clinical practice within a country, let alone between them. For example, Rappley *et al.* (1995) found that the rate of diagnosis varied by a factor of ten from county to county within the same state (in the United States). There are also significant differences between raters when raters rate children from different ethnic minority backgrounds (Sonuga-Barke *et al.*, 1993). One replicated finding is an apparently high rate of hyperactivity in China and Hong Kong (Shen *et al.*, 1985; Luk and Leung, 1989). In these studies nearly three times as many Chinese as English children were rated as hyperactive. A more detailed assessment of these results suggested that most of the 'hyperactive' Chinese children would not have been rated as hyperactive by most English raters and were a good deal less hyperactive than English children rated as 'hyperactive' (Taylor, 1994). One suggestion for such a consistently large disparity in hyperactivity ratings between Chinese and English children is that it may be due to the great importance of school success in Chinese culture leading to an intolerance of much lesser degrees of disruptive behaviour (Taylor, 1994). Whatever the reason(s), it demonstrates that hyperactivity and disruptiveness in boys is a highly culturally constructed entity.

That ratings of hyperactivity, inattention and disruptiveness are highly culturally dependent is not surprising as inattention, impulsivity and motor restlessness are found in all children (and adults) to some degree. Diagnosis is based on an assessment of what is felt to be developmentally inappropriate intensity, frequency and duration of the behaviours, rather than on its mere presence. All the symptoms described in this disorder are of a subjective nature (e.g. 'often does not seem to listen when spoken to') and therefore highly influenced by the rater's cultural beliefs and perceptions about such behaviours. After all how do you operationalize, define and understand non-specific words like 'often' and 'excessive', which are invariably found in ADHD rating questionnaires?

Then there is the whole thorny question of co-morbidity. Numerous epidemiological and clinical studies demonstrate the high frequency with which supposedly separate child psychiatric disorders occur in individuals with ADHD (Caron and Rutter, 1991). In children with ADHD, co-morbidity with other child psychiatric conditions is common no matter what definition is used (Beiderman *et al.*, 1991). It is estimated that about half the children with ADHD also have a conduct disorder, about half also have an emotional disorder, about one-third have an anxiety disorder and another third have major depression (Barkley, 1994). Co-morbidity is so prevalent that at least three quarters of ADHD-diagnosed children will have at least one other diagnosable child psychiatric condition (Hazell, 1997). The co-occurrence of the symptoms that make up oppositional/defiant and conduct disorders with those that make up hyperactivity and attention deficit disorders is so strong (Szatmari *et al.*, 1989b; Beiderman *et al.*, 1991; Fergusson *et al.*, 1991, 1993) that many commentators have questioned the reality of the distinction between them (Hinshaw, 1987). What does this all mean?

Psychiatrists have adopted co-morbidity as a way of trying to explain clinical reality when it does not appear to tally with research-generated views of mental life. It is a way of maintaining a fantasy that there is a natural, probably biological, boundary where no natural boundaries exist (Tyrer, 1996). This may be because in conditions such as ADHD, like many other psychiatric diagnosis, the extent to which neuronal circuits in the brain are involved vary individually and do not have an obvious one-to-one causal relationship with the psychiatric diagnoses (Van Praag, 1996). In other words if, or when, we get to the stage where we are able to do reliable tests to pick up some sort of chemical imbalance in the brain, we may well find that there is no obvious correspondence between say (for the sake of argument) a dopamine imbalance and the symptoms of ADHD. Some children with a dopamine imbalance will have symptoms of ADHD, which may well be causally related to this imbalance, and others with symptoms of ADHD would not (and therefore in these children dopamine imbalance could not be causally related). Furthermore the massive amounts of co-morbidity present suggests that our current diagnostic framework does not reflect boundaries between 'naturally' occurring syndromes related to a biological cause. To take up my example of a dopamine imbalance again, this means that if you suffer from a dopamine imbalance it is likely that what we will discover is that in one child this imbalance causes ADHD-type symptoms, in another it causes more anxiety-type symptoms, in another it causes a mixture of ADHD-type and depressive-type symptoms, in another it causes no symptoms at all and so on. In such a scenario, the current diagnostic system would in a medical sense become redundant; instead we would have more clearly physically valid diagnosis (e.g. Dopamine Imbalance Syndrome) and a medical way of establishing the physical component to a mental health problem. Furthermore, we would have a clear rational scientific basis for the physical component of any treatment and for building coherent scientific research-based knowledge of this physical component. Only when there is a clear test to establish this physical component is a medical linear argument valid. Until then, in any individual child, it is pure speculation. Castles built on sand, if the foundation assumption is wrong the castle collapses.

This lack of a coherent concept is reflected in the lack of consensus on the question of possible causal mechanisms. Thus the condition was initially viewed as being due to an underlying, excessive motor activity in the child (Schachar, 1991) and later as being due to an underlying central attention deficit (Douglas, 1972, 1983). Others have suggested that the central deficit is one of generalized intellectual impairment (Werry *et al.*, 1987a) or of motivation (Draeger *et al.*, 1986). The conviction held by a number of influential researchers about the likely central deficit has had a big influence on the behavioural definitions of the disorder. For example, Douglas's belief (1972) that attention, not hyperactivity, was the essential feature distinguishing these children from other difficult and disruptive children led to the establishment of the 'Attention Deficit Disorder (ADD)' definition in DSM-III. There is not even consensus on whether the core behaviours (of inattention, impulsivity and hyperactivity) need always be present (i.e. pervasive) or need to be observable in only one situation (e.g. school or home) for a diagnosis to be valid. Some suggest that the behaviours need to be pervasive (e.g. Taylor *et al.*, 1991) and others conclude that pervasiveness is not a necessary condition of a valid definition (e.g. Szatmari *et al.*, 1989a).

Claims have been made that neuro-imaging studies have confirmed that ADHD is a brain disorder. Closer examination of the quoted studies not only reveals a more complex picture, but also actually suggests the opposite, as the studies demonstrate that there is no characteristic neuro-physiological pattern that can be found in children diagnosed as having ADHD. Brain scan studies have not uncovered a consistent deficit or abnormality, with a wide variety of brain structures being implicated, for example: Striatal, Orbital, Prefrontal, Fronto Posterior and Medial Orbital areas, Caudate Nucleus, Corpus Calosum and Parietal lobe (see Rapport, 1995). The sample sizes in the studies have all been small and in none of these neuro-imaging studies have the brains of the ADHD-diagnosed children been considered to be clinically abnormal in any way (Hynd and Hooper, 1995) nor has any specific abnormality been convincingly demonstrated (Baumeister and Hawkins, 2001). Interestingly, after almost 25 years and over thirty studies, researchers have yet to do a simple comparison of unmedicated children diagnosed with ADHD with an age-matched control group (Leo and Cohen, 2003). Most worryingly, animal studies suggest that any differences observed in these studies could well be due to the effects of medication that most children in these studies had taken (Breggin, 1999, 2001a; Moll *et al.*, 2001; Sproson *et al.*, 2001).

What we end up with is speculative 'biobabble'. Even if consistent differences in neuro-imaging studies were found, unidirectional cause and effect cannot be assumed if there is an absence of anatomical abnormalities. This is because neuro-physiological measures may reflect different children's different reaction to the same situation causing differences in brain chemistry rather than different brain chemistry causing different behaviour (Christie *et al.*, 1995). Thus, differences in brain function have been demonstrated in normal healthy children who have different temperaments (Fox *et al.*, 1995). There is also much evidence to show that changes in brain physiology can result from psychological factors. Thus Schwartz *et al.* (1996) demonstrated that when individuals suffering from obsessive compulsive disorder were successfully treated with cognitive behavioural therapy similar changes in brain physiology took place when compared to those successfully treated with an anti-depressant. Rappaport (2003) demonstrated that changes can be seen in the brain physiology of pupils with a diagnosis of dyslexia after undertaking a two-week course in remedial reading; and Leuchter *et al.* (2002) showed that changes can be seen in brain function of depressed patients successfully treated with a placebo. As things stand we really do not know enough about what any differences in brain function-measures/size really mean. At the turn of the century doctors used to measure the size and shape of the part of the skull housing the brain. They came up with all sorts of statistical differences and used these to justify a 'scientific' basis for, amongst other things, the prevailing racist views of the time. This now-discredited 'science' was known as phrenology. If we cannot stop ourselves from impulsively jumping to unwarranted conclusions about the reasons for differences found in brain-scanning studies, we will create modern day phrenology.

In the rest of medicine, what has made diagnosis a useful way of categorizing health problems is that the diagnoses point to unique aetiological process. There is nothing strange about this opinion as many commentators have pointed out that ultimately useful categorizations in medicine are ones that point to unique aetiological processes (Taylor, 1988; Beiderman *et al.*, 1991; Klein and Riso, 1994). These unique aetiological processes are completely absent from most psychiatric diagnosis and similarly in ADHD no unique aetiological processes have been identified, very much the reverse in fact as the evidence above appears to demonstrate. Indeed, the National Institute of Health, a government body in the United States, concluded that there is no evidence to support the proposition that ADHD is a biological brain disorder (NIH, 1998). This conclusion is further supported by a large body of family (Cantwell 1972; Welner *et al.*, 1977; Stewart *et al.*, 1980), twin (Graham and Stevenson, 1985; Stevenson and Graham, 1988; Goodman and Stevenson, 1989; Gillis *et al.*, 1992; Eaves *et al.*, 1993; Rhee *et al.*, 1995; Thapar *et al.*, 1995) and adoption studies (Cantwell, 1975; Cunningham *et al.*, 1975) that support the idea that a genetic component contributes to hyperactivity, conduct disorder and other externalizing behaviours in a manner that suggests a common genetic mechanism underlies all these disorders (Silberg *et al.*, 1996). Presumably this common genetic mechanism has something to do with being boys. Unfortunately for the enthusiasts who wish on the basis of their 'bio-babble' to turn a blind eye to worrying cultural trends of increasing intolerance and hostility we in the West show towards children, as soon as you get into specifics their arguments start to fall apart. Thus professor Taylor argues that molecular genetic variations have been robustly replicated (Timimi and Taylor, 2004), in the chapter by Schachar and Tannock (2002) that Taylor sites, they conclude that ADHD is associated with the dopamine transporter gene (DAT1) and the dopamine receptor gene (D4), yet a more recent study of 126 sibling pairs concluded that these two genes if they are involved in ADHD aetiology at all make only a minor contribution to overall genetic susceptibility (Fisher *et al.*, 2002).

The assertion that ADHD is a genetic condition is another of those culturally constructed ideas that has developed as a result of advocates of the diagnosis, either deliberately or through ignorance, ignoring matters of context. If we take our starting assumption that behaviours such as motor activity, attention and impulsivity are normally distributed temperamental characteristics, then the evidence fits. Viewing these behaviours as temperamental characteristics as opposed to signs of a medical condition allows more attention to context. Research on children's temperament has shown that problems result from a mismatch between the child's temperament and their environment (Chess and Thomas, 1996; Thomas and Chess, 1977). Even children who are highly difficult temperamentally can become well adjusted behaviourally if their family and other social circumstances are supportive (Mazaide, 1989). Indeed a difficult temperament (such as high levels of activity and low attention span) is a poor predictor of future problems at school, the best predictors being parents' and then schools' ability to cope (Carey and McDevitt, 1995). What the genetic studies have been discovering is that the behaviours we call ADHD are probably inherited in much the same way as other personality traits, whether these behaviours come to be perceived as a problem is mediated by social factors. In their international consensus statement on ADHD, Barkley and 78 co-endorsers (2002) virtually admit this, when, in a spectacular own goal, they compare the genetics of ADHD to the genetics of height. Since when has height been considered a medical disorder?

Genetic studies on children diagnosed with ADHD suffer from many other inadequacies. Concluding that the higher rates of diagnosis in the identical twins as opposed to non-identical twins is evidence of genetic transmission ignores the substantial psychological difference involved in being an identical as opposed to a non-identical twin. For example, substantially more identical as opposed to non-identical twins report identity confusion and are more likely to be reared 'as a unit' (Joseph, 2003). Similarly research comparing incidence of ADHD and other psychiatric disorders in relatives of a child diagnosed with ADHD fails to consider the impact of environmental factors that could explain familial clustering. Research on possible environmental causes of ADHD-type behaviors has largely been ignored, despite mounting evidence that psychosocial factors such as exposure to trauma and abuse can cause them (Ford *et al.*, 1999, 2000).

Children described as having ADHD do not appear to have cognitive deficits in attentional mechanisms (Van Der Meere, 1996). The conclusion that children described as ADHD have inhibitory deficits due to abnormal brain functioning, which leads to them performing poorly on standard neuro-psychological tests of inhibition, has been undermined by studies that demonstrate that the impulsiveness is reduced when the link between fast responding and the length of the research session is removed (Sonuga-Barke *et al.*, 1994) (In other words when the possibility that these children where getting bored with the experimental test is taken into consideration). A very frequent clinical observation of children with poor concentration and impulsiveness is that this picture changes dramatically when they play their computer games or watch their favourite video, where many so-called ADHD children demonstrate a high ability to concentrate for extended periods of time (another example of typical boy behaviour).

Most 'middle-of-the-road' ADHD review articles thus conclude with broad sweeps that have little to offer the clinician in the way of aetiological explanation. For example, Hinshaw (1994: 64) concludes that 'the development of most cases of ADHD is more likely to constitute a complex intertwining of intra individual, familial and broader systems factors than a purely environmental or purely genetic causal route'. Schachar (1991: 181) concludes, 'Hyperactivity is thought to represent the behavioural manifestation of various underlying psychological, biological and social processes acting singly or in concert'. A British Psychological Society review paper (1996: 24) concluded, 'It is probably not useful to think of ADHD as a mental disorder given the current understanding of the psychological basis of the concept.'

In the rest of medicine this lack of ability to establish a cause would lead to the label 'idiopathic' (meaning without apparent cause) being applied to a disorder. Thus more a medically accurate label for these children would be 'Idiopathic inattention' or 'Idiopathic hyperactivity'. Despite the overwhelming evidence that ADHD cannot be conceptualized in a simplistic, linear, uni-causal way, authors in influential journals still write completely unsupported statements such as 'attention deficit hyperactivity disorder is a condition of brain dysfunction…it is a genetic, inherited condition' (Kewley, 1998: 1594). Articles such as this and many others in both the medical and the popular press, which offer propaganda for an opinion masquerading as fact, contribute to the process of the ADHD construct being passed on from the medical profession to the general public and into general cultural consciousness as if ADHD were an already understood biological condition.

These conceptual difficulties are no less problematic for those more 'moderate' of believers. In their article Recognising Hyperactivity: A Guide for the Cautious Clinician, Hill and Cameron (1999) stumble along in a clumsy manner not quite knowing how to conceptualize this construct. They conclude, 'in other words a primary hyperactivity disorder is a serious mental health problem, largely biologically determined' (Hill and Cameron, 1999: 52). A couple of pages later they have changed their mind 'Hyperactivity is a reflection of an underlying deficit that may have several ultimate causes but a common final path at a behavioural level' (Hill and Cameron, 1999: 54). The serious conceptual problem for the authors of how to separate this apparent multi-factorial hyperactivity from the biological condition is not tackled.

All those who take part in research and use the diagnosis of ADHD without questioning its basis have already taken the first leap of faith in accepting that 'There now appears to be little doubt about the validity of the concept' (Toone *et al.*, 1997: 489). Then there are the, in my opinion, religious fanatics like Dr Kewley quoted above. These fundamentalists see ADHD wherever they look. They view ADHD in a cult-like fashion believing it to be a biological and genetic condition that is more common than internationally recognized (Kewley, 1999). Dr Kewley believes that this medical illness undiagnosed and untreated (primarily by medication) leads to just about every psychosocial problem you could think of including; criminality, school exclusion, substance misuse, conduct disorder, lack of motivation, learning difficulties, poor self esteem, depression, obsessionality and so on. He then has the cheek to accuse others of perpetuating 'trite and simplistic explanations for the symptoms of the disorder'! (Kewley, 1999: 18).

In *Understanding ADHD: A Parent's Guide to Attention Deficit Hyperactivity Disorder in Children* (Green and Chee, 1997), everything seems to be explained in terms of ADHD. Thus children with ADHD can be 'superb at sports…One of Australia's rugby greats was recently in trouble for impulsive outbursts on the field' (Green and Chee, 1997: 33). On the previous page it is mentioned that children with ADHD are poor at sports because 'they have difficulty in coordinating a sequence of movement' (Green and Chee, 1997: 32). A whole host of social problems are also put down to ADHD, 'A common pattern for ADHD disordered men is to conceive then leave' (Green and Chee, 1997: 56) and 'the genes of ADHD predispose families to more restless, mobile, unsettled lifestyles. When I visit the remote mining towns of Australia I see many isolated mothers with challenging children. The busy men folk love the twenty four hour action of the mine' (Green and Chee, 1997: 56). Thus for the fanatics, even context is interpreted as being the result of a biological condition.

Such loose, unsubstantiated and easy option definitions (if only there was a quick diagnosis and instant cure for life's problems!) have many cultural knock-on effects (as well as golden opportunities to make some quick bucks). Rates of diagnosis in the United Kingdom have been increasing exponentially over the past decade. Private and NHS ADHD clinics are proliferating. It is even possible now to get a diagnosis of ADHD without ever being seen by a professional as some paediatricians, child psychiatrists and educational psychologists in the United Kingdom offer diagnosis over the phone or via the Internet (Baldwin and Anderson, 2000).

Fortunately, not everybody associated with the medical profession accepts unquestioningly the trite simplistic explanations put forward by the fundamentalists. For example professor Rose of the Brain and Behaviour Research Group with the Open University writes, referring to ADHD, 'This sudden emergence of a genetic disorder is puzzling. The result of mass mutations? Scarcely likely... All part of the medicalization of daily life. Naughty and disruptive children have doubtless always existed. In the past their unruly behaviour might have been ascribed to poor parenting, poverty, impoverished schools, or unsympathetic teachers... Now we blame the victim instead; there is original sin in them there genes.' (Rose, 1998: 317).

ADHD as Culture-specific Solution to Culture-specific Problems

The cultural preconditions for ADHD to become a popular idea have come about in the United Kingdom as it did in the United States. In response to the current cultural anxieties the types of solutions attempted are by and large culture specific. In this culture it means a market place commodity/consumer-driven solution. Anyone who works in the health service in the United Kingdom these days knows how much the culture in the health service has shifted towards a management-driven culture with management 'speak' being evident in the decision-making bodies. This in turn leads to a way in which the practice of medicine itself is influenced by issues of the hierarchy and power. In a health service becoming dominated by market-driven thinking (which has obviously influenced the private sector for a long time) service developments have to adapt their thinking to fit into this powerful influence on its own development.

ADHD, in the United Kingdom, has recently received a lot of coverage in the popular media. Most articles/programmes have advocated using this label (explicitly and implicitly by referring to ADHD, not for example 'hyperkinetic syndrome' or 'conduct disorder'), often citing examples of medical practice in North America for comparison (although there is some sign of a fight-back with some newspaper articles raising serious concerns, although they have tended to be in the middle-class read broad sheets). UK Pressure groups such as ADDIS have taken up ADHD as a medical concept and have become increasingly vocal in advocating the use of the American Diagnostic Statistical Manual label ADHD and the prescription of stimulant medication. In North America the national parent support group, Children and Adults with Attention Deficit Disorder (CHADD) has become a very powerful body defining ADHD as a 'neuro-biological thing'. CHADD, not surprisingly, receives significant funding from the drug company that makes Ritalin (Merrow, 1995). The process of the powerful medical establishment passing on the idea of there being a discoverable, biological disorder to the public having taken place, the effects of the consequent consumer pressure is already showing. Demand from parents, teachers, educational psychologists and general practitioners for ADHD assessments and for consideration of prescription of stimulants have increased enormously in the past few years.

The notion of ADHD is seductive and influential on practitioners as well as consumers. The encounter of doctor and patient follows a well-known cultural script involving a dependent sufferer and a healthy expert who is assumed to possess the skills and knowledge to diagnose an illness, have information about that illness and provide a treatment. In child psychiatry, practitioners have had to largely work outside this script in attempting to engage with the ambiguities and anxieties that children, their families and other professionals bring; a process that can be slow and stressful for the practitioner as well as their clients. ADHD is the biggest of a growing number of the so-called childhood psychiatric disorders where the traditional cultural script for doctor and patient can be followed. It thus has the potential to be packaged and marketed as a commodity.

As Freud (1930) noted, all cultures struggle with the difficult question of how to gain control over that source of suffering that comes from inter-personal relationships and all cultures develop ways of trying to regulate this complex area of life in an effort to try and reduce the suffering and negative emotion that comes with it (see Chapter 4, Timimi, 2002). In this sense I believe that ADHD can be seen as one of the most recent cultural defence mechanisms that has been invented as a cultural way of trying to deal with the growing anxieties about childhood development that are present in modern, Western culture. In such a scenario where no real expert knowledge on ADHD can be said to exist, the wish to define this disorder becomes complicit with the client's and families' wish to be controlled, to feel that there is certainty, an answer where really there is only uncertainty and questions.

The push towards greater use of the diagnosis and stimulants for mainly naughty boys has been hugely influenced by the macroeconomics of drug company (more about that later) and doctor's financial interests. In the United States, with the managed healthcare system being the bread and butter of the majority of psychiatrist's and paediatrician's work, when the more labour-intensive psychotherapies lost favour with healthcare insurers, doctors soon realized they could make more money by going down the psychopharmacology route than that of psychotherapy – much more. Doctors can earn three times more by 15-minute medication review follow-ups than a 45-minute visit with the child's family. Managed healthcare has meant an economic system has come to be built around DSM-IV diagnoses. In order to obtain a legitimate ticket to a service, you need a DSM-IV diagnosis. Thus DSM-IV has become a more than a mental health diagnostic manual; it is a legal, financial and ideological document, driving thinking about all sorts of emotions and behaviours, including those of our children towards evermore pathologization.

ADHD is a popular and popularized construct because it comes from the medical profession, which continues to have a high status in this culture. The belief amongst those scientific priests of ADHD is that it is a discoverable condition on which we can build scientific knowledge, even though they have started building the institute without first building the foundations. A jump in logic has taken place. Basically, some observable behaviour in children (such as inattention and hyperactivity) has changed in status from behaviours containing no more or less information (in isolation) than the inattention or hyperactivity as described by an observer, to becoming the basis of a primary diagnosis. The biomedical template is applied and the behaviours are interpreted as disorder. This leaves out several layers of experience and context that could contribute to any observed behaviour as well as the meaning given to the behaviour. This medical explanatory model has enormous cultural power. Naturally, most of the population will assume that once doctors have named these behaviours as a disorder, such a categorization must have a natural, scientific basis. This leads to the huge differences in the experiences of children with the label being interpreted as being of lesser importance when compared to the assumed similarity that children with a disorder are felt to possess. Once the cultural idea of the ADHD construct becomes rooted in everyday culture, children experiencing difficulties due to a variety of complex processes can now be given the label of an illness, with the accompanying illusion that with such a label, information, advice and scientific understanding of the child's condition is now available.

Anxieties about children's development and behaviour have grown enormously in modern, Western societies in recent times. In the hierarchy of professional relationships, medicine is in a strong position to influence other professions also trying to deal with this growing anxiety about children. In America, behavioural psychologists, trusting that neurologists will, in time, discover the characteristics of the central nervous system that makes behavioural categorizations valid (Homans, 1993) took up the disorder and along with medical institutions passed the concept on to educationalists and eventually policy makers (United States Department of Education, 1991). The medical profession has been ideally placed to influence other professions and eventually government policy, leading to the popularization of the concept and ever-widening boundaries of its definition. Once there has been greater cultural popularization of this idea, children, particularly boys, who are either failing academically or exhibiting behavioural problems at home or at school are suspected by a wide variety of professionals, parents, relatives and other influential people in the child's life of having ADHD. The highly subjective nature of the DSM-IV definition allows for some very liberal interpretations, making ADHD well placed as a potential dumping ground for a whole host of problems. Wolraich *et al.* (1990) showed that in only 30 per cent of already diagnosed children in their study did the home and school report that both fulfil the DSM-IV diagnostic criteria.

In addition to the ADHD construct being in an ideal position to act as a cultural defence mechanism, its popularity has been further strengthened through the growing interests in the merits of prescribing stimulant medication to children. There is little doubt that in the short-term methylphenidate, commonly known as Ritalin (the stimulant most frequently prescribed to children) results in clinical improvement in many children who show hyperactivity and poor attention, with decreases in motor activity and defiance frequently reported (Schachar and Tannock, 1997; Greenhill, 1998). This observation has acted as a powerful re-enforcer of the ADHD construct, many interpreting this as confirmatory evidence of the suspected physical causation (and therefore treatment) of the disorder. Baldessarini (1985) calls this sort of reasoning *allopathic* logic, meaning that because a drug produces an effect, there must be a disease. He sees this type of reasoning as false, misleading and invalid.

The evidence suggests that stimulants' central nervous systems effects are not limited to those children who can be defined by the boundaries of this disorder. Thus stimulants have been found to have the same cognitive and behavioural effects on otherwise normal children (Rapoport *et al.*, 1978, 1980; Donnelly and Rapoport, 1985; Garber *et al.*, 1996), aggressive children regardless of diagnosis (Campbell *et al.*, 1982; Spencer *et al.*, 1996) and children with co-morbid conduct disorder (Taylor *et al.*, 1987; Spencer *et al.*, 1996). This is not surprising. The pharmacological action of Ritalin on the brain is basically that of amphetamines (or its street name – speed) and cocaine (Volkow *et al.*, 1995). Adults who abuse drugs like speed get a high, one of whose components is a capacity to hyper-focus into very particular and intensely experienced sensory inputs (e.g. music). This psychochemical effect occurs in most of those who take speed. Similarly, when given to children this psychochemical effect is not diagnosis-dependent.

Research has focused almost exclusively on short-term outcomes. Why so little long-term studies from the manufacturers? Outcome research in Ritalin treatment has been shown to have serious shortfalls in methodology such as small samples, inadequate description of randomization or blinding and not accounting for withdrawals or drop-outs (Joughin and Zwi, 1999; Zwi *et al.*, 2000). A recent meta-analysis of randomized controlled trials of methylphenidate found that the trials were of poor quality, there was strong evidence of publication bias, short-term effects were inconsistent across different rating scales, side effects were frequent and problematic and long-term effects beyond 4 weeks of treatment were not demonstrated (Schachter *et al.*, 2001). Huyuh *et al.* (1999) in their medium-term outcome study discovered that about 30–50 per cent of children treated for an average of 64 weeks on Ritalin had a poor outcome. This was particularly so for the group receiving significantly higher doses of the stimulant medication. This fits with my clinical experience of children becoming tolerant to increasing doses of Ritalin. The few long-term studies that have been conducted suggest that stimulants do not result in any long-term improvement in either behaviour or academic achievement (Weis *et al.*, 1975; Rie *et al.*, 1976; Charles and Schain, 1981; Gadow, 1983; Hetchman *et al.*, 1984; Klein and Mannuzza, 1991). This concurs with the clinical impression that sometimes you can get a positive gain from a cautious approach to prescribing Ritalin, by approaching it as a window of opportunity and using it for a limited time in combination with non-drug approaches, and little by treating it as a wonder drug. Despite the complete lack of evidence for any long-term effectiveness, Ritalin is most usually prescribed continuously for seven, eight or more years, with children as young as two being prescribed the drug in increasing numbers despite the manufacturer's licence stating that it should not be prescribed to children under six (Baldwin and Cooper, 2000; Zito *et al.*, 2000).

A big fuss has been made about a large multi-centre trial in the United States, testing the efficacy of Ritalin (MTA, 1999a, b). I recently heard an eminent professor of child psychiatry in this country (the United Kingdom) state, at a large conference attended by child psychiatrists and paediatricians, saying that the implication of the results of this study is that we should be treating children with ADHD with medication as the first-line treatment and possibly without any other intervention. This extraordinarily narrow interpretation of the results, shows how some clinicians are hell-bent on stripping all context and controversy to bolster their beliefs (and their pockets) and without regard for the enormous impact such statements will have on clinical practice.

The study in question compared four groups of children who were given: medication only, intensive behavioural treatment, combined behavioural treatment and medication, and standard community care. The study concluded that the medication only and combined behavioural and medication groups had the best outcome, with the combined group having only a marginally better outcome than the medication only group. A closer look inevitably brings up important questions of how to interpret their results. As with other studies, serious methodological issues have been pointed out in relation to this one (Boyle and Jadad, 1999; Breggin, 2000; Leo, 2002). First, it was not a placebo-controlled double-blind clinical trial, in other words participants (patients, their parents and those treating them) knew they were taking active medication, nobody was taking a placebo (a non-active drug substitute) and so it is impossible to know how much any positive response was due to the expectation for a positive response. All the principle investigators were well-known staunch advocates of medication with long-established financial ties to the pharmaceutical industry, a conflict of interest that seriously compromises their judgements. The parents and teachers who participated in the study were exposed to pro-drug propaganda at the start of the study, putting them in a mindset of positive expectation for change in those children receiving medication. Interestingly there was one group who rated symptoms through observing children in the classroom, who were blind to the treatment status of the children they were observing (in other words they did not know which children were taking medication). These raters found no difference between any of the treatment groups on the behavioural measures they were using. Not surprisingly this important finding was given no importance in the study conclusions. There are also many question marks with regard to the selection and recruiting process, the behavioural interventions used and the lack of attention to the number of children experiencing side effects (up to two-thirds experience some side effects) and the dismissing of some reported side effects as probably being due to non-medication factors (Breggin, 2000).

Even if we accept the conclusions at face value, the findings are not particularly remarkable and only confirm what we already know, namely that this powerful medication has the potential to bring about large changes in behaviour in the short term. (this study was for 14 months, a long way off the many years Ritalin is usually given for). The comparison psychological treatment of behaviour therapy is another based on a medical linear construct and therefore of questionable quality. Presumably all those (researchers and their subjects) in the study are assuming there is such a 'biological' thing as ADHD and so are already being cultured into a disability mode. Then there is the small print, the bits that you do not notice if you only advertise the particular bias of the researchers in their conclusion. All four groups in the treatment programme showed sizable reductions in symptoms. The conclusion could have read 'Children not on medication made enormous improvements'. In none of the treatment groups was there a significant improvement in academic performance and there was little effect on social skills. Two thirds of the community treated group were also receiving stimulant medication during the period of the study, yet were placed in the poorer outcome category. The conclusion of the study that medication only is the most efficient and cost-effective treatment for ADHD clearly reflects the interests and agenda of the researchers and their paymasters.

The dogma from ADHD priests stating that Ritalin is a safe drug with few harmful side effects could not be further from the truth. Troublesome and frequently reported side effects include poor appetite, weight loss, growth suppression, insomnia, depression, irritability, confusion and mood swings, obsessive compulsive behaviours, psychosis, explosive violent behaviour, personality change, a flattening of the emotions which, when observed, looks like a zombie-like state, stomach ache, headaches, staring, disinterest, tachycardia, pituitary dysfunction, dizziness (Barkley *et al.*, 1990; Breggin, 1999, 2002; Cherland and Fitzpatrick, 1999; Adrian, 2001) and occasionally death due to its toxic effect on the heart (Baughman, 2002). Cramond (1994) has also reported that treatment with Ritalin is associated with a lowered self-esteem and suppression of creativity in some children. Ritalin may also have long-term adverse effects in as many as one-third of those treated, including subtle cognitive effects such as perseveration, preoccupations, sombreness and deterioration in performance on complex cognitive tasks (Sprague and Sleator, 1977; Solanto and Wender, 1989). The lack of long-term studies into the effects of Ritalin and other stimulants is a concern, as we do not really know what sort of effect giving an amphetamine-like substance has on the developing brain. Animal studies have found that that taking stimulants can cause a long-lasting change in the brain biochemistry of rats (Breggin, 1999, 2001a; Moll *et al.*, 2001; Robinson and Kolb, 2001; Sproson *et al.*, 2001). We often forget that stimulants are powerful amphetamine-like drugs with potentially addictive properties. Children become tolerant to its effect resulting in gradually increasing doses being given to children as years on a stimulant clock up. The potential for tolerance and addiction is further demonstrated by withdrawal states (known as the rebound effect, which manifests in increased excitability, activity, talkativeness, irritability and insomnia) seen when the last dose of the day is wearing off or when the drug is withdrawn suddenly (Zahn *et al.*, 1980). Stories of adults becoming addicted to prescribed stimulants are becoming more prevalent by the day (e.g. Wurtzel, 2002).

More difficult to assess is the possible socio-cultural effects such widespread use of stimulants in children may have. Doctors may be unwittingly convincing children to control and manage themselves using medication, a pattern that may carry on into adulthood as the preferred or only way to cope with life's stresses. Clinically I often come across children on stimulants that have admitted that they were secretly self-medicating at times of stress. Parents, teachers and others may lose interest in understanding the meaning behind an ADHD-labelled child's behaviour beyond that of an illness internal to the child that needs medication.

In North America, concern has been voiced about ADHD being diagnosed more frequently amongst children from families of low socio-economic status leading some authors to conclude that Ritalin is being misused as a drug for social control of children from disadvantaged communities (Kohn, 1989; McGuiness, 1989). The National Association for the Advancement of Colored People in the United States has offered strong testimony that young blacks are over-represented in the ADHD category and over-medicated and has been campaigning for black parents to reject such a diagnosis (British Psychological Society, 1996). The dynamics of Ritalin prescription in North America have changed in recent years, however, with the majority of those who get the prescription coming from white middle-class families (Olfson *et al.*, 2002). In this context the dynamic appears to be middle-class parent's fears about their children's education. The anxiety is that that if their children do not get into college or university, they are 'sunk'. Thus parents and the middle-class teachers of their children are converting this anxiety into more and more requests for the perceived performance-enhancing properties of stimulants, and with more children in classrooms taking stimulants many parents end up feeling their child is at a disadvantage if they do not (Diller, 1998, 2002).

This dynamic is reflected in the trend where stimulants are being prescribed to children without making a diagnosis. This trend has now become so established that in many areas of the United States, less than half the children prescribed stimulants reach even the broad criteria for making a diagnosis of ADHD (Wasserman *et al.*, 1999; Angold *et al.*, 2000).

Ritalin is a drug of abuse as it can be crushed and snorted to produce a high (Heyman, 1994). Surveys have shown that a significant proportion of adolescents in the United States self-report using Ritalin for non-medical purposes (Robin and Barkley, 1998). Accounts of abuse of Ritalin and other stimulants are increasingly being reported in the lay press (Ravenel, 2002). A national survey in the United States found that 2.8 per cent of high-school seniors had used Ritalin without a physician's prescription the previous year (Sannerud and Feussner, 2000). The neuro-chemical effects of Ritalin are very similar to that of Cocaine, which is one of the most addictive drugs. Cocaine users report that the effect of injected Ritalin is almost indistinguishable from that of Cocaine (Volkow *et al.*, 1995). Biederman's (1999) study on the likelihood of substance misuse amongst those with a diagnosis of ADHD treated with a stimulant concluded that they were less likely to abuse substances when compared to those with ADHD who were not treated with stimulants. However, Biederman's study has been criticized on a number of grounds including having a small number in the non-medication control group and an unusually high rate of substance abuse amongst the control group suggesting that this group was not representative (Ravenel, 2002). A much larger, community-based study (Lambert and Hartsough, 1998) found a significant increase in cocaine and tobacco dependence amongst ADHD subjects taking stimulants when compared to 'untreated' controls; furthermore, they discovered a linear relationship between the amount of stimulant treatment and the likelihood of either tobacco or cocaine dependence. Ritalin remains a controversial drug for reasons that go well beyond simply its side effects. Yet these important issues that should be important information for all parents trying to make the difficult decision as to whether or not to agree for their children to take a stimulant is information that is rarely given by prescribers (Baldwin and Cooper, 2000).

Despite these contradictions and concerns, the availability of a drug that is believed to treat a childhood biomedical illness has proved so attractive that prescription levels, certainly in North America and more recently in the United Kingdom, have spiralled to reach what can be considered epidemic proportions. General practitioners and paediatricians as well as child psychiatrists routinely prescribe stimulants to children in North America. National surveys of paediatricians (Copeland *et al.*,

1987) and family practitioners (Wolraich *et al.*, 1990) in the United States have found that over 80 per cent of children they diagnosed as having ADHD were treated with Ritalin. National consumption of Ritalin in the United States more than doubled between 1981 and 1992 (Drug enforcement Administration, 1994). Prescriptions of Ritalin have continued to increase in the nineties, with over 11 million prescriptions of Ritalin written in 1996 in the United States (McGinnis, 1997). The amount of psychotropic medication prescribed to children in the United States increased nearly threefold between 1987 and 1996, with over 6 per cent of boys of ages between 6 and 14 taking stimulants in 1996 (Olfson *et al.*, 2002), a figure that is likely to be much higher now. There has also been a large increase in prescriptions of stimulants to pre-schoolers (aged 2–4 years) (Zito *et al.*, 2000). One study in Virginia found that in two school districts, 17 per cent of white boys at primary school were taking stimulants (LeFever *et al.*, 1999). Despite this alarming evidence, advocates of diagnosis and medication still claim that the majority of children who warrant this diagnosis are not getting it or the (drug) treatment they need (e.g. Barkley and 78 co-endorsers, 2002). Of the children placed on stimulants, 80–90 per cent are boys (Zachary, 1997).

This phenomenal rise has led to the suggestion that ADHD has been conceived and promoted by the pharmaceutical industry in order for there to be an entity for which stimulants could be prescribed (McGuiness, 1989); after all the pharmaceutical industry knows that the way to sell psychiatric drugs is to sell psychiatric diagnoses. It is after all a multimillion dollar industry, with the National Institute of Mental Health (Karon, 1994), the US Department of Education (Merrow, 1995) and the Food and Drug Administration (Breggin, 1994, 1997) all having been involved in funding and promoting treatment which calls for medicating children with behavioural problems. It is claimed that the pharmaceutical companies Ciba & Novartis conspired and colluded to develop and promote the diagnosis of ADHD in a highly successful effort to increase the market for its product, Ritalin. This effort has included funding parent support groups, pro-medication research and payments to professionals to act as spokespeople for their companies or products (Breggin, 2000). The situation with drug companies controlling the agenda of scientific debate has become so bad that it is virtually impossible to climb up the career ladder without promotional support (e.g. to fund research, to speak at conferences, to write articles for journals) from drug companies. Thus we have reached the situation where most senior academics have long-standing financial links with drug companies, which inevitably seriously compromises the impartiality of their opinions (Burton and

Rowell, 2003). Similarly the impartiality of patient support organizations has to be questioned. In recent years it has become apparent that drug companies are using such consumer-lobbying groups to their advantage not only by (often secretly) generous donations, but also on occasion by setting up patient groups themselves (Herxheimer, 2003). The main pro-medication pro-ADHD consumer support group in North America is CHADD. CHADD has long received substantial amounts from drug companies, receiving an estimated $500,000 in 2002 (O'Meara, 2003). There are other support groups, for example in the United Kingdom the parent support group 'Overload', who have been campaigning for prescribing doctors to provide more information to parents about the cardiovascular and neurological side effects of stimulants, believing that many more parents would be likely to reject such medication if they were being properly informed about it by the medical profession. However, without the financial support of the multinational giants, their message rarely gets heard.

The Influence of Culture in Causing ADHD-type Behaviours, is Western Culture ADHD-ogenic?

Attention deficit hyperactivity disorder is being diagnosed in epidemic numbers in North America, an epidemic that is spreading to other parts of the Western world. There are two possible reasons why the rate of diagnosis of ADHD has increased so dramatically in recent years. First, this could be due to the way we view children's behaviour such that behaviours previously felt to be normal or given another meaning are now felt to represent a medical disorder (which I have explored above). Secondly, the increase could be due to a real increase in ADHD-type behaviours amongst children, in which case there must be an environmental cause for this. Of course it is possible and probable that the increase is due to a combination of both reasons. Either way, an exploration and understanding of environmental, social and cultural factors that could lead to a change in the way we view childhood behaviours or/and cause ADHD-like behaviours is central to the task of understanding the current epidemic.

Some of the reasons behind the epidemic can be found by looking at the nature of cultural, political and social changes that have occurred in Western countries in the past few decades (see also Chapter 4).

Our conception, in the West, of children's impulses has undergone several transformations in the last 100 years. Over the first half of the twentieth century, children were viewed as being endowed with strong and dangerous impulses that necessitated parents to wage a relentless battle against the child's sinful nature to control these. Post-Second-World-War children had been transformed into being almost completely harmless and parents were now being advised to allow babies and children to explore the world and to provide them with plenty of stimulation and opportunity for their impulses to have full expression (Wolfenstein, 1955). The right-wing backlash towards the end of the last century, together with a powerful children's rights culture, resulted in a contradictory view of children's impulses emerging. On the one hand, trying to control a child's impulses is viewed as potentially abusive of that child's human rights, on the other children's impulses are viewed as a danger to society and a threat that has to be controlled.

Life got tougher for American families. From the mid- to late 1970s, a marked shift in social welfare policies took place. American businesses became less profitable and so began cutting wages, speeding up production, increasing automation, weakening unions and curtailing welfare programmes. Efforts were made to lower taxes to boost businesses resulting in re-distributing income upwards by providing tax cuts for those in the highest income brackets. Losses in government revenues were partly offset by cuts in social welfare programmes (Harvey, 1990; Phillips, 1990). The gap between rich and poor increased, with families bearing the brunt of the worsening social conditions.

Being a parent in North America has become more and more difficult. Issues such as violence, poverty and the breakdown of the family unit have been affecting ever-increasing numbers of families (Long, 1996). The index for the social health of the United States, which is produced by Fordham University's Institute for social Policy, is based on 16 measures including infant mortality, homicide, teenage suicide, unemployment and drug abuse (Miringoff, 1994). This index gives a score ranging from 0–100 (with 100 being the best). The index score declined from 74 in 1970 to 41 in 1992 indicating growing adversity facing US families. In 1994, there were over 4000 children murdered, over 15 million children living in poverty and over 14 million children living in single-parent families (Children's Defence fund, 1994).

At the same time as successive American governments were introducing policies to favour the business sector at the expense of a welfare safety net, an ideological shift was taking place in order to justify these actions. Social programmes were no longer viewed as humane or necessary, but as a potentially counter-productive effort that causes dependence and indolence amongst its recipients. An increased hostility developed towards the notion of dependence on the state, creating a new marginalized 'under-class' crowded into no-go urban areas where underground economies (such as the drug trade) developed (Cohen, 1997).

American right-wing policies of a similar nature were imported into the United Kingdom in the early 1980s by the then British Prime Minister, Margaret Thatcher. The sense of social breakdown in the lives of children in this country (the United Kingdom) is also evident in the daily recurrent media reports and debates about school crises, discipline problems, expulsion, violence in the young, crime in the young, bullying, drug abuse, break-up of the family and breakdown in parent–teacher relationships. A study on what was loosely termed psychosocial disorders amongst the young (such as suicide attempts, alcohol and drug abuse, and criminality) concluded that there has been a sudden and sharp rise in these disorders throughout Europe and North America over the past couple of decades (*British Medical Journal*, 3 June, 1995). In the United Kingdom this has been occurring within the context of a dramatic widening of the social inequality gap over the recent decades, with by far the biggest group effected being lower-income families with children (Bradshaw, 1990).

As I discussed in Chapter 4, changes in social, political and economic circumstances are intimately connected with our common cultural beliefs and value systems. The last couple of decades of the twentieth century saw North America lead the way in promoting masculine competitive free market ideology and placing this at the centre of our value system. Socialism became a bad word, dependence and nurture came to be viewed as promoting passive helpless individuals who were of no use to society, and the cult of individualism blossomed. Notions of social responsibility diminished, to be replaced by worship at the mantle of the individual, Margaret Thatcher once famously saying, 'There is no such thing as society.' Social mobility was encouraged as the best way to defeat the massive levels of unemployment, with Norman Tebbit (a member of Margaret Thatcher's government) telling people they should 'get on your bikes' to go to where the work is. As in the United States, an under-class developed in the United Kingdom, with areas of urban deprivation that attracted an underground economy that often revolved around drugs and gangs.

The knock-on effect for children and families of this right-wing capitalist ideology has been appalling. These social stressors are likely to have contributed enormously to the sadly negative experiences so many children in the West experience from the moment they are born. Children are growing up in families with no fathers, looked after by mothers who have no support networks and whom the state believes should be working (there is no esteem or importance attached to the work of a mother in Western society), in communities where drugs are sold at their school gates and rival gangs shoot at each other in next door flats.

Could these increased life stressors for the young cause an increase in ADHD behaviours such as impulsivity, hyperactivity and distractibility? Perry and his co-workers (1995), pursuing a neuro-biological approach, note how the symptoms of ADD/ADHD closely parallel those that occur during trauma – the hyper-alertness, the need to act quickly, the need to be on the go at all times in the expectation of danger and the inability to turn attention to matters other than those of physical safety. Their hypothesis is that in a critical period in infancy some children experience trauma which initiates a habitual automatic response as though to some external threat. When older such children are sensitive to threat to a much greater extent than other children and revert, as it were, to a state of 'red alert' very easily. Thus as with post-traumatic stress, such children react quickly, over-actively, and not so much to their ordinary life as to anticipated threat.

Other 'brain development' researchers agree with this idea as more evidence is accumulating that shows that experience has physical/biological effects on the brain which is now seen as an organ capable of undergoing reorganization in response to experiences, particularly in childhood but right up into adulthood (Greenough *et al.*, 1987; Valenstein, 1998; Bloom *et al.*, 2001). This model is not intended as a parent blame model nor does it seek to avoid the interpersonal realities of life, but it does point out that what is traumatic to an adult may not be traumatic to a child and vice versa (Offord, 1998). Empirical support for this idea can be found in the little bit of research that has been done on possible environmental causes of ADHD-type behaviors (not surprisingly this area has largely been ignored by the drug company–funded ADHD gurus), which has found that psychosocial factors such as exposure to trauma and abuse can cause them (Ford *et al.*, 1999, 2000).

Breggin (1994, 1997) has put forward a strong case for the missing role of the absent father causing the ADHD-type behaviours seen in children with the diagnosis and has renamed the syndrome DADD (Dad's Attention Deficit Disorder). He believes that loving attention from their fathers is an effective curative factor for these children. In a similar vein attachment theory suggests that the modern stressful social situation is having a dire and negative impact on the ability of parents to provide the sort of strong, secure and positive relationship children need with their parents. An accumulation of stresses on a family (such as lack of support, unresolved loss, poor relationship with father, insufficiently positive maternal model, pregnancy and birth complications and difficult infant temperament), in some families, it is hypothesized, causes increasingly negative interactions to develop between a child and their parent(s) leading to exhaustion, frustration and irritability in the parent and challenging and hyperactive behaviour in the growing child, which in turn leads to a reinforcing demand-dissatisfaction cycle (Stiefle, 1997).

Lieberman and Pawl (1990) argue that impulsivity, recklessness, negative attention seeking, hyperactivity and poor concentration may represent a defensive adaptation on the part of a child in the context of an insecure attachment relationship. Similarly, Speltz (1990) interprets the dyscontrol and non-compliance of young insecurely attached children as an attempt to control the proximity of the carer via problem behaviour. Putting the two above hypotheses together – that is increased life stressors in modern society and the resulting weakening of family structures leading to insecure attachment amongst children – we have a powerful culture-specific explanation for the current epidemic of ADHD. But there are plenty more.

A post-modern analysis of discourse and power suggests that a mother-blaming culture maybe another important factor in the rise of ADHD diagnoses. In this explanatory model mothers who hear the negative judgements of school and other parents experience a profound sense of self-blame, failure, guilt and helplessness as well as anger and frustration at the child. When put in contact with the ADHD industry such a mother may, at least temporarily, feel freed from the mother-blaming context that has been so oppressive. She is no longer a failed mother, but a mother battling against the odds with a disabled child. In this analysis, the primary problem is not seen as residing in the mother or the child (or the often absent father), but in the effects of the dominant discourses of psychology, psychiatry and patriarchy, which render parent and child as passive and separated from their abilities, competence and strengths (Law, 1997).

Another culture specific set of ideas relates to our modern lifestyle. The increasingly centre-stage role of electronic media that are fast paced, non-linguistic and visually distracting that young children spend so many hours sitting in front of may literally have changed children's minds, making sustained attention to verbal input such as reading or listening, far less appealing than faster-paced stimuli (Healy, 1998). Exposure to TV and computer games from a young age could then lead to a form of sensory addiction, leading to problems when children are asked to adapt to less stimulating environments such as school (De Grandpre, 1999). Interestingly, among the Amish, who are well known for their rejection of most modern indulgences such as computers and television, symptoms of ADHD appear to be uncommon (Papolos and Papolos, 1999).

Other modern lifestyle issues may also contribute to more ADHD-type behaviours in our children. Advertising not only creates young consumers who pressure their parents, but by its short, snapshot nature could be training our children to have a short attention span (Hartman, 1996). Children are not being taught to control their impulses. In the past, with parents having limited disposable income and there being fewer readily available sources of instant gratification, children had to learn through necessity to control their impulses. Nowadays, with instant gratification being such a big feature of the consumer culture, children are no longer being forced to learn early self-control of their impulses, a problem made worse by the belief that a diagnosis of ADHD means the child can not learn self-control (Timimi, 2002).

Fears about children's safety, together with more 'in-house' entertainments such as computers and TV, has also led to many children growing up with a lack of fresh air and exercise, leaving those more active boys to behave like 'caged animals' (Panksepp, 1998a, b; Timimi, 2002). Indeed there is evidence from animal experiments to show that access to what the authors call 'rough-and-tumble' play promotes brain maturation and reduces levels of hyperactivity and impulsiveness in later life (Panksepp *et al.*, 2003; Gordon *et al.*, 2003).

Children's diets, which have become high in sugar salt and low in natural unprocessed ingredients may also be causing ADHD-type behaviours (Jacobson and schardt, 1999). This may be due to variety of causes including allergies to certain foods or additives (Feingold, 1975; Rapp, 1996), heavy metal toxicity (Tuthill, 1996), low protein and high carbohydrate diets (Stein and Sammaritano, 1984), mineral imbalances (McGee *et al.*, 1990), essential fatty acid deficiency (Stevens *et al.*, 1995), amino acid deficiency (Nemzer *et al.*, 1986) and essential vitamin deficiencies (Greenblatt, 1999).

Hartman (1996) has an interesting cultural perspective on ADHD. Although he convincingly deconstructs ADHD as a medical disorder, sadly he is unwilling to dispense with it completely. Nonetheless, taking an evolutionary approach he argues that traits such as impulsivity, distractibility and hyperactivity were once adaptive traits. Amongst our hunter/gatherer ancestor's adaptive characteristics would have been constant scanning of the environment for signs of danger (distractibility), quick decision-making (impulsiveness) and a willingness to be active and take risks. These traits then only appear as a problem within settings such as classrooms where such characteristics are mal-adaptive. Although I disagree with this hypothesis (it seems to me that hunters would have required a great capacity for patience, perseverance and concentration), in taking a positive view of these traits Hartman also sees the potential, creative and change-inducing value that ADHD-type behaviours possess, seeing on the go adventure-seeking risk takers as individuals who have the potential to push the boundaries of possibility, to invent through lateral thinking and to produce social change. He sees modern culture as having little appreciation of or tolerance for such 'difference'.

Other theories relate to parenting. Life has become difficult for parents who are caught in a double pressure when it comes to discipline. On the one hand there are increased expectations for children to show restraint and self-control from an early age. On the other hand there is considerable social fear in parents generated by a culture of children's rights that often pathologizes normal, well-intentioned parents' attempts to discipline their children. Parents are left fearing a visit from the SS (Social Services) and the whole area of discipline becomes loaded with anxiety. This argument holds equally true for schools. Parents often criticize schools for lack of discipline. Schools often criticize parents for lack of discipline. This double bind has resulted in more power going to children. Thus, for many children with ADHD the basic problem is a breakdown of their relationship to authority (Timimi, 2002). Parents are being given the message that their children are more like adults and should always be talked to, reasoned with, allowed to make choices, and so on kids can not be kids anymore, dependent, helpless, in need of rules, protection, values and authority, and there is nothing more likely to set a kid on the path to being out of control than giving him/her more power, responsibility and independence than they need.

There is also a lack of common ownership of rules and values with regard to upbringing of children, therefore children learn that only certain individuals have any right to make demands and have expectations with regard to their behaviour. Thus children can more easily play adults off against each other these days (Timimi, 2002). The basic problem here relates to the way in which the task of parenting has come to be viewed in Western culture, as one that needs childcare expert's advice in order to get it right. A form of 'cognitive parenting' has arisen whereby parents are encouraged to give explanation and avoid conflicts (Diller, 2002). This hands-off, excessively verbal model of parenting is both more taxing and less congruent with children's more action-based view of the world. In addition, some parents may be motivated by discovering that ADHD is a new convenient way of getting a label from which you can get extra disability benefits (Breggin, 2002; Timimi, 2002).

School is another big part of children's life where considerable changes have occurred that could promote ADHD-type behaviours. Modern teaching methods emphasize self regulation and reject spoon feeding (dependency), resulting in a poor environment for children who have problems with organizing, ordering and learning and whose restlessness – in classroom environments that are over stimulating, offer too much choice and therefore encourage distraction and poor concentration – is subsequently intensified (Timimi, 2002).

Emphasis has changed in schools in North America and in the United Kingdom. Schools are now expected to demonstrate better levels of academic achievement amongst their pupils and often have to compete with other schools in national performance league tables. As a result there are more standard tests and much of the curriculum is being pushed down-wards from older to younger children, with less time being set aside for more energetic and creative activities such as gym and music (see Chapter 4 and Sax, 2000). Schools are anyway better set-up for girls' development. Thus special needs support is four times more likely to be given to boys who lag behind girls in the development of core school adaptive abilities such as reading and social skills. These latter two factors put together – more emphasis on academic achievement and differential rates of development – have put young-for-grade boys at a particular disadvantage with as many as four-fifth of young-for-grade boys being prescribed stimulant medication in some areas of North America (LeFever *etal.*, 1999; Ravenel, 2002).

Taken together, the above all suggest that the origins of the current epidemic of ADHD lies deep in cultural machinery of Western society. We have become child-blaming societies that have lost the interest or capacity to reform our medical, education and other social institutions and challenge our cultural ambivalence towards children, family and community life.

Developing Non-toxic Solutions for ADHD-type Behaviours

As with non-medical theories of causation, non-drug-based solutions to the problems children with ADHD-type behaviours present have been marginalized by the more politically powerful, drug company-supported medical and consumer bodies. A comprehensive set of therapeutic strategies and approaches needs to be able to tackle the issues cited above, from the adverse effects of labelling, therapy with the child concerned right up to working with parents, schools and the local community of professionals. This does not mean doing all of these with all children referred, this is neither practical nor desirable, what it does mean is a wholesale shift in attitude away from the self-defeating lunacy of labelling kids with a medical disorder, in the absence of any evidence that they are suffering from a physical defect.

In my opinion, the starting point for offering a holistic, integrated, multi-perspective model has to be the rejection of ADHD as label that offers anything meaningful or useful to clinical practice. Paradoxically, although the use of the ADHD diagnosis and stimulant medication may appear to offer a cheap, labour-saving way of helping these children and their families, as with stimulants effectiveness it does the opposite. In other words although it appears that you get quick results in the short term, in the long term you create a group of children who are dependent (on the drugs and the doctors who prescribe them) and need to carry on seeing their doctor for years (some say the rest of their lives), without ever having dealt with the original difficulties. My experience is that if I see my basic role as that of empowering children, parents and schools to find their own solutions, the dependency on doctors does not happen and my clients can be discharged from my clinics in a comparatively short time and with a better outcome than going down the more labour-intensive (in the long-term) diagnosis and medication route.

In mainstream practice the treatment most usually mentioned in addition to drugs is that of behaviour therapy where parents are given advice on how to manage their children's behaviour. There is no magic to this for, hiding behind the pseudo-scientific jargon, is a modern version of the centuries-old, common-sense, carrot-and-stick method (see Chapter 3). Most modern Western behaviour therapy-based parent training methods tend to emphasize more carrot (rewards for good behaviour) than stick, the main stick used being that of 'time out'. Behaviour therapy-based parent training methods used with children diagnosed with ADHD vary from this in emphasizing more immediate and stronger rewards for appropriate behaviour as well as using more prompts, cues and reminders (in other words giving children more attention). Use of more stick (punishments) as in many other cultures' approaches to parenting is considered to be counter-productive. This is nonsense, in many schools and families this professional discourse has unintentionally resulted in them developing a state of learned helplessness in the face of more actively disobedient children (usually boys) who are then felt to have a medical disorder because the children are thought to be unable to respond to normal parenting and behaviour management strategies (their brains would not let them).

Stein (1999, 2001) has described an approach that challenges the wisdom of conventional behaviour management approaches that emphasize carrot and warn against stick. In Stein's method, called the Caregivers

Skills Program (CSP), the assumption is that children with ADHD-type behaviours can be enabled to develop more adaptive behaviours without using conventional carrots (such as monetary rewards). Indeed Stein criticizes the current behavioural therapies used in children diagnosed with ADHD, accusing them of encouraging ADHD-type behaviours rather than reducing them. Stein in many ways is appealing to what might be considered more old-fashioned values. He emphasizes the importance of love and copious positive attention in a natural and unforced manner. The approach to 'time out' is to target all unwanted behaviours and impose sanctions at the slightest sign of inappropriate behaviour. All accountability for appropriate behaviour is transferred onto the child, and parents are responsible for implementing the programme in the home environment, with schools being involved only occasionally. According to Stein (1999), in a group of 37 children fulfilling DSM-IV criteria for ADHD, children's ADHD-type behaviours improved dramatically or disappeared within four weeks of starting the programme and this improvement was stable at one-year follow-up.

In a more 'ordinary' vein, Breggin (1997, 2002) appeals to more old-fashioned wisdoms by emphasizing the importance of re-establishing the moral authority of the parent in the home setting. He steers away from modern behaviour therapy-based parent training's pseudo-scientific preaching and advocates a more common sense-based approach that places greater importance on the parents developing their own sense of responsibility, recovering and developing their own value system and reawakening their faith in their ability to influence the conduct of their children. He points out that yelling, screaming and hitting do not increase a parent's or teacher's moral authority, they undermine it, at the same time too much reliance on rewards affects a child's sense of values and self-direction and can also undermine the adult's moral authority.

Oas (2001) also claims that therapeutic efforts with children who present with ADHD-type behaviour should be directed towards working with the child's parents. Using the simple idea that parents are responsible for their children's behaviour as his starting point, he narrates how through a process of guided introspection, reflection, discussion and free association, parents can learn to understand just how they actively and passively shape their children's behaviour. Parents then learn to discover their own solutions to their children's problems by understanding their own problems and their own patterns of behaviour with their children. Oas is so confident about his method that he challenges skeptics to send him their most difficult ADHD child, claiming that if the parents decide they can work with him, their child will always be cured, according to the parent's own definition of 'cured'.

Oas's (2001) emphasis on parents developing an understanding of the nature of their relationship with their child(ren) is similar to the theme Neven and colleagues (2002) write about in their book *Rethinking ADHD – Integrated Approaches to Helping Children at Home and at School*. Criticizing the conventional view that ADHD-type behaviours need to be managed rather than understood, they instead propose that therapeutic efforts should be directed at helping the development of relationships. The authors devote considerable space to voice concerns about the impact on children of the modern system of childcare and criticize the modern concern with establishment of routines. By helping parents deepen their affectional bonds with their children, the authors believe that children show greater internal security and develop the capacity to act instead of react.

Armstrong (1995), another ADHD skeptic believes that ADHD research is fundamentally flawed by lack of attention to context and by seeing the child labelled with ADHD in terms of their deficits, not strengths. Armstrong offers a whole list of ways to improve children's behaviour without the need for labels or pills. Most are to do with lifestyle changes and include: a balanced diet, limiting television and video games, encouraging a child's interests, plenty of exercise including martial arts classes, background music to focus and calm, use of colour to highlight information, removing allergens from diet, giving instruction in attention-grabbing ways, using stimulating learning activities, providing positive role models, providing plenty of hands-on activities, spending positive time with the child, valuing achievement through personal effort, teaching problem-solving skills, offering the child real life tasks to do, giving children choices, letting children teach a younger child and holding family meetings.

In my last book (Timimi, 2002, Chapter 7), I described the setting up and running of an ADHD clinic in East London and the guiding principles we used to help develop a multiple-perspective approach to helping these children and their families. Since that time I have moved jobs and now practice in the county of Lincolnshire in the United Kingdom where I have continued to develop this multi-perspective approach. As a consultant in the UK National Health Service, I do not have a choice about the clients I see as I serve as a consultant to geographical area and therefore accept all appropriate referrals (that come mainly from the client's general practitioner). At the same time referrals for children with behavioural problems also go to the local community paediatrician. In my over three years in Lincolnshire I have been the child-and-adolescent psychiatry consultant to two community patches, each with its own particular dynamic.

In both of the above jobs, my experience has been that the other professionals in my team (nurse therapists, social workers, psychologists and psychotherapists) are sympathetic to my views and approach and it is the other child psychiatrists who are most at odds with my clinical practice. Consequently my approach remains one that is much localized to the areas where I have consultant responsibility. I have set out in more detail elsewhere the guiding principles I use to help children who could be diagnosed with ADHD and their families (Timimi, 2002, Chapter 7). Below is a summary of these principles (which I have called a multi-perspective approach) and which continue to evolve. Indeed, since my first book the need to use medication has steadily diminished to the point where, at the time of writing, it has been nearly two years since I last started a child under my care on a stimulant.

Slow Down the Assessment Process and Engage the System

Ideally a three-stage assessment is helpful. The first appointment is a clinic-based appointment and a first opportunity to meet with the family and the child. At this meeting I can get the history and get some understanding of the family's stories. It is also the first opportunity to try and engage the child, find out their viewpoint and what (if anything) they would like to see change. The second stage is to do a school visit as for many children school is the main concern of the parents. The third stage of the assessment is to do a home visit where I have the opportunity to meet with the family on their territory. Finally an appointment back at the clinic completes the assessment. Since moving to Lincolnshire, pressures of time and geography have meant that I am unable to routinely offer a school and home visit as part of every assessment. Instead I have developed a standard letter to send to schools, which asks about a number of areas including behaviour, academic level, peer relationships, relationship with teachers, extra help given, strategies used by the school, changes noticed over time and in particular strengths and positive qualities of the child. I do not use any rating scales. I carry out school visits and more occasionally home visits only if, in my judgement, the above is not sufficient. From the first appointment I show an interest in the family's and their children's own ideas about what the problem is. Frequently opportunities for what might be considered treatment arises during the assessment, thus I also view the assessment period as the first opportunity to begin interventions. Sometimes just the whole process of bringing different bits of the system together can, in itself, make all the difference needed. By trying to slow down the process from the start, I am covertly introducing the idea that my job is not to simply focus on a 'yes he has it' or 'no he doesn't' medical test kind of approach.

Put a Lot of Effort into Trying to Engage Children and Their Families

Some families who come to see me have had previous referrals to child-and-adolescent mental health services and other agencies (social services, education psychology, educational welfare, private clinics, paediatricians, other psychiatrists, etc.). Many of these families feel ambivalent about helping agencies, possibly experiencing them as blaming or perhaps even fearing that these agencies are going to take their children away. A patient, sympathetic, long-term approach is needed. Steering clear of any suggestions on how to parent may be important in the initial stages of engagement. Instead picking up on any examples of good parenting or examples of how dedicated the parents appear to be towards their children that I hear or see in a session can be experienced as positive and trust building. Obviously, there are important precautions to be taken, as I do not want to be condoning abusive situations. In my experience, however, the vast majority of these difficult-to-engage clients are not abusive to their children, but perhaps because of class or cultural issues, their style of parenting and the way they express their love for and dedication to their children may have been misinterpreted as abuse by the predominantly white middle-class agencies (e.g. teachers, psychologists, social services). Even if such a thing had not happened, the parents themselves may fear it will. There are other simple things that can be done to help the parents feel that you're on their side such as letters to social services, letters supporting a recommendation for extra support at school and so on. Children too may come in a suspicious, defensive frame of mind, fearing more telling-off and blame. I try to look for the positives in any account and show much more curiosity and interest in these aspects. I try to talk to the referred child first (in the company of their parent(s)) and like to focus questions and comments on the more functional, coping and thoughtful aspects of the child. If a child is completely hostile, then a more playful approach can be rewarding, for example give them easy challenges and tell them that you bet they can not do it and express surprise when they do.

Take a Multi-factorial Approach

I try to move families from single explanation approaches (ADHD is often approached as if it is an explanation whereas I have mentioned above that it is only a description of behaviour) to including all other explanations available. These may come up through my own opinions during the assessment but often are explanations that families, schools and others have put forward, whose significance has been pushed down in status as being less meaningful than ADHD as an explanation. Thus clinically I am continually trying to rehabilitate complexity. The alternative explanations that are put forward include: learning difficulties with consequent low threshold of frustration and low self-confidence, a child full of energy who is not getting enough exercise, emotionally troubled but will not express himself (e.g. no longer having contact with father, witnessed domestic violence, a victim of bullying, etc.), uses his intelligence to work out how to get round people, is not getting enough sleep, finds the only way he can get attention is to be the class clown, likes being hyperactive, is copying his father, has no respect for the authority of females and so on. It is very easy to miss these everyday explanations that many parents and children have about why they are the way they are and it is very easy to give these explanations no significance at all. Once you look out for these simple, everyday explanations, in every case that I have come across so far, one or more of them exists but need to be actively searched for as they are relegated to a lower status than the assumed possibility of ADHD as an explanation, particularly if they are meeting a doctor!

Take a Slow Process Approach to Deconstructing the Meaning Behind a Diagnosis of ADHD

I try to be open with clients about the controversies relating to ADHD in a straightforward manner. For example, I might explain quite early on that there is no such thing as a test for ADHD and in that sense it is different to diagnoses such as pneumonia or diabetes where you can take a blood sample or an X-ray, in other words do physical tests to help substantiate the diagnosis. I explain that the diagnosis is not based on any 'rocket science' but on clinical judgement and explain about the types of behaviours we look for in making the diagnoses. I also explain that there is substantial disagreement between professionals not only on how to arrive at the diagnosis, but also on whether such a condition exists in the first place. The aim of taking this approach is to get the idea across that the ADHD label does not provide an explanation; it does not answer the 'why' question. If the meaning behind an ADHD diagnosis is not opened up you can get that dreadful situation that often arises in those who have been too vigorously cultured into the ADHD faith that when a problem arises with a child who has a diagnosis of ADHD, the first question on the lips of the faithful (be they the parents, teachers or even the child themselves) is, what is happening with the medication? (Has he taken it? Does he need more?) This is a very understandable reaction but leads to a rather disastrous, no-win situation, where the only way to deal with problems becomes that of increasing the medication or adding a new prescription. As a result, a number of the more religious clinicians have found themselves going well beyond the licensed maximum dose for Ritalin. (I often hear of adolescents who are on two to three times the maximum licensed dose for Ritalin. To me this is no different than the medical profession creating a drug addict.)

Look for the Positives and for Solutions the Family have Already Generated

When families come to the clinic they are there because of problems they or someone else (e.g. the school) is having with the child. Thus the session(s) will be dominated by problem talk usually in front of the child concerned. Of course, it is important to listen carefully and try to understand the nature of the difficulties the child, family and others are experiencing. However, I often make an active attempt right from the first session to look for the positives and/or descriptions of the child that do not fit with the dominant story being given. It is not unusual for families to take a while before they can adjust their frame of mind to start talking about positive qualities and the 'silver lining' that comes out of their experience and often I have to gently persist. I have yet to come across a family (where there were not any child protection concerns) who, given a bit of space, time and a touch of persistence on my part, have not come up with something positive. I often do this type of thing again in later sessions and refer back to the original session to compare how their child is now and see what has changed over time. Keeping hold of the big picture is, I believe, very important. For example six months or a year after you first started seeing a child and their family you may be bogged down in a rather hopeless feeling session where the family is telling you about a particular incident or difficulty they are currently trying to deal with in relation to their child. Yet overall you know the child has made significant progress. Keeping the good news alive is important in all cases but particularly where there seems to be a history of major attachment-type issues (in other words a lot of built-up hostility and negative feeling between a parent and child). Noticing solutions and amplifying them can also be of great benefit. By paying attention to a time, however small or seemingly insignificant, when the child was not all over the place and out of control, and getting everyone to think about what might have been different about this time (what was the child doing, what were the parents doing, what else was going on, etc.), you can begin to help parents and children rediscover their own competence and expertise. I often make a special effort at showing surprise at moments when coping or solution stories emerge, 'hang on a minute run that past me again', 'really? Is that really what happened?' 'Wow, that's amazing how did you accomplish that?' I often come back to these solution stories during a session in the hope that at least one participant might have experienced at least one part of the session as a time when they showed me what they were capable of, as opposed to what is wrong with them.

Be Open and Informative and Allow the Parents to Make the Decision About Medication

I see my main duty where the use of medication is being considered, whether it is an issue that has been raised by myself, another professional or by the parent(s), as that of providing adequate information to allow the parent(s) to make an informed decision. This is particularly so for stimulants like Ritalin, which after all is a controlled drug (prescriptions for controlled drugs have much stricter guidelines than non-controlled drugs). Providing information means telling the clients about how the drug works, the evidence for its effectiveness, the side-effect profile and the types of controversies there are. For me, it also means telling clients what is factual, for example side-effect profile, and what is my opinion. I also encourage those families who decided to have (or keep) their child on a stimulant to be flexible and creative in their use of medication. For example, many families can cope without giving their child medication during weekends and school holidays. This approach to medication also includes the idea that medication is not diagnosis-dependent. Many parents are helped by the attitude that medication is a window of opportunity, not a cure and from the outset develop the notion that medication is being used to allow a breathing space for everyone to find better more long-lasting solutions to the child's difficulties. Most parents seem to understand my approach and, I believe are happy to be treated as the expert best placed to make decisions about their child. In my experience, most parents want to avoid their child having to take a stimulant and if their child is on medication would like to see them come off it as soon as is practical. There are, however, occasions where I do not feel it is appropriate to prescribe a stimulant even though the parent(s) want me to and I have no child protection concerns. Although I am aware that in these situations I am taking a 'modernist' stance (see Chapter 8 on the tension between working in a modernist and post-modernist style) I sometimes conclude that the child's parent(s) are not trying out the interventions we have agreed and are looking towards medication as the cheap and easy solution. In those situations I am open with the parent(s) that I will not be recommending a stimulant until I am convinced that they are making a proper effort to try out the alternatives to medication that we had agreed.

Be Prepared to be in There for the Long Haul

Be patient – time often brings unexpected coincidences and new things to explore in a natural unforced manner. I now feel less inclined to jump into theorizing and trying to find out too much information about a family (particularly things like the parents own histories) until opportunities naturally present themselves and when there is a reasonable sense of trust being established between the family and myself. Then I can start being more openly challenging and curious if necessary. Opportunities for looking at new explanations and new solutions frequently happen by chance. By being involved with cases over long periods (sometimes years) I am no longer concerned if solutions and improvements do not happen in the short term. Events such as changes of teacher or school, re-involving an uninvolved father, changes in lifestyle (such as attending a martial arts class) are continually occurring and can have dramatic effects on a child's behaviour and well-being.

Be Prepared to Consider Alternative Approaches

Diet is frequently an issue that is brought up by parents. Where parents are interested, I give them any information I have on this topic. For some parents this has meant trying their children on supplements, most commonly a multi-vitamin and mineral preparation such as 'Forceval junior' and a fish oil-based preparation such as 'Efalex', at the same time as developing a healthier diet for their children (e.g. cutting out sugary foods and increasing the amount of raw fruit and vegetables they consume). Others, depending on the child and family history, wish to try exclusion diets such as an additive- and 'e-number'-free diet, a lactose-free diet or a gluten-free diet. I often refer such children to a dietician for more detailed advice on particular exclusion diets. Many other lifestyle issues are explored in sessions including the amount of time parents are spending with their children, exercise, sleep routines, limiting television and computer game, social activities, peer contact and encouraging children to attend clubs such as scouts, army cadets and other activity-based groups.

Challenge and Deconstruct the Hierarchy

I give greater importance to client's own knowledge and less importance to my own. Local knowledge is searched for, opened up and explored wherever possible. ADHD would in this context be an example of professional knowledge, given that it is a concept created by professionals and requiring the so-called specialist expertise to diagnose. Common-sense, grandparent, old-school-type advice is important to pick up on and follow through. Ideals like children require nurturing, firm discipline, plenty of exercise, plenty of time to play, plenty of fresh air, good diet, routines and good sleep have been known about for hundreds of generations. This common-sense everyday knowledge will always be relevant. I encourage parents to talk about their value system and to teach this and impose it on their children. As far as professional knowledge is concerned, this is provided in an open non-prescriptive and non-top-down sort of manner. One obvious example is parenting. Professionals all too often act as if there is only one way to parent and any other way is harmful. The current convention in professional circles is for a white middle-class style of parenting as enshrined in the cognitive behavioural, learning theory approach. I have no particular problems with this version of how to parent, indeed, like most mental health professionals; I often use some of the principles in my own practice. What I believe to be important, however, is to consider how this fits in with things like: the practical reality for families (it seems to me cognitive behavioural therapy for behavioural problems in children has been designed for reasonably well-off families who have no more than two children), the nature of the families' relationship to the institution (or the institutional transference if you prefer that concept) and how this fits in with the families own style of parenting. In working with families on parenting issues it is quite frequent to pick up in the conversation a principle from a behavioural intervention. If I do I move in quickly to make sure the family or the individual owns that bit of knowledge, for example by saying 'Are you sure you did not write the books that I learnt from? Because this is exactly what the psychology books say' I might try and elaborate from there and say in the form of information some other things that are said in these psychology books. Sometimes I feel very strongly that a certain principle from theory needs to be put across (e.g. if there is a cycle of negative reinforcement), in which case I will say that (i.e. I feel very strongly that such and such is happening and we have to find a way to break this cycle). At this point, if we are in agreement, I would ask for their ideas and tell them what the books say and perhaps something from my own experience both as a parent and as someone who has worked with other families who have had similar problems with their children. Another important aspect of deconstructing the hierarchy is that of deconstructing the professional identity. These days I feel I am a similar person at home and at work. I engage in a lot of chitchat and small talk with clients. If anyone (client or other professional) wants me to call them by their first name, then I insist they call me by my first name. Given that I spend so much time prying into other people's personal business, if someone asks me a personal question I will answer it honestly.

Transparency

I try not to keep ideas secret. If I have an idea then I share it, however difficult it might be. For example, if it occurs to me that the child has worked out that if he plays up he might keep his parents from splitting up, then I would wait for a convenient moment and start off by saying something like, 'can I be devils advocate' or 'would you mind if I put the cat amongst the pigeons'. Similarly if I get strong emotions when with a Family or individual (or counter-transference if you prefer that term), I will usually share it or even act it out. For example, with families who are nice to each other and afraid of the boat being rocked, I may find myself wanting to say something that maybe difficult to hear, but then back away from saying it because I feel too guilty about upsetting a family who have been so nice to me. As soon as I realize this I might say, 'I've just realized something which I've got to tell you', this might

Chapter 6

Multi-perspective Approaches 1: The Influence of Culture on Defining a Problem

We therapists sometimes unwittingly create self-fulfilling prophecies (or perhaps we should call them other-fulfilling prophecies, in this case). If we believe that there is a deep, underlying problem, we might prompt the creation of one in the course of therapy. If we believe clients are sick and incapable, they may begin more and more to fulfil our expectations.

O'HANLON and WEINER-DAVIS, 1989: 32

In this chapter and the following two chapters I explore how a cross-cultural perspective can be used in the clinical situation to enable access to multiple frameworks and diverse approaches that can be used to help families with naughty boys.

In this chapter, I will consider approaches that involve trying to help change the perspective of the child, their family and other professionals through searching for new meanings to give to the problem. This can include finding ways of reducing (or sometimes increasing) how much of the behaviour is seen as a problem, as well as looking for alternative explanations or meanings for the behaviours that individuals or families have come to seek help about. In the next chapter, I explore the more formal therapies currently being marketed as specific to children with behavioural problems. In the third chapter of these 'multi-perspective approaches' chapters (Chapter 8 of this book) I consider how our own beliefs and values (as doctors, therapists, other professionals and parents) impact on not only the clients we deal with but also the wider culture we are a part of.

Mental health is a peculiar area of medicine. As a child-and-adolescent psychiatrist, I work as a doctor with no medical tests to back my hypotheses.

In the absence of objective facts to back our opinions the essence of what we deal with is our subjective interpretations of our clients' difficulties. We are basically dealing with systems of meaning as our clients and ourselves construct them. A good mental health therapist, like a good shaman or traditional healer, is able to join with their client's system of meaning and transform or manipulate this in some way to produce a positive outcome (Kleinman, 1988). In their ability to manipulate these culturally meaningful symbols, a good therapist acts like a cultural interpreter who can take the meaning provided in one cultural frame, interpret a new meaning for it by referring to another cultural frame and then reinterpret that new meaning back to the client in the client's own cultural frame and in a way that provides new opportunities and possibilities for a positive change (Timimi, 2002).

The problem in Western institutionalized thinking is that cognitive theories provide the dominant framework around which institutions such as schools, psychology, psychiatry and the therapies construct their accounts of meaning. In the cognitive cultural framework, meaning shows up as something to be investigated in a broadly similar way to other 'things' in the natural and human world. It is something generated within individual minds through the interaction of personal 'schemas' with sensory experience. This is understood as being amenable to causal explanation and scientific investigation (Bracken, 2002). Furthermore, centuries of political, economic and military dominance of Western powers has meant centuries of embedded Western cultural dominance. This has left a legacy of superiority and arrogance in Western belief systems and cosmology, an arrogance, which feeds through into the institutions born out of Western thought such as psychiatry. These institutions naturally go on to develop a conceptualization of mental health and illness that is riddled with racism and belittles and marginalizes alternative systems of thought (Fernando, 1988). This cultural oppression is just as apparent in the concepts and systems of meaning used in child-and-adolescent psychiatry and its allied institutions (Timimi, 2002). For professionals trying to break out of the restrictions of their professional constructions of meaning, it can be a lonely, frightening and crazy making experience. Nonetheless, such journeys where you feel the ground beneath you begin to shift as you enter new unknown worlds will not only help the practitioner be able to incorporate new perspectives which can be used to help the clients they work with, but in addition can help teach humility, keep you ordinary and be a personally enriching process.

It is not just the doctor or therapist who arrives at the consulting room bounded by a belief system that will influence what they do and the way they do it, but also the client. When a client arrives for a session they come with their own belief system not just about the possible meanings of the difficulties they have come to consult you about but also about who they think you, the doctor or therapist, are and what they think you expect from them. We all structure our lives around specific meanings. Meanings attributed to events influence our behaviours and our understanding of that event. Thus it could be said that in order to make sense of our lives we 'story' our experiences. This 'narrative' perspective has been known for thousands of years and is being re-discovered in post-modern Western culture. This narrative perspective that explores the 'storying' process that brings meaning to our lives is being independently developed in many apparently disparate areas. These include social linguistics (Linde, 1993), models of science and human action (MacIntyre, 1980, 1985), social science research (Sarbin and Kitsuse, 1994), family therapy (White and Epston, 1990) and medicine (Muir-Gray, 1999).

Some, whose lives have been surrounded throughout their growing years by Western materialist, cognitive discourse, will come ready to play the traditional, Western, doctor/patient script. It goes something like this: the client who is ill or unhealthy in some way comes to see the healthy expert who has scientific knowledge about particular group of medical conditions. The doctor then asks a series of questions to elicit the information they need to make their diagnosis, examines the patient and organizes any medical tests that are needed. In this encounter the client remains essentially passive, waits for the doctor's diagnosis and then has a treatment plan prescribed by the authoritative expert. Many in the world of child psychiatry, feeling insecure about their professional identity as a doctor wish to return to a traditional doctor/patient cultural script (e.g. Goodman, 1997).

In these post-modern times many patients are questioning the continued acceptance of a passive role in their encounter with doctors and wish to see the medical profession being able to deal with them as intelligent people with knowledge to bring to any consultation (Muir-Gray, 1999). In adult psychiatry there is plenty of research that suggests that users of adult mental health services do not like the medicalizing approach of psychiatrists and would prefer more active participation in the decision-making process and more talking therapies to be available to them (Rogers *et al.*, 1993; Pilgrim, 1997).

In child-and-adolescent mental health, of course the situation is compli-cated by the fact that usually the referred patient (the child) is not the main person(s) that the doctor will be discussing their opinion with.

Inevitably this means that often, consciously or unconsciously, the parents (particularly mothers in this mother-blaming culture) are seeking reassurance that they are not to blame for their child's difficulties. The medical model, with its focus on a within-child, context-deprived explanation may seem an attractive and seductive way of dealing with this covert or overt, conscious or unconscious guilt and fear of blame. Whilst the diagnoses-based industries (e.g. the ADHD industry) have been able to exploit this particular dynamic to great monetary profit, my personal experience has been that parents are very open to and interested in diverse perspectives, providing these can be married into their own belief system. Furthermore, the underlying sense of guilt that many parents experience does not disappear with a diagnosis. In my experience almost all the parents I see are positively motivated and concerned about their child's well-being. They wish to understand their children's difficulties, have their own important opinions to pass on and if treated like capable people tend to respond as capable people.

Normalizing Boy Behaviour

Whilst being careful not to appear as if you are belittling or not taking seriously parental concerns there are often many opportunities during clinical sessions, from the first session onwards, to try and detoxify some perceptions about boy's behaviour. How and when to introduce these ideas depends, of course, on clinical judgement and conversational style.

Here is a version of a familiar story I heard and some of the normalizing responses that can be made. (This case example and others in the book are, for the sake of confidentiality, fictional but based on real situations I have encountered in clinical practice.)

George's Story

George is a 10-year-old boy who has been referred by his general practitioner after George's mother and stepfather asked for further help following an incident at school where George had sworn at one of his teachers and ran out of the classroom. The parents were called into school and George was threatened with suspension. In the referral letter it states that George's parents complain that he has always been short-tempered, is fidgety and that teachers have previously voiced concern about his poor concentration. He is also aggressive to his sister at home.

When I meet with George and his family, after introductions, I start talking to George. He comes across as a pleasant, co-operative young man and starts to explain to me his version of recent events. He admits that what he did at school was wrong, at the same time complaining that he feels that his teacher does not like him, is always picking on him and following a relatively minor incident where this teacher had told him off for talking to a fellow pupil he felt he could no longer 'stand it' and got up from his seat, shouting at his teacher, ran out of the classroom and went to hide in the toilets. George's family explained to me that they were very upset about this incident and that they also have a number of other concerns about George's behaviour at home, including fighting with his sister, not doing his homework and poor concentration when he does get down to doing it. He is often oppositional and seems to lose his temper 'big time', including physical aggression towards his sister and mother such as kicking and punching them and this tends to happen when 'he can't get his own way'. His parents are also concerned about George's school reports that mention that he has a tendency to be easily distracted and sometimes annoys others in class. School believes that George could achieve a lot more if he showed more willingness to work. He has been assessed as about a year behind in his reading skills.

Here are a few comments and directions to take the dialogue that can be slipped in at convenient moments whilst we discuss George's situation.

With regard to the school's poor opinion of George: 'I noticed that George feels his teacher is always picking on him, whether this is true or not it suggests that George and his teacher do not see eye to eye, a situation that George seems, understandably, unhappy about. You know, in my work here I hear this sort of story again and again. I don't know if you would agree with me, but it seems to me so much of how children get on at school has to do with whether they get on with their teachers or whether the teachers get on with them. A familiar story to me goes something like this, a boy and his teacher find that they don't get on, soon the boy finds himself being labelled a troublemaker. I have come across many reasons why once somebody is labelled a troublemaker in the eyes of a teacher they become a scapegoat. For example, it could be that the teacher is under a lot of stress due to changes within the school, the teacher's performance being assessed, lack of support from the special needs section in the school, a lack of a special needs section in the school, a school environment that is hostile and divided and so on. Once the young boy finds himself in that situation it becomes very hard to get out of it and day after day that boy goes to school feeling more and more unhappy, less and less willing to try and soon a vicious circle builds up with every now and then the young boy's frustrations blowing up. In between the blow-ups the boy has sometimes learned to switch off, using the "I don't care" attitude to help him get through the day.'

A comment like the above would be specifically chosen to fit in with my impression of what sort of boy George is. The aim is to introduce another possibility, another potential story, which opens the door to thinking in terms of normal people involved in complex relationships. Often versions of the above are introduced or hinted at by the parents, in which case the therapeutic task is to open up a conversation on a more relationship-orientated footing. It should be noted that developing this line of thinking does not mean excusing unacceptable behaviour, nor does it mean blaming the teacher.

By enquiring about school, children and their parents start offering other school-related stories that can be developed, which have the aim of implying a response, on behalf of the youngster, to an environmental situation they find themselves in. For example, it may be that I get a story of a small school with many staff changes, who have been unable to build up or enforce discipline in which case the story might be about the child having learned that they can have fun in that environment because they have worked out that this is a system they can easily get round. It could be that the child is being bullied and teased and is then bringing its frustrations home. There could be a gender issue where the child has a female teacher(s) whose use of verbal techniques such as praise and restriction demands are ignored by the youngster who sees no power of influence over him. A conversation about gender may result, which may uncover gender issues and dynamics elsewhere, for example in the home environment or in the child's history (such as witnessing domestic violence).

With regard to the behaviours at home I often use anecdotes from my own childhood or my current struggles as a parent with my own children with the aim of suggesting that some of these behaviours are common in a family's everyday life. This is not the same as saying they are acceptable (George's behaviours described above are in my opinion not acceptable), but bringing them to a more 'ordinary' level makes them easier to deal with.

For example, fighting with his sister, 'I think I know what you mean. It is such a struggle knowing how to deal with sibling rivalry and I am speaking now as a parent myself. I have got a boy and a girl who are just over a year apart and sometimes it feels as if my wife and I spend all our time trying to stop them from killing each other. My boy often takes great delight in winding his sister up, particularly if he is bored, and watching her snap so that a fight then follows. My girl, on the other hand, will come running to us complaining about her brother's behaviour, presumably hoping that we will tell him off such that it is impossible to tell how much of what she is saying is the truth and how much is an exaggeration, as I am sure she takes great pleasure in getting her brother into trouble sometimes.'

Or, 'My mother seems to insist that I and my wife have got it easy compared to what she had to deal with. I was one of three boys and I do remember the three of us running rings around her when we were younger, such that she was literally left in tears sometimes, not knowing what to do with us other than the "wait until your father gets home" threat which at the time would have absolutely no impact on what we were doing. I also remember that sometimes we could be really vicious with each other. You see this scar just next to my right eye; my older brother inflicted it on me when he threw a stone, which cut me there. Meanwhile, my younger brother managed to crack and chip one of my older brother's teeth by pushing him off a table and I too was not innocent as I remember one day breaking my younger brother's prized toy violin, smashing it to pieces in a fit of anger. Now that I am a parent myself, I am beginning to see my mother's point and I'm glad that we don't have three boys to deal with', or with regard to homework 'I rarely come across children who enjoy homework. I am told such children do exist so I am still hopeful and looking forward to the day that I do meet a young person who loves doing their homework. I went to school in Iraq, which has a very different system to this country, and I had to start doing homework from the age of five and I remember this quite vividly from my first year at school. I hated school, but more than anything else I hated doing homework and to start with I would not do it. Then one day, after a lot of patient attempts from my mother and father to get me to start doing my homework, my father finally lost his temper and gave me several hard smacks that made me cry. Eventually I realized that I was going to have to do the homework whether I wanted to or not. For the rest of my schooldays homework stayed as an unwanted, unwelcome chore which I had to do and often had to be pushed unwillingly to complete.'

Or with regard to tempers if George does not get his own way, 'Oh, God, tell me about it. My children get into such a state if they cannot get their own way. They shout, cry, throw things, we get called everything under the sun to the point where I wonder what has got into them. Surely I was not like that as a child, but my mother assures me that I was. She tells me that on some days when I was in the mood, nothing would be right, I would say my food was too cold and when they heated it up I would say it was too hot, I would refuse to go out with them somewhere and when they finally dragged me out, I would refuse to come home again, such that whatever they did or asked me to do, it was not right in my eyes. I guess now that I have had some time working in this field as well, I have heard this story so often that I have begun to realize that these are familiar situations that families up and down the country are dealing with as they struggle to do their best to bring up their children. Nowadays, I do tend to think of these problems as middle of the road, fairly common sort of problems.'

With regard to George being a year behind with his reading, as well as possibly putting an alternative frame for this, for example, 'his unhappiness at school may have led to a switching off of his motivation rather than him having an inability to learn', I find it helpful to have a discussion with parents about the differential development of boys and girls. For example, 'George is a year behind in his reading at the moment which must be upsetting for you and probably frustrating for George. However, the good news is that there is a strong likelihood that in time George will catch up and I will tell you why. Boys and girls develop different skills at different rates. Unfortunately for boys, the education system is particularly geared towards the skills that girls are naturally good at and learn quicker than boys, for example: language, reading and verbal skills. Unfortunately for boys, the stuff that boys are good at such as physical activities, doing things with your hands and things that require quick reactions seems to have less of a place in the current curricula being used by schools. What has happened as a result is that there are four or more times as many boys receiving special needs help in schools, as girls. These special needs are most of the time for reading and writing problems or behaviour problems. Now I cannot believe that this is because boys are somehow more stupid than girls and indeed this is not the case, because what you find is that boys slowly catch up and when you get to the world of work there are plenty more opportunities for boys to exercise those practical skills that are not as highly prized in our current education system.'

There are also plenty of opportunities of noticing normality 'live' within each session. For example, 'I must say I have really enjoyed meeting you and talking to you today. I think George is a credit to you. He's shown me that deep inside he has a good understanding of how to behave in public. He's been polite, listened to my questions, thought carefully about his answers and didn't shy away from trying to answer any of them. You know I deliberately tried to give him some very tough questions and kept this up for nearly half an hour to see how he would handle it. He handled it beautifully and showed that he can concentrate even when the going gets tough. Fantastic.'

And, 'I can see that you're really very caring parents. Its always difficult to come and see a doctor like me as it can make you feel like the way you parent is being put under the spotlight or that somehow you've failed as parents. To me there's no better indication of being a good parent than coming to a place like this in the knowledge that family life will be put under the microscope but you are willing to do this for the sake of your son's happiness.'

Reframing

To reframe means to change the conceptual setting or viewpoint in relation to a situation which is experienced and to place it in another frame which still fits the situation equally or sometimes even better and thereby changing the entire meaning that is given to that situation (Watzlawick *et al.*, 1974). In their book Watzlawick *et al.* (1974), discussing the philosopher Epictetus, point out that our experience of the world is based on the categorization of the objects of our perception into classes and that once an object is conceptualized as a member of a given class it is extremely difficult to see it as belonging to another class. However, once we see alternative class memberships (in other words, reframing) it becomes difficult to go back to our previously limited view of reality.

The process of reframing is a subtle one. It is a way of retelling the story that clients are telling you, in such a way as to allow new possibilities and new ways of understanding the situation to unfold. The professional has to listen actively, shift an emphasis here and question a conclusion there, in order to allow for the possibility that a new meaning could be offered. In many ways all therapies offer a degree of reframing, asking the client to believe in the practitioner's preferred theoretical frame. Making this process explicit allows access to more diverse multi-perspectives.

One of the masters of using reframing in the therapeutic process was the American psychiatrist, psychotherapist and hypnotherapist, Milton Erickson (see for example, Rosen, 1982; Erickson, 1980a–d; Zeig, 1980). Erickson used a huge variety of sources including personal experiences, dealings with patients, scientific research, literature and so on and often through the use of stories in a highly intuitive way would give clients' problems an alternative context and meaning in a way that enabled access to a greater variety of therapeutic interventions. Indeed, although I am putting reframing under its own heading it is arguable that in the field of mental health our therapeutic interventions all have a lot to do with the process of reframing as we are giving our clients' difficulties a particular meaning or set of meanings which we hope will be of therapeutic value to them. My particular criticism of the dominant models used in our therapeutic institutions, such as the medical model, is that they limit the potentially limitless possibilities by which a situation can be given a meaning that is potentially helpful to our clients. Furthermore, medical model psychiatry emphasizes what's wrong with you and tells you that this is inside you and biologically fixed (e.g. in your genes). This often makes it a profoundly anti-therapeutic story to give to clients.

Thus, to some degree all the approaches explored in this and the next two chapters are to do with reframing the meaning given to the presenting problem. For example, the preceding section, which looks at normalizing boy behaviour, is an example of reframing whereby the therapist is attempting to give a less toxic meaning to the child's problems by reinterpreting the child's behaviour as normal responses of a normal boy to particular environmental situations. Later in this chapter I look at the process of noticing and amplifying strengths within the client. This too can be seen as an attempt to reframe the way a problem is viewed. By ascribing positive or noble motives to the behaviour of family members, symptoms that have previously been considered by all concerned to have a negative value and to be bad or undesirable can be given a positive connotation (a kind of every cloud has a silver lining). Palazzoli and her colleagues (1978) set out the value of positive connotation in all, including the most difficult of families. What they point out is the importance of not just describing and ascribing negative labels to problematic behaviours, but also trying to understand the intention behind them, which can often be given a more positive connotation. For example, the mother who owns up to often giving in to her child's demands because she feels guilty and mean if she acts towards him/her in a withholding way can be reframed as being positively motivated by commenting that she is showing how powerful her love towards her child is and how important its happiness is to her.

Steven's Story

Steven is a 10-year-old boy when he is brought to see me by his mother. His mother complains that at home he is rude, swears a lot, will not do as he is told, has been stealing money from her purse and has done 'bizarre' things such as cutting up new clothes she bought for him with a pair of scissors. He is regularly in trouble at school, mainly during playtime when he fights with other children. Teachers are concerned at his progress and describe him as 'moody'. Steven's mother says that she thinks Steven is attention-seeking and sometimes she feels as if Steven 'is out to get her'. During our conversation together I have noticed that Steven is trying to answer honestly and keeps steeling a look towards his mum while he is answering, as if he is looking to see what reaction she will give. I comment on this and wonder out loud if Steven is a sensitive boy who takes things to heart. At this point Steven's mother tells me about the break-up of her marriage (to Steven's father) a few years ago. She tells me that she felt really low at this time, but knew she had to keep going for the sake of her kids. She also remembers that Steven used to lay the table for breakfast in the mornings 'as if he was trying to look after me'. This leads to a conversation about the effects of not only the marriage break-up, but also the stress at home before the marriage broke up, on Steven. As Steven's mum talks about her marriage breakdown, she becomes tearful. Steven holds her hands. This gives me the opportunity to talk about how the past is still with them (emotionally) and issues such as role changes in the family as a result of what has happened to them. By the end of this session the frame of reference has changed from that of the observable behaviours to that of underlying emotions.

Mark's Story

Mark is a 13-year-old boy living with his father. His father has brought Mark to see me for 'anger management'. Mark loses his temper and becomes physically violent at home and at school. He is a bright boy, but school is now considering expelling him because of his behaviour. Mark's father tells me that Mark's mother died some years ago from liver failure. She was an alcoholic. We talk about life with an alcoholic. They both tell me how they tried to stop her from drinking but could not. We talk about habits and how ingrained they can become. 'Old habits die hard' becomes the dominant metaphor for our therapeutic work. Mark's relationship to and his father has got stuck in a set of habitual responses that they repeat and will lead to their destruction if they do not change it. But 'old habits die hard', so in addition to giving them suggestions to help change their relationship (e.g. dad not giving in so easily, a contract of expectations and consequences) we talk about how vigilant they must be to prevent the old habits returning. We conceptualize the 'old habits' as being like a supernatural 'spirit' constantly trying to trip them up to get them back into the destructive cycle. They decide that fighting the 'old habits' is the best way they can do to honour the memory of Mark's mum, 'It's what she would have wanted.'

Simon's Story

Simon is a 15-year-old boy who comes to see me together with his mother, father and 13-year-old sister. At home Simon and his dad, or Simon and his sister, or dad and Simon's sister frequently argue. Simon's mother feels like she is 'piggy in the middle' trying to negotiate between the warring parties. School is concerned about Simon's poor concentration and 'day dreaming'. Simon's father was an agricultural worker. Some years ago the family bought a cottage attached to a farm that Simon's father worked on. Then Simon's father had an accident at work, injuring his back. He has been unable to return to work since then. The family faces huge financial problems and an ongoing and unresolved court case in relation to compensation following this accident. I put to them that they are a family 'under stress'. I describe their situation as one where it is as if there is a stress cloud that hangs over their home and that as soon as someone walks through their front door they feel this stress cloud weighing down on them. They relate to this description and we talk about how the stress cloud has affected their relationships at home. I ask them if they ever get opportunities to enjoy each other's company these days. They tell me they rarely do. We start the task of reducing the stress cloud's influence on them by suggesting they start going out together as a family once a week with each person in turn deciding where they should go.

One of the most important things to look for when reframing is the local explanations that exist for the problem. By local I mean explanations that the child and family already have, which will have been picked up through the cultural discourse that the family is surrounded with. By accessing the child's and the family's belief systems you can access potentially helpful therapeutic directions at the same time as confirming that child's and family's own abilities to understand the problems that confront them in life.

Local explanations often have to be actively searched for as children and families come with a particular set of expectations with regard to the consultation. When they come to see me they know they are seeing a doctor who is a consultant and their expectations may well be that the script they need to follow would be the traditional doctor/patient script that I outlined above. They would expect me to be asking relevant questions to gain relevant information and arrange for relevant tests in order to diagnose the relevant medical condition from which their child is suffering and then start the appropriate treatment. If they come in that frame of mind they will, often quite unconsciously, be privileging particular sorts of information that they think I will need in order to arrive at my diagnosis.

Naturally, they will assume that this sort of information will be more important for me to know about than any of their own particular ideas and theories that they have had about their child's problems during the time they have been experiencing them. These local explanations then become relegated to a position of lesser importance in the child's and family's mind and will need reorientation to their importance to bring them into the therapeutic conversation right from the first meeting.

Common local explanations for the naughty boy syndrome includes the child having learning difficulties, getting easily frustrated, being bright kid who is getting bored, knowing what buttons to push to get their own way, missing their father, not able to express themselves and bottling up their feelings, clashing with particular teachers, anxious and this comes out in lots of energy, poor discipline at the school, poor discipline at home, does not want to grow up, is desperate to please and goes over the top, is looking for attention, is suffering following a marriage break-up, is lonely and does not know how to make friends, has difficulty coping with changes, is copying others, is easily led, has low self-esteem, got off to a bad start and now does not know how to get out of it, his teachers only like girls, there are no male role models, the parent gives in too easily, knows how to play one person off against another and so on.

Michael's Story

Michael is an 11-year-old boy brought to see me by his mum. Michael had already been diagnosed as suffering from ADHD and had been taking Ritalin for a year. He continued to have major behavioural problems at home and at school, including running away, aggressive outbursts, rudeness and defiance. He presented as sullen and refused to talk to me at our first meeting. Michael's mum believed that this is because he did not want to see doctors because he did not like taking the Ritalin. Michael confirmed this saying there is nothing wrong with him. Michael's mum also tells me that she has felt guilty and blamed by professionals whom she thinks see her as an incompetent mother, but she also felt that Michael's problems have been caused by what happened with his dad who moved out of the area a few years ago and hardly ever sees Michael now. Michael refused to talk about his feelings towards his dad and instead kept pestering his mum to leave. Michael's mum also told me that she has tried to talk to Michael about this issue but he cannot seem to do it. She believed that he is bottling his feelings up. I decided to make the following intervention. I told Michael he is being rude and that I do not accept such rude behaviour in my office. I told him that I expect him to apologize for his behaviour and then tell me in a respectful way about his relationship with his dad. I insisted that he would not be leaving my office until he has done this. Michael refused to co-operate and so with his mum's permission I asked her to wait outside until Michael had co-operated and shown some respect. She readily agreed to do this. Michael became tearful, agitated and abusive. I stuck to my guns and insisted that his mum will only be invited back in once he had apologized and agreed to talk about his dad and if this takes all day, so be it. It took Michael half an hour before he apologized and agreed to co-operate. He explained that he misses his dad and thinks his dad does not love him anymore. By doing this I was hoping to impart several messages. First, I am broadly agreeing with Michael's mum's explanation that the problem lay in what happened with his dad and Michael's subsequent bottling up of these feelings. This also meant that I am not seeing her (Michael's mum) as the root of the problem. Secondly, I was also modelling an intervention that gave Michael boundaries that his mum's sense of guilt made difficult for her to feel it was fair to do to Michael. I also showed by doing this that being firm with Michael can deliver results and I did this without needing to sound one note of criticism that could make Michael's mum feel worse (she had in effect already warned me that criticism would be counter-productive to our therapeutic relationship). Following this session I phoned Michael's father to discuss with him what Michael had said. His father agreed to meet with me and eventually he started seeing Michael more often. When the situation began to improve I was able to tell Michael that indeed there was nothing wrong with him and his medication was discontinued.

Aden's Story

Aden is a 9-year-old boy brought by his parents because his school was saying that he is distractible, hyperactive and distracts others in his class. There are no reported problems with his behaviour at home. Aden's parents tell me that they think his teacher has no patience with him, that she is unduly critical and that they are not supporting him at school. They think Aden has now gone off school and no longer wants to co-operate. I visited Aden's school to observe him in class and talk to his teachers. Aden was in a class of thirty children with one teacher and no classroom assistants. The young teacher looked and sounded stressed. She spent a lot of the time making ineffective pleas for the class to be quiet. During my half-hour observation she sent three different boys (but not Aden – who was pleased to see me and on his best behaviour) to stand in the corner for 'time out'. I could not see any particular reason why these three boys were singled out when, compared to the chaos in the rest of the class-room, I could not see anything that particularly stood out about their behaviour. I met with Aden's teacher and suggested a home–school diary was started in which daily they noted Aden's good as well as problematic behaviours. I explain that following this I can then work with Aden's parents with regard to appropriate rewards and sanctions for his school-based behaviours. The parents showed me this diary at a later session. In it Aden's teacher is only noting his problematic behaviours; there are no entries commenting on positive aspects of his behaviour. I now had ample evidence to fully agree with Aden's parents' original explanation that his behaviour reflects school-based rather than Aiden-based difficulties. I helped them find a different school for Aiden and he soon flourishes in his new school.

Noticing and Amplifying Strengths

In mainstream Western psychiatry and psychology the professional language revolves around notions of 'deficit'. We have created frames of reference (such as the Diagnostic Statistical Manual or DSM) by which events, experiences and behaviours can be categorized and compartmental-ized into fixed entities that are generally assumed to have a neurological/biological origin. As professionals we are trained to search for deficit, to uncover 'psychopathology' to diagnose any aberration that does not fit our cultural opinion of 'normal'. This is not just an academic point. These cultural beliefs have consequences – huge consequences. They compel us to act in certain ways and to pass highly loaded and powerful messages to our clients and their families. They take our attention away from functional stories, from noticing the exceptions, from seeing strength, courage and resilience.

Post-modern therapies such as narrative therapy and solution-focused therapy challenge such constructions. By searching for exceptions to the problem-saturated story, finding strengths and building on them, a form of therapy that challenges the dogma of deficit can be constructed. Such a 'building health'-orientated (as opposed to 'getting rid of illness') therapeutic strategy is not only potentially empowering, but can also be viewed as an important way of demonstrating cultural/political resistant to the dominant discourse.

Daniel's Story

I first saw Daniel shortly after his 14th birthday. He came with his mother, father and older sister. Daniel attended a school for children with mild learning difficulties. Daniel's school had been complaining for many years about his oppositionality, lack of effort and frequent tempers. At home he would not do as he was told, stayed out later than he was allowed and would get violent if challenged. For several months he had been sleeping in his parent's bedroom, complaining that he could see ghosts in his room. Daniel had seen many professionals over the years and been tried on different medicines, which he did not like taking and often refused to take. When speaking to Daniel I noticed that he seemed eager to speak to me about all these issues (taking medication, seeing ghosts, school and home life, etc.). On more than one occasion I expressed surprise that he had learning difficulties, telling him that he was coming across as a very thoughtful young man. We spoke about the ghosts. He told me that he started seeing them after watching a horror film at a friend's house. Eventually he told me that he thought he had seen one on one occasion after seeing this film and now he was too scared to sleep in his bedroom. Daniel's sister said that their parents are too soft with Daniel and that she was sure Daniel would manage if he went back to his bedroom. I asked about other things Daniel was scared of. Amongst the things the family mentioned was being away from them (school trips and sleepovers). I then asked Daniel if he had ever managed to go on a school trip or a sleepover. He told me of a few occasions he had. I asked him all sorts of questions about his last school trip and how he had managed. As I listened I said frequent 'wow's and made remarks about how there was a very brave bit inside of him. At the end of this session I gave his parents some suggestions as to how they could wean him off sleeping in their bedroom. The next time I saw them, the parents told me that Daniel had gone to sleep in his own bedroom straight away on the night of our last meeting. He had told them he was going to do it himself and he did.

William's Story

William was 8-years old when I started seeing him. His parents adopted him when he was four. Between the ages of two and four he had stayed with several different foster carers, having been removed from his family of origin at the age of two on the grounds of neglect. William could be a real handful, on the one hand oppositional, violent and hyperactive, on the other sensitive to criticism and easily made tearful and 'clingy'. He had seen several professionals and had been diagnosed as suffering from Asperger's syndrome and ADHD. He was also taking a prescribed stimulant and an anti-psychotic. During the first meeting his parents told me that William had written a poem about having Asperger's syndrome and ADHD. William read it out loud at my request. It was a sad poem about being lonely and empathizing with others who felt hurt inside. I kept commenting on how moving I had found the poem and how it did not fit for me with a diagnosis of Asperger's syndrome, as I felt William was demonstrating a profound imagination and capacity to empathize with feelings at a level well beyond his age (the capacity for imagination and empathy are meant to be poor in Asperger's syndrome). I asked about other things he was good at and his parents told me about William's model building, sometimes from odds and ends he finds, sometimes from Lego and sometimes from model building kits. I asked them to bring some of his models to the next session. William brought three of his models. I commented on the fine detail and asked how long they took to build. I told William that he has fantastic creativity and that it had taken an amazing feat of concentration to build such marvellous models. I suggested to William and his family that such levels of sustained concentration suggests that William does not have ADHD either. I worked with William, his family and his school over the following year, building on his strengths, courage and capacity to survive adversity. By the end of the year he no longer needed to take any medication and was diagnosis-free.

Deconstructing Expertise

The traditional doctor/patient script creates unnecessary dependence on the perceived expertise of the doctor. More often than not, our clients know the solutions, and it is up to us professionals to show them that they do. This calls for a different sort of knowledge or expertise, one that is more subtle and grounded in an understanding of the culturally scripted nature of our perceptions. From a purely technical point of view the importance of this more subtle knowledge quickly becomes apparent once we realize that psychiatry and psychology is hardly what could be considered 'rocket science'. Indeed, one of the comments I frequently make as a way into deconstructing perceived expertise is along the lines of, 'Let me let you into a professional secret. Psychiatry is not based on any rocket science.' By putting client's wishes central, they can be the guides for what they would like to see change, whether change has occurred, how often they wish to meet and when they feel our work is finished. This does not diminish my responsibility as a therapist or my therapeutic confidence, quite the reverse. Another useful metaphor I use to try and convey this way of thinking is that I may have the Knowledge but it is they – parents/carers/child – who know the child.

Edward's Story

Edward was aged seven when he was brought by his parents to see me. Edward was a right terror at home, ruling the roost and riding roughshod over any rules. His parents were kind, gentle and compassionate. They did not believe in physical punishment and told me that they both had unhappy experiences as children with their parents, which they associated with being physically punished. Edward's father told me he was a prison officer. I was very curious about this and asked him about prison rules and discipline for inmates. Edward's father explained to me a three-level system that prisoners could move up or down on depending on their behaviour, earning more privileges if they were compliant with the rules and having them taken away if they weren't. I suggested to Mr Edward that he already knew how to manage his son's behaviour and that he and his wife should discuss how to implement a system similar to the one Mr Edward was used to at his work but more geared to home life. The Edwards worked out a three-tier system at home with privileges that could be added or withdrawn, and within two weeks Edward was behaving himself.

Charlie's Story

Charlie was 15 when I first met him. His parents were professionals who came from Hong Kong. They brought Charlie to see me as he had been caught smoking cannabis at school and suspended for a week as a result. His parents felt ashamed, but also wanted some 'expert' guidance on how this problem should be handled. I asked them for their opinion and asked them what they had done. They told me they had 'grounded' him as punishment, but they were concerned he was not talking to them. They were also aware that Charlie had grown up in a culture different to them and had different expectations. They were afraid that their 'punishment' would lead Charlie to reject them. I asked Charlie for his opinion about what his parents had said. He said he was sorry for what had happened, and although he agreed that he had values different to his parents, he thought their punishment was justified. In fact he thought they should have been more severe with him than they were. Charlie's parents said they wanted to continue with some degree of restrictions on his going out, until trust had been rebuilt. They expressed surprise at my wholehearted agreement with their way of handling the situation with Charlie, stating that they were expecting that I would disapprove of their methods and suggest alternative ones. We met a few more times at their request mainly to confirm what I suspected – that Charlie and his family were doing well.

Chapter 7

Multi-perspective Approaches 2: Developing Diverse Solutions

The popularization of the disease notion had other ramifications... Treatments were not designed to make these children think and function fully. Instead because children were viewed as diseased, handicapped and helpless, behaviour treatments were designed to augment the efforts of drugs, rather than to truly ameliorate the problem... All of this, actually, only helps to convince the children that they are sick and helpless. These behavioural techniques reinforce and handicap their inability to think or behave without constant outside assistance.

DAVID STEIN, 2001: 6

In the last chapter, I looked at how, when confronted by a human problem, there are diverse possible meanings we can give to this problem. Furthermore the meaning we give the problem has a huge impact on what we choose to do as doctors and therapists. The process of interpreting and re-interpreting the meaning given to a problem can, in itself, be a therapeutic process and sometimes it is all that is needed. In this chapter, I would like to explore a range of possible approaches to trying to solve a particular problem (in this case children's 'naughty' behaviour) once some common meaning has been established between the therapist, child and their family. The approaches I look at in this chapter are not mutually exclusive with the ideas explored in the last chapter – merely a convenient way of organizing my thoughts. I have also previously detailed many useful interventions in Chapter 5.

I start with the current mainstream practice in Western child-and-adolescent mental health ideology for dealing with naughty children. Following this I touch upon other approaches from more diverse perspectives that can be helpfully used by clinicians. Incorporating and considering the potential helpfulness of non-Western culture's systems of medicine and psychology, lies in the wish to promote the usefulness to all of us of reversing the process of colonization.

Western mental health treatment technologies are justifiably subject to constant criticism. They have proved themselves to be pretty ineffectual and there is ample evidence to suggest that some of the more 'ordinary' (such as family support-based) approaches employed in the developing world contribute to a better outcome for those with major mental health problems, when compared to Western mental health technologies (Fernando, 1988; Timimi, 2002; Whittaker, 2002).

Perhaps an excessive focus on materialistic science, research, evidence, statistics and so on has become part of the problem rather than part of the solution. The process of trying to objectify and de-contextualize human subjectivity is always in danger of atomizing our humanity as we construct the individualized person splintered from that which troubles and more importantly enriches our social milieu. In this respect the more intuitive, spiritual and experiential approaches of many non-Western forms of treatment can provide a welcome antidote to failed Western mental health technologies. It is sad to see the cultural colonization of superior and more effective local ideologies by Western-inspired ones, and gratifying to see an awakening interest in this issue amongst some in the mental health movement. We still have much to learn from the so-called 'developing countries'.

The Use of Medication

The most commonly used medicine for naughty boys in Western culture is via the route of a diagnosis of ADHD, leading to a prescription of a psycho-stimulant such as Ritalin or Dexedrine. I have covered psycho-stimulant prescribing to children and adolescents in Chapter 5.

In addition to psycho-stimulants, many other medicines are used in the Western child-and-adolescent mental health world to try and control naughty children. The extent of medicalization of naughtiness becomes apparent when we consider that paediatricians hand out a large proportion if not most of the prescriptions that are handed out for the purpose of 'treating' naughty children. Within the medical profession ADHD is now viewed as and classified as a 'neuro-developmental' disorder. This means that ADHD is conceptualized as being due to a biological problem in the development of the nervous system, despite the lack of medical evidence or tests to identify this supposed biological problem (see Chapter 5). Thus, by virtue of a trick of categorization, paediatricians and not psychiatrists have become a, if not the, professional group given the responsibility to diagnose and 'treat' ADHD (usually by prescribing medication). When leading medical journals publish articles purporting to represent an 'evidence-based' approach to managing children with behaviour problems in which paediatricians argue that about 7 per cent of children, mainly boys, have ADHD for which the first line of treatment (and possibly the only treatment needed) is a psycho-stimulant (Guevara and Stein, 2001), the depth of the problem of medicalization becomes apparent.

As many paediatricians and child psychiatrists have become comfortable with prescribing psychoactive drugs for naughty children, this having become an important component of their cultural belief system (at least in Western culture), these professionals began to experiment with many other psychoactive drugs. Most of these experimental treatments are with drugs that have not been licensed for use with under-16s. In most Western countries pharmaceutical drugs have to go through certain trials and tests and following this obtain a licence from governing authorities. The licence usually shows the indications for which the governing authority feels the drug has shown acceptable standards of efficacy and safety. That doctors are allowed to prescribe out of licence, however, does mean they are prescribing drugs in situations where safety standards, efficacy and side effects have not been tested for and established, a fact not always explained to the recipient and their family. This hasn't stopped doctors from trying out every class of psychoactive drugs on children and adolescents, to the point where many of the drugs I mention below are commonly prescribed by many child psychiatrists and paediatricians for the 'treatment' of naughty children, often using several at once (known as 'polypharmacy') and usually for many years.

Thus in addition to the use of psycho-stimulants, neuroleptics (also known as anti-psychotics), which are extensively used in adult psychiatry for the treatment of those considered by adult psychiatrists to be severely mentally ill, are increasingly used in children with a diagnosis of ADHD, in children who show aggressive behaviour and in children diagnosed with autism or learning difficulties who have (or are perceived to have) behavioural problems (Connor *et al.*, 1998; Campbell *et al.*, 1999). Neuroleptics, including older drugs such as Chlorpromazine and Haloperidol and newer drugs such as Risperidone and Olanzipine, are used mainly for their 'dumbing down' effect on the nervous system (another name for neuroleptics is 'major tranquilizers'). The available studies on children taking such medication have been of poor quality, having had small samples followed up for a short time such as a few weeks or months (e.g. Mandoki, 1995; Simeon *etal.*, 1995). Of concern is the dreadful side-effect profile that neuroleptics have, which makes them unpopular with adult patients. Given that children are prescribed these toxic drugs and kept on them for many years, there is an enormous potential for inflicting on these children many unpleasant and sometimes irreversible side effects. Indeed chemically this class of drug has been blamed for causing, rather than ameliorating, psychiatric problems, given their potential for causing irreversible brain damage (Breggin, 1991; Whittaker, 2002). The most obvious and troublesome side effect is a permanent untreatable movement disorder that many on long-term treatment get, that involves involuntary movement of certain muscle groups such as involuntary chewing type movement of the face and jaws (known as tardive dyskinesia). Other common side effects include; weight gain, sedation, breast enlargement, muscle spasms, urinary retention, sweating, diabetes, heart disease, convulsions, depression and sometimes death. It is likely that, given their biological immaturity, children are more sensitive to these side effects than adults. Shockingly, I have come across children in their pre-school years who have been prescribed neuroleptics to control their behaviour. I have seen children who had been taken to a private consultant when they were 3-years old, been diagnosed as having ADHD and prescribed both a Stimulant and a neuroleptic.

Anti-depressants are also used to 'treat' ADHD, aggression and other naughty behaviours in children. Anti-depressants such as Bupropion, Imipramine, Trazodone, and Paroxetine are amongst those that have been used in this regard (Emslie *etal.*, 1999; Geller *etal.*, 1999). Whilst the safety and efficacy of anti-depressants in treating naughty children has not been established, as with neuroleptics, this has not prevented doctors from using them in increasing numbers with children (from as young as 18 months) and adolescents (Olfson *etal.*, 2002; Zito *etal.*, 2000). Like other psychoactive drugs, anti-depressants expose the body to a multitude of possible side effects including: blurring of vision, sedation, urinary retention, heart disease, nausea, vomiting, headache, dizziness, agitation, weight gain, convulsions, mania and sudden death. The selective serotonin re-uptake inhibitors class of anti-depressant (or 'SSRI's) like Fluoxetine, Sertraline and Paroxetine, can lead to suicidal or violent impulses in as many as a fifth of those who take them, a flattening and deadening of emotions, as well as a withdrawal syndrome on discontinuation (Healy, 1999; Breggin, 2001b). Following a review of safety and efficacy of SSRIs, the UK committee on safety of medicines, in December 2003, advised that most SSRIs should not be used in the under-18 age group due to emerging evidence (suppressed by the drug companies for a long time) that there is little evidence to demonstrate efficacy and that this age group is more sensitive to potentially serious side effects (Ramchandani, 2004).

The so-called 'mood stabilizers' such as Lithium, Valproate and Carbamazepine (the latter two are mainly anti-convulsants) are also used for 'treatment' of naughtiness. As with neuroleptics and anti-depressants, studies on the use of mood stabilizers with naughty children have had small samples that were followed up for a short time (e.g. Rifkin *et al.*, 1997; Donovan *et al.*, 2000; Malone *et al.*, 2000). Side effects of Lithium include: stomach upsets, tremor, kidney damage, weight gain and intoxication if prescribed in too high a dose that can lead to circulatory failure and death. Side effects of anti-convulsants include: nausea, blurring of vision, dizziness, headaches, poor concentration, confusion and occasionally liver and kidney failure and blood disorders. Other medications that have been experimented with to try and control naughty children include: Clonidine, Guanfacine and beta-blockers (all are used primarily for treatment of high blood pressure), and Buspirone (a minor tranquilizer) (Connor, 2002).

Unfortunately, all too often within this context-deprived medical culture, many children will end up on more than one drug as the effects of the first prescribed medicine begins to wear off over time, particularly if everyone in the system has been cultured into a medical model view of the child's problems. Sometimes this 'polypharmacy' (use of more than one drug at a time) happens right at the start, with some clinicians feeling that using more than one drug is clinically necessary. For others drugs are added to combat the side effects of the original drug. For example, a child may be prescribed a psycho-stimulant, but this keeps him up at night and so a sedative is added to the regime, but unfortunately both the psycho-stimulant and the sedative make the child feel depressed and so an anti-depressant is added to the cocktail.

With consideration of context so often absent and alternatives to the use of medications which inevitably have side effects, pushed to the back of the shelve, I am left wondering what impact this blind use of powerful chemicals has not only on our cultural competence when it comes to dealing with boys, but also biologically on the developing brains of the now millions of children being exposed to these potential toxins.

Teaching Parenting Skills

In a reflection of the stuckness of mainstream psychiatry in the nature-versus-nurture argument, a debate that is highly polarized seems to go round and round in endless fruitless circles. Historically, the two dominant and competing models in mainstream child-and-adolescent mental health ideology with regard to naughty children are causation as nature (child's fault to be treated by medication) and causation as nurture (parent's fault to be treated by teaching parenting skills). Teaching parenting skills often goes under the heading of Parent Management Training (or PMT for short). Most of these PMTs are about teaching parents a version of the carrot and stick that is particularly popular in and congruent with a white Western middle-class value system. The language of the popular theories is wrapped in the pseudoscience of psychology technical speak, to give the illusion of a high-status theory that requires a scientifically trained expert to understand it. To my mind, however, the principles behind most PMTs are pretty straightforward, and are about noticing and rewarding good behaviour in the child (carrot) and having some sort of sanction to deal with unwanted behaviour in the child (stick). Having said that, the setting up of the various rituals that occur when you formalize the strategies suggested in PMTs are undoubtedly helpful for many parents as is the process of bringing parents struggling with similar difficulties together in the group format that many PMT programmes use.

Parent management training provides a set of procedures for parents designed to alter the pattern of their interaction with their child. It helps parents to establish clear and consistent rules for a child to follow, provides positive reinforcement of desired behaviour (carrot) and methods to try to suppress unwanted behaviour (stick) as well as helping parents find ways of negotiating compromises with their children where appropriate. The basic teaching style is that of careful instruction by the therapist as well as modelling, role-playing, behavioural rehearsal and often some structured homework exercises for parents to do (Kazdin, 1987, 1997). Carrot strategies include star charts to monitor desired behaviour, catching the child being good and praising them and reward systems in the form of treats and extra individual attention from a parent. Stick strategies include ignoring unwanted behaviours, 'time out' procedures, withdrawal of privileges and distraction.

The first formal parent management training programmes with a particular, as it were, curriculum was developed by Hanf (1969) and Patterson (1976). Such programmes have subsequently been modified and developed by several independent groups. For example, the 'helping the non-compliant child' programme for children aged three to eight years (Forehand and McMahon, 1981) is a two phase programme in which the parent learns to break the cycle of coercive interchanging and focus on building a positive relationship with the child in the first phase (carrot). In the second phase of treatment the programme consists of teaching the parent to use various 'stick' strategies such as 'time out' procedures and appropriate commands to decrease a child's non-compliant behaviour.

Another popular parent management programme for 3- to 8-year olds is called 'Basic' (Webster-Stratton, 1996). This programme uses videotape modelling and group discussion format. There is a standard package of ten videotape programmes illustrating parenting skills and common pitfalls, which are shown by a therapist to a group of parents and then discussed with them. There are approximately two hundred and fifty videotape vignettes that each last about two minutes and include examples of parents interacting with their children in what is considered inappropriate and then appropriate ways. These vignettes are then used by the therapist to lead a discussion with the parents who are often given homework assignments to practice various parenting skills with their children based on what they had learned through the videotapes and the ensuing discussion. This Webster-Stratton package is now used widely for PMT and the programme has recently been expanded to include a videotape programme for children, focusing on children's social skills (McMahon and Wells, 1998).

The Oregon Social Learning Centre (OSLC) programme for children from 3 to 12 years of age is another popular PMT programme based upon the work of Patterson and his colleagues (Patterson, 1975). In this programme, parents are first given reading assignments so that they acquire background information that the programme considers necessary for the further skills training. Parents are then taught to track the children's behaviour problems and are assisted in developing a positive reinforcement system (carrot) and a consequence programme for non-compliant behaviour (stick). As the treatment progresses, the parents are encouraged to become increasingly responsible for designing and implementing their own behaviour management programmes at home in a way that promotes the parents' own problem-solving and negotiating strategies.

Another variant is Barkley's 'Defiant Children' programme (Barkley, 1987, 1997). This programme consists of ten steps taught to parents individually or in groups. The steps emphasize progressive skill building, including instruction in making positive or negative consequences immediate upon a child's behaviour, making consequences consistent across time, settings and between parents, establishing incentive reward programmes for desired behaviours and mild punishment for undesired behaviours, anticipating and planning for unwanted behaviours, and recognizing that each member of the family has a role to play.

All the particular programmes mentioned above were developed in the United States and have then been exported elsewhere. Groups in other countries have sometimes adapted some of these programmes in order to be more suitable for their country's population. For example the Webster-Stratton programme of videotape vignettes has been adapted in the United Kingdom by Scott *et al.* (2001). This group produced their own videotape vignettes but this time using British actor's voices, having encountered difficulties in running parent groups with the American videotapes, because of parents' not understanding the language or being able to relate culturally to the actors.

A more innovative spin on the Webster-Stratton training package has been developed in Ireland. This programme known as the 'Parent Plus Programme' not only uses its own videotape vignettes with Irish actors but also has changed much of the emphasis. The philosophy behind the 'Parent Plus Programme' is that it is for good parents who want to become better parents (instead of implicitly giving the message that a parent training programme is for failed parents). To support this approach they eliminated all the vignettes in which examples of inappropriate ways of parenting were shown and included only vignettes of the suggested methods. In addition, more acknowledgement of context was made by introducing into the videotape and the parenting group discussions about the way modern life has changed the family and the sorts of new pressures that parents and children experience as a result (Sharry, 1999).

The majority of the programmes mentioned above are designed for teaching parent management skills to the parents of pre-adolescent children. In recognition that adolescence can be a more complicated life stage in modern, Western culture, PMT programmes specifically geared towards helping parents with adolescent children show a bit more variety and complexity.

Patterson and colleagues have modified their OSLC parent training programme for use in families of adolescents (Patterson and Forgatch, 1987; Forgatch and Patterson, 1989). Adaptations in this programme include expanding the list of target behaviours for parental monitoring and tracking to include any activities that put an adolescent at risk of further misbehaviour (e.g. school truancy, substance misuse), a strong emphasis on parental monitoring and supervision of the teenager, more age-appropriate forms of stick strategies including restriction of free time, restriction of activities and repayment of stolen/damaged property, asking parents to report legal offences to juvenile authorities and then to act as advocates for the adolescent in court as a way of decreasing the risk of the youth's removal from home, and greater involvement of the adolescent in the treatment programme (McMahon and Wells, 1998).

Functional family therapy (FFT) is a family intervention programme, which includes elements from systemic, behavioural and cognitive therapy ideology (Alexander and Parsons, 1982). Clinical problems are conceptualized from the standpoint of the functions they serve for the family as a system as well as for individual family members. The underlying rationale is that an adolescent's behaviour problem serves some interpersonal function, such as intimacy, distance and/or support among family members. The goal of FFT is to alter interaction and communication patterns in such a way as to foster more adaptive functioning amongst family members. The FFT programme itself consists of five components (Alexander *et al.*, 1988). The introduction phase is concerned with family members' expectations prior to therapy. The assessment phase involves the therapist identifying the behavioural, cognitive and emotional expectations of each family member and exploring family processes that need to change. In the induction/therapy phase attributions and expectations among family members are modified. In the behavioural change/education phase various behavioural techniques are employed, including improving communication or skills using behavioural contracts and other management techniques to try and promote change in the behavioural patterns within the family. In the generalization/termination phase, the clinician's task is to facilitate maintenance of the therapeutic gains while fostering family independence and gradual disengagement from the therapeutic context.

Multi-systemic therapy (MST) is a family systems approach for families with naughty adolescents that emphasizes both the interactional nature of adolescence and the role of multiple systems in which the adolescent lives, such as the family, school and peer group (Hengeller and Borduin, 1990). MST views the family as just one of a number of systems that have the potential to affect the teenager. Thus, in treatment, MST employs many different treatment techniques that are flexibly deployed with the adolescent and their family to try to promote change within different parts of the system. Several family therapy techniques are used in MST and, depending on the individual family, MST will also include other domains within its therapeutic purview beyond the parents and their difficulties with their adolescent, such as marital difficulties, unemployment, school difficulties and so on. Therapists are guided by a set of treatment principles (e.g. focusing on the system's strengths and keeping interventions developmentally appropriate) that serve to integrate the different treatment strategies used in a coherent approach that is individualized for each family. MST, when compared to most other approaches discussed so far in this section, offers the most context-rich thinking in terms of its treatment ideology.

Another programme gleaned from more context-aware family therapy approaches is the 'Seven Steps Programme' for re-establishing authority and reclaiming love over the out-of-control teenager (Sells, 2001). The programme grew out of the author's own research, watching hundreds of videotapes of successful family therapy interventions for out-of-control teenagers and taking the common elements from these interventions and incorporating them into a step-by-step programme that the author considers has a clarity that it easy for families to follow. Step one of the programme is aimed at allowing parents to vent their feelings and therapists to explore with parents the question of why their particular teenager has problems. Step two looks at the question of how teenagers defeat parents. Parents are introduced to the concept that out-of-control teenagers know what buttons to push with their parents, and parents consequently lose because they do not understand the 'rules of the game'. Using role-play and other techniques, the teenagers' game playing is explained to parents and home assignment tasks are given. Step three involves an exploration of why current contracts and any home assignment tasks have failed and is often combined with step four which looks at helping the family to mobilize outside helpers like friends, neighbours and schools who can be enlisted to help with developing strategies that can re-enforce parents' authority. Step five looks at troubleshooting and how to start thinking two steps ahead of the teenager by predicting which buttons the teenager is likely to push in order to try and re-establish their power at home and how the parent may respond to that. Step six consists of a menu of techniques to stop the teenagers' so-called 'seven aces' (the aces include various techniques teenagers may use to restore power over their parents, such as truancy, running away, threats or acts of violence and threats of suicide). Finally, step seven is an exploration of how to restore lost nurturance and tenderness within the family system once some authority has been re-established over the teenager. The sessions are conducted with either the parents or the parents and their teenager and sometimes all the family.

All the above programmes are backed up by claims that outcome research shows them to be effective in reducing naughtiness among children and adolescents, including, in some of the family therapy approaches, quite severe behavioural problems and delinquency (Gordon *et al.*, 1995; Borduin, 1999). However, a number of criticisms can be levelled at the PMT ideology, particularly those that are context-deprived. PMT makes several demands on parents such as mastering educational material, systematically observing the child's behaviour, consistently implementing specific procedures at home and attending weekly therapy sessions, which can lead to high drop-out rates. Furthermore, many programmes are experienced by parents as having unrealistic expectations and an unrealistic understanding of the home circumstances of the family with regard to issues such as pressure of time, number of children to manage and other external pressures such as pressures of resources, pressure from school, employers, housing and so on. Thus, in clinical situations many families are unable to respond or consistently attend PMT programmes. There is also evidence to suggest that PMT programme's effectiveness tends to diminish as the child grows older (Barkley, 1997; Kazdin, 1997). In addition there is the whole question of therapist variables and the ability of non-relationship-grounded approaches to therapy in using the interpersonal skills of therapists to help the therapeutic process along, particularly if they do not pay attention to cultural discourses that marginalize certain groups (such as mother-blaming and cultural belittling of non-Western beliefs and practices).

Behavioural therapies such as PMT rely too heavily on Western psychiatric metaphors, in other words conceptualizing human relationship problems in terms of symptoms-diagnosis treatment (aimed at eliminating symptoms). This medical paradigm has enormous cultural power and has been exploited by the pharmaceutical industry. Research in psychological therapies, especially cognitive behaviour therapy, has been shaped by the medical model 'drug metaphor'. The drug metaphor has also had a distorting and potentially damaging effect in psychological medicine. Psychotherapy is essentially concerned with people, not conditions, disorders or symptoms, and its methods arise out of an intimate relationship between people that cannot easily be reduced to a set of prescribed techniques (Holmes, 2002). One of the most robust findings in psychotherapy research is that a good therapeutic alliance is the best predictor of outcome in psychotherapy (Horvath and Symonds, 1991).

Therapy with the Child

In mainstream mental health practice, medication is not the only method that targets the child in order to promote change. The most popular of other methods used is the cognitive behavioural approach whose aim is to teach the child better ways of behaving. As with PMT, cognitive behavioural therapy sits comfortably within modern, Western cultural ideology and has a basic compatibility with the medical model approach. In this paradigm too, a symptom profile is collected and a diagnosis is made. A Western, cognitive framework emphasizes logical analysis, gathering of evidence and teaching skills through logical reasoning with the young person concerned.

Behavioural social skills training focuses on poor social skills with the underlying theory that children who display problematic social skills often do so to get rewards from the environment, therefore direct training in more adaptive skills to get what one desires can help reduce the need some children may feel for mal-adaptive social behaviours such as fighting. The approach typically involves the modelling by the therapist of appropriate skills, role-playing with the young person, practising interpersonal skills and positive reinforcement, by the therapist, of any achievements the youngster makes. Follow-up studies on outcome of such approaches have, as a generalization, shown only moderate, short-term effectiveness for this approach which seems to benefit youngsters who present as more anxious rather than those who show more features of aggression in their presenting problem (Schneider, 1992).

As a result of the limited success encountered with purely behavioural approaches, behavioural approaches that incorporate more cognitive elements have been developed with the assumption that what is necessary is to change the young person's perceptions and appraisals of events rather than change the events themselves (Kendall, 1985). Cognitive approaches aim to help the child identify triggers for bad behaviour (such as aggression), map out habitual thoughts, feelings, actions and consequences and construct a plan to replace these with more useful ones. An attempt is made to help the child identify what is termed 'cognitive distortions', in other words thoughts that misinterpret reality (presumably as constructed by others such as the therapist) and find alternative thoughts that can be used instead, such as 'I don't have to rise to the bait', 'I don't need to prove myself', 'its not worth it', 'by doing this I will be the loser' and so on.

Coping Power is a 33 sessions, school-based programme, developed to teach cognitive skills to schoolchildren (Lochman *et al.*, 1987; Lochman and Wells, 1996). The format is for primary school–aged children. The children meet once weekly in a group where they practise examples of social encounters and discuss their and other people's motivations in these social encounters. As well as practising social skills directly the young people are encouraged to look at the thought processes going on, generate alternative solutions and thoughts to any problems encountered and then to evaluate the solutions. According to the authors of this programme, there is evidence showing continued benefits for children for at least three years after completing the programme (Lochman, 1992).

Problem Solving Skills Training (PSST) has been developed to teach cognitive skills to help children identify problems, evaluate the situation, generate a solution and enact this solution (Kazdin, 1996, 1997). PSST is given over twenty sessions to pre-adolescent children. According to the authors, there is evidence to support the effectiveness of this approach in reducing mild to moderate naughtiness in children referred for treatment (Kazdin and Wassell, 2000).

Cognitive behavioural approaches are the most popular of the psycho-therapies in mainstream mental health ideology for any perceived mental health problem. The emphasis on logical reasoning within the cognitive behavioural approach means that younger children and children with particular learning difficulties (and in both cases by virtue of their slower verbal reading and language development) (Kazdin, 1997) are less likely to be able to make use of such an approach, and with this approach being context-depleted it is also of limited use to children who are living in situations where there are multiple other social pressures on them such as poverty, bullying, broken families, mental health problems in the parents and so on. In addition they rely on a culturally constructed idea concerning social norms and so need adaptation and more careful thought when involving children from ethnic minority backgrounds. There are, of course, a multitude of other individual therapies that have developed out of Western culture that can be and are used to try and help naughty children. Unfortunately, mainstream medical and mental health culture in their enthusiasm to develop the so-called evidence-based technologies to be applied to mental health problems have spent too much time searching for universals (or rather creating their own universals within their ideologies) and ignoring the subtleties of subjective human life. Thus, certain therapies such as psychoanalysis for naughty children have been written off as ineffective (Kazdin, 1996) prematurely. Similarly, other ways of thinking about and researching effectiveness such as qualitative research, feedback from users about their experiences of therapy and the single case study have been unnecessarily marginalized. If, as I believe we must, we are to keep our minds open to the potentially infinite possibilities for human behaviour, beliefs and therefore interventions, then we should con-sider not only the potential usefulness of depth psychology treatments such as psychoanalysis but also the potentially useful ways of thinking about and framing a problem, which can be gained from a depth psychology approach that explores emotional states and their connection with thought and behaviour. In addition, there is much within psychoanalysis as a value system that is of benefit to therapists, such as the long-term perspective, the patient as opposed to the 'Jim will fix it' approach to change and the emphasis on the importance of relationships in sustaining our humanity. Although I believe there is much to criticize about psychoanalysis, particularly in its emphasis on pathology rather than strengths and resilience, the potential for a psychoanalytic perspective to enrich our understanding of naughty children and how to help them is enormous. For example, attachment theory which was developed by the psychoanalyst Bowlby (1969, 1973), following his studying the effects that mass evacuation had on children's sense of security and belonging, has been embraced by most psychoanalytic psychotherapists and has generated a huge amount of research into the deleterious consequences for the child of a poor early relationship with their carers. From this perspective, it can be understood that some naughty children are trying to retrieve the lost, pain-producing relationship, even if there is a more soothing and loving carer that has taken their place, for example through adoption (Novick and Novick, 1987; Fineman, 1995).

In a society where psychological trauma and loss through the diminishing value ascribed to children, the breakdown of the extended family and even the nuclear family, and the cultural promotion of self seeking (or in psychoanalytic terms, narcissistic) goals for existence – the clinical perspective that comes from an ideology that explores the cyclical result of such loss and trauma – should be supported. Just as the ideology behind a psychoanalytic approach may no longer fit in with mainstream, Western mental health ideologies so a treatment approach that involves labour-intensive, prolonged therapy, where the therapist develops an ever-deepening relationship with their client, does not fit in with the current mainstream. Nonetheless, many of the components of such an approach that includes the explicit recognition that patients enter into a relationship with a therapist are as useful today as they have always been. In some ways the psychoanalytic, ideological approach to therapy seems to come from an older time in Western history when people had more time for each other and did not find their lives so consumed by the rat race. In the words of Donald Winnicott, 'psychotherapy has to do with two people playing together' (Winnicott, 1971: 38).

Other Western Therapies

Of course there are a whole host of other psychotherapies that can be used with children such as play therapy, art therapy, drama therapy, neurolinguistic programming, transactional analysis, hypnotherapy, gestalt therapy, relaxation techniques, education therapy and so on. There are many interesting and innovative approaches that have been developed utilizing children's imaginative capacities. For example, Gardner (1993) developed the 'mutual storytelling technique' where a child is invited to make up a story and the therapist helps in this process with prompts and suggestions. When the story is finished, the therapist asks the child about the lessons that can be learned from the story. The therapist may then tell a similar story with complimentary therapeutic lessons which can be discussed with the child. Similarly Brooks (1993) invents stories based on a character that is named by the child, but whose nature is intended to address a therapeutic aim.

One of the most innovative psychiatrists/psychotherapists of the last century was Milton Erickson (see for example Haley, 1973; Erickson and Rossi, 1980 a–d; Zeig, 1980; Rosen, 1982). Erickson's intuitive approach to treating mental health problems can be considered a forerunner of many approaches that have since developed mainly within the family therapy field, such as strategic therapy, narrative therapy and solution-focused brief therapy. Erickson brought his insight and experience from using hypnosis in clinical practice, incorporated the principles of how to influence the unconscious in hypnosis and applied this to psychotherapy without formal trance induction. For example by taking an approach or making a comment that the client does not expect, the client's habitual patterns of thinking are disrupted for a brief period giving the therapist a window of opportunity to make therapeutic suggestions that may not be otherwise accepted by the client. This can be seen in many clinical examples of Erickson's work, such as in the case of the 'Cinnamon face' (Rosen, 1982) where Erickson surprises an unruly 8-year-old girl who has been brought by her mother for a consultation with him. As part of her problem this girl hated her facial freckles. On bringing her into his office, Erickson looks at this girl and accuses her of being a thief. Naturally the girl protests; however, Erickson persists with his accusation and adds that he has proof that she is a thief. The girl continues to protest and Erickson continues to build up the tension now adding that he even knows where she stole and what it is that she has stolen. By the time the girl was thoroughly angry with Erickson, he told her that she was in the kitchen and setting the kitchen table when the crime happened. She had then stood on the table to reach up to the cookie jar, which contained cinnamon cookies, cinnamon buns and cinnamon rolls. The jar then fell off the shelf and spilled cinnamon all over her face. Not only had Erickson surprised the girl but also he had got her to build up towards him the same emotion (of anger) that others had been complaining of. He then resolved this situation with humour that turned the therapeutic encounter into something very different for this girl (thereby surprising her again). Through this brief encounter Erickson effected an important therapeutic change for this girl and her family. Erickson often used stories such as the above, both in therapy and in teaching, as a device for metaphorical communication of potential solutions. Using stories as a therapeutic device for metaphorical communication of therapeutic messages is now used extensively in various forms of psychotherapy (see for example Madanes, 1981; Barker, 1985; Mills and Crowley, 1986).

In addition to 'treatment packages' that are specific for treatment of children with behavioural problems and that have been influence by family therapy approaches (see pp. 186–188), there are whole ranges of family therapy approaches that can be utilized flexibly by practitioners.

'Strategic family therapy' is a general term used to describe therapy that incorporates a plan that may be quite complex, to produce change, as opposed to a simple directive on the part of the therapist or a mutually agreed task (Madanes, 1981; Barker, 1998). Strategic therapy is a broad church and as a generalization it can be described as a style of working that can encompass a range of interventions including: reframing, the use of metaphorical communication, giving paradoxical instructions (in other words, instructions that involve the therapist advising families to do the opposite of what the therapist would like them to do), prescribing rituals, declaring therapeutic impotence, using humour, staging a debate and so on. Thus strategic therapy is not a specific method to be applied to all cases but rather an approach that depends on devising a strategy for each clinical problem. The therapist generally takes responsibility for developing the strategy, which often involves some sort of intervention in the client's social context. In many instances the social context target area is the client's family, and thus strategic methods are most commonly used as a means of intervening in families. Many of these strategic techniques can be found in the book *Paradox and Counterparadox* (Palazzoli *et al.*, 1978).

The setting of tasks and the performing of rituals can be used as devices to promote change. This can include providing new rituals for members of the family to follow or altering pre-existing ones (Hart, 1983; Wolin and Bennett, 1984). Rituals can be used as strategic devises to help individuals or families gain a sense of mastery and control over behaviour. For example, a boy with temper tantrums may be given the ritual prescription that his tantrums must continue to happen but he is to have them at a certain time, a certain place and for certain duration, such as everyday at home at 4 pm for at least 30 minutes (Hare-Mustin, 1975). By prescribing this paradoxical ritual, the boy and his family can begin to feel that the tantrums, rather than coming at them to try and destroy them, are at least partly under their control.

The 'systemic approach' to therapy was developed from general systems theory first articulated by Von Bertalanffy as a general theory of how parts organize into whole systems with the system becoming a complex of interacting elements (Bertalanffy, 1968). Perhaps the best-known group promoting the use of the systemic view in therapy is the 'Milan systemic therapy group' (Boscolo *et al.*, 1987). In a systemic context, it is not just the client and their immediate family that need to be considered but also other important influences in 'the system' in which a person is embedded, such as the extended family, the neighbourhood and of course for children their school. This way of thinking recognizes that we all live within a complex network of relationships and institutions. The essence of the systemic approach to children and their families is the belief that a family system is more than the sum of its parts and that the system as a whole can be the focus of therapy. The symptoms of individual members of the family can be seen as manifestations of the way the family system, or other institutions in which the client and their family are embedded, is functioning as a whole. The approach developed by the Milan systemic therapy group (Palazzoli *et al.*, 1978; Boscolo *et al.*, 1987) emphasizes working as teams. The usual way of practising this model is for one or more colleagues to observe a therapy session through a one-way screen so that they can offer input to the therapist either during a session by use of a telephone or an earpiece, or by having breaks in a session during which the team discuss their observations. Taking a systemic perspective is of course itself a form of reframing; in other words, rather than seeing the problem as being a mother's depression or a naughty boy's genes, the symptom is conceptualized as rooted in the way the system as a whole is functioning. Interventions are then conceived in order to try and bring about changes in the way the system functions as a whole, resulting hopefully in an improvement in the individual client's symptoms as a by product of changes in the system. Interestingly, one of the cornerstone pieces of research in modernist Western child psychiatric ideology, the Isle of Wight study of 10- and 11-year-old children (Rutter *et al.*, 1970), provides a lot of support for the systemic view point when it comes to the issue of naughty children. In this large-scale epidemiological study, little overlap was found between the group of children categorized as being naughty at home and those categorized as naughty at school. Evidently much of children's behaviour depends on their social context. Similarly it is also common to find that children's behaviour differs according to which family members are present. For example some boys will be well behaved in the company of their dad or a certain aunt, but become unruly in the company of their mum or a certain grandparent.

In 'structural' family therapy, the therapist works on the boundaries between systems and sub-systems, helping to erect what the therapist considers to be appropriate boundaries and a necessary sense of separation and hierarchy, for example, within the family unit. According to this approach, it is conceptualized that families require a well-functioning parental system where there should be clear, but not unduly rigid, boundaries between the parental and the children sub-systems. In larger families, there may be more than one children sub-system and there may also be, for example, a grandparental sub-system, which is having an important impact on the way the family works. In the structural approach (see for example Minuchin, 1974; Haley, 1976), therapy often revolves around re-establishing effective sub-systems and hierarchies where these are felt by the therapist to have become dysfunctional. The therapist also tries to promote communication and emotional interchange where it is felt to be inadequate, at the same time as they are trying to erect functional barriers where necessary. Thus in a situation where the therapist perceives that the parents are no longer the 'bosses' in the family system with the result that a particular child or children sub-system has too much power, the structural therapist's task would be that of re-establishing the parents as the boss in the system, allowing the child or children to go back to a position that the therapist would consider more age-appropriate with regard to power and responsibility.

In their book *Narrative Means to Therapeutic Ends*, White and Epston (1990) describe a number of original ideas for helping individuals and their families achieve change. Narrative therapists criticize traditional Western therapies that are largely based on the approach of trying to get rid of 'pathology', feeling that this results in clients internalizing social discourses, including those from the medical and other Western professions that pathologize much of our behaviour, thoughts and feelings thereby scripting problems into our lives. For example, a family may come with a naughty boy whom they feel has a problem with his temper, and our dominant culture (including in the medical profession) would then speak as if the child him/herself is the problem, in other words 'this is an angry child' or 'this is a conduct disordered child', rather than talking in terms of the child facing or dealing with his/her anger. In the narrative approach, the client's identity is separated from the problem by having 'externalizing' conversations with them and their family. In the case above, the therapist's externalizing reframe might be in terms of, 'so it sounds like your parents are concerned about what happens when temper is around' or 'do you think it's possible for you to be angry or sad without letting temper get the better of you?' This model, which to me is very similar to a 'possession' model (where the evil doings are the result of possession by an outside force), frees the client to take more responsibility for coping successfully with their problems without feeling that it is their very personhood that is being challenged (White, 1989; White and Epston, 1990; Freeman *et al.*, 1997).

Another narrative approach with a slightly different emphasis to the 'externalization' approach is the 'hermeneutic' approach. In contrast to the re-authoring focus of the therapist who is trying to help clients free themselves from oppressive cultural stories, the hermeneutic approach assists clients in moving from stuck monologues to facilitate the client's dialogue with many different internal and external narratives or voices. The premise here is that there are many different selves or voices that can be called forth in different relationships or situations. By providing a setting to explore these different voices and selves, the therapy can help with exploring and sorting through these diverse selves so that the client can select alternative and more flexible ways of responding to their problems (Anderson and Goolishian, 1988, 1992; Andersen, 1991, 1993). The therapist often begins by being curious about what sorts of discussions and thoughts have led up to the client or family seeking further help. By being curious about this process therapists can often then open up many different versions of the referred client right from the first session. For example with the boy above referred for his temper, the therapist may discover that the father believes he is lazy but has good reflexes, that his teacher feels he does not get enough attention and so is seeking attention, that his mother feels he is a sensitive boy and thinks he has got a medical problem, that his brother believes he is selfish and that his friends think he is a brilliant footballer. Thus from the first session many versions of this boy are present to talk about, expand and explore in a way that can subtly change a client's and their family's familiar assumptions.

Another therapeutic approach, which like the narrative approach has roots in Milton Erickson's techniques and in post-modern philosophy, is the solution-focused brief therapy approach. Solution-focused therapy emphasizes people's competence rather than their deficits, their strengths and possibilities rather than their weaknesses and limitations (De Shazer, 1985, 1988, 1991, 1994; O'Hanlon and Weiner-Davis, 1989). Some of the key assumptions of solution-focused brief therapy are: understanding the cause of a problem is not necessary to resolve it; doing something different and changing the familiar patterns of response is a key strategy; clients have resources and strengths which should be brought to bear in resolving a problem; clear, salient and realistic goals are a vital factor in eliciting a successful outcome, a small change is all that is usually needed to start change as a change in one part of the system can effect change in another part of the system; it is the client who defines the goals and decides when the therapy should end and that each client is unique in their skills; resources and the way they view their problem resulting in no one-size-fits-all solution. A solution-focused therapist uses active listening to the complaint, but then tries to steer the client and their family towards what it is that they would like to see change. This can be discovered through use of strategies such as the miracle question (an exploration of what the client would like to see different in their life if a miracle happened), three wishes for younger children and the crystal ball question (exploring what the client would like to see if the therapist had a crystal ball which they could look into to see the client in six-months time or a year's time). Once it is clear what the client and/or their family would like to see change in their life, a search is made for the exceptions. For example if an 'out-of-control' teenager has said that they wish to have a better relationship with their mother so that they can talk to their mother about everyday things more often, then the therapist can explore exceptions, in other words how often already there are times, however brief, where this teenager does talk about everyday things to their mother. By going through this process, the therapist is sowing the seeds for change. Now the therapist can explore what else could be done to make it possible to increase the amount of time this teenager spent talking about everyday things to their mum, by just a tiny fraction. This can be done by asking this teenager if they can think of anything different, or perhaps a bit more of something or a bit less of something they already do that they could try that could make a small difference to this first goal of talking to their mother about everyday things. The emphasis in therapy is therefore on the client's existing abilities. By setting the framework of looking for only small changes, it becomes easier to frame the therapy as being devised and implemented successfully by the client with any large changes that may occur being viewed by the therapist as a surprising bonus, confirming the client's amazing abilities.

Another technique that has been used for over a century in Western culture is that of hypnosis. Children can make excellent hypnotic subjects not only because of their imaginative powers, but also because of their ability to 'switch off' from adults around them (Benson, 1989). Various methods of induction can be used with currently popular ones including: concentrating on an imaginary TV programme, general relaxation, imagining doing a favourite activity, or imagining walking into a secret garden known only to the subject. Treatment often utilizes guided imagery, for example the child can be asked to imagine a video in which the problem can be replayed and then the video reprogrammed, or an imaginary desk which contains everything to do with that child's life, which the child is then asked to imagine sorting through the drawers and tidying the desk. Guided imagery can also be used within hypnosis to help planning goals for the future, for example the child can be asked to imagine walking down a path or maze in which the child encounters obstacles before reaching the desired goal. Guided imagery can also be used to help with raising self-esteem and a child's belief in their inner resources, for example the child can be asked to imagine making the mixture for biscuits into which the child is asked to put happy memories, strengths and so on, once the imaginary biscuits are baked the subject is asked to eat a biscuit and feel the strength it gives them and then go into an overgrown garden where all the weeds can be cleared leaving the strong beautiful plants growing healthily. There are potentially limitless possibilities as to how trance could be utilized and what guided imagery may be helpful (see for example Gardner and Olness, 1981; Benson, 1984; Gibson, 1984).

As I hope can be appreciated from above, psychotherapeutic approaches are as rich and varied as human personalities. This diversity should be welcomed and is a welcome antidote to the decades of chronically unsuccessful attempts at finding foolproof ways of uncovering universal human truths through categorizing mental life into rigid, stifling, diversity killing psychiatric constructs and rule bound therapy protocols. All the approaches described above have a potential contribution to make as part of having access to a diverse set of perspectives to help the equally diverse population of naughty children we see. Perhaps the most important thing not to overlook is that any therapy process involves a relationship between the therapist and their client. There is much evidence to suggest that it is these personal qualities of therapists and the subsequent relationship they develop with their clients that has the biggest impact on the success of any therapy, and that this influence is much bigger than that of par-ticular techniques or types of therapy (Miller *et al.*, 1997).

The Influence of Non-Western Psychologies

There is hardly any technique used in modern Western psychotherapy that has not already been discovered by the more ancient psychologies (Hoch, 1960; Shamasundar, 1997). The above could just as easily be a summary of Eastern therapeutic approaches as they are of Western ones, with some important differences. These include less emphasis on the notion that behavioural problems are the result of fixed inner qualities (such as the child's genes), greater emphasis on establishing a balance/harmony with body, environment and spiritual world, the promotion of health and capacity for resistance, greater use of metaphor, rituals and family/community, and a different construction of self.

Buddhism as a philosophy has had a strong influence on some Western psychotherapy practitioners. Buddhist texts are littered with examples of stories offered as metaphors to enable solutions to 'the problems of living' to be found. For example: A Buddhist monk asks his master 'I have a terrible temper and I can't cope with it. Please help'. The master says, 'Well bring it to me and I'll see what I can do'. The monk hesitates 'I am sorry, I haven't got it at the moment'. So the master suggests, 'Next time, when you have got it bring it to me' and the monk confesses, 'I am not sure I can do that'. The master then declares 'In that case it is not yours', and suggests that if it comes again the monk should get hold of it and then beat it away with a stick! (Dwivedi, 1997). This story has echoes of the technique of externalization as used in narrative therapy (see pp. 195–196).

Another Eastern story that has echoes of techniques used in strategic family therapy and cognitive-behaviour therapy points out how actions can lead to unintended consequences: An anger-eating demon went around annoying people and making them angry. Once he went to the 'plane of the thirty-three gods', gatecrashed up to the throne of the king of the gods and deposited himself on it. The king Sakka was away at the time. When the other gods found out, they became furious with the demon. The more they became angry, the more the demon grew bigger, shinier and brighter. When Sakka arrived, the gods informed him of what was going on. Sakka, to everyone's surprise, approached the demon with great humility, without any sign of anger, and prostrated himself in front of the demon three times and appeared most welcoming. Thus the anger-eating demon was starved of feeding on any anger and could not survive. He kept on shrinking until he became almost negligible and went somewhere else in search of people whom he could make angry and whose anger he could relish (Burlingame, 1991).

Another Eastern story resonates with some aspects of learning theory (the theoretical basis of behaviour modification programmes based on the idea that the child's behaviour is learned), and structural family therapy. In this story a yogi with extraordinary powers discovers that a cat is chasing a nearby mouse. The yogi, feeling pity for the mouse, turns the mouse into a cat. On some other day the yogi discovers that this cat is being chased by a stronger beast, the yogi again feeling pity turns the cat into a stronger beast. This process continues until the mouse has finally become a tiger. The tiger begins to lead a fearless life in the jungle. One day the tiger thinks to himself that he is essentially a mouse although, except for the yogi, the whole jungle thinks of him as a tiger. He decides that if the yogi weren't there then he would really be a tiger and sets out to kill the yogi. Fortunately the yogi realizes what was happening and turns the tiger back into a mouse (Dwivedi, 1997).

The above stories illustrate that not only had non-Western psychologies already anticipated and known about Western psychological concepts long before they were 'discovered' in the West, but also that the preferred framework for presenting the ideas is very different. Use of metaphor and narrative is more explicit in many non-Western psychologies when compared with the more technological rule-bound 'scientific' approach of most Western therapies. This may be a presentational difference, as much of Western psychologies claims to objectivity dissolve under close scrutiny, leaving us with another metaphorical system of thought that simply borrows from different metaphors to interpret the meaning it gives its ideas and practices (Stainton-Rogers and Stainton-Rogers, 1992; Goonatilake, 1998).

Complimentary medicine has become widely used in most Western countries, reflecting the dissatisfaction many peoples experience of Western techno-medicine, together with the ancient wisdoms inherent in older systems of medicine. Therapies such as herbal medicine, homeopathy, acupuncture, reflexology, osteopathy and so on have become popular and available in most Western cities. Although most Western practitioners are likely to be providing a Westernized version of Eastern techniques, it is worth noting that the organizing principles of the system of knowledge these therapies rely on is different to the mind/body split, linear, organ-centred knowledge systems of Western medicine.

In Ayurvedic medicine, psychic and somatic complaints and components of health are integrated (Langford, 1995). Ayurvedic medicine conceives the body and person as fluid, penetrable and engaged in continuous interchange with the social and natural environment (Kakar, 1982; Zimmerman, 1987). Whilst biomedicine sees illness as a discrete entity, Ayurvedic philosophy sees illness as a disruption in the delicate somatic, climactic and social system of balance (Kakar, 1982; Trawick, 1991). Causes are not located as such but seen as part of a system out of balance with symptoms being viewed as being a part of a process rather than a disease entity (Obeyesekere, 1977).

Another ancient system of medicine is the Unani (or Tibb) medicine practised over the centuries in many Arab countries and Indo-Pakistan. Unani medicine also believes that the body should be viewed as a whole because harmonious life is possible only when there is proper balance between physical and spiritual functions. In the Unani system of treatment great reliance is placed on the power of self-preservation and adjustment with the aim of the practitioner often being to help develop these natural functions (Said, 1983).

Whilst complimentary and traditional medicine and healing can offer direct, helpful, alternative interventions, their usefulness is in more than just their techniques. These systems of thought contain attitudes and ideas that have the wisdoms born out of hundreds of generations of practitioner's observations, contemplations and reflections on the nature of human life and suffering. With regard to understanding children, their behaviour, problems in their behaviour and how to solve them, the value of understanding harmony and balance (within the body and with the environment), increasing health and the nature of the processes that cause symptoms seem to me to be far more enlightened than the organ-obsessed, context-deprived, linear treatments developed in the West.

Chapter 8

Multi-perspective Approaches 3: Examining Our Values

*The ambivalent adult relationship with children is a suppressed
feature of the cultural landscape, rarely, if ever, addressed in
even the professional schooling of child welfare professionals,
child psychologists, or elementary educators. These silences
must end.*

JOE KINCHELOE, 1998: 176

In the last two chapters I explored the issue of what meaning we give to
a problem and then presented an array of diverse approaches that can be
used with naughty children, their families and communities. Just as the
previous two chapters represented a convenient way of organizing the
ideas presented rather than mutually exclusive categories, so the issues
explored in this chapter are intimately tied up with those of the last two
chapters. In this chapter, I would like to explore a question that has
received far too little attention in the world of psychiatry and psychotherapy – the question of what cultural values and beliefs we take into
our work and how this then affects our clients and the local populations
that we deal with. This chapter is, in other words, an exploration of who
we are as clinicians when we meet with clients, rather than the presentation
of a set of clinical techniques.

Boyd-Franklin (1989) emphasized the need for therapists, when
dealing with families from ethnic minority backgrounds, to be aware
that these families will always see them as the agents of white-dominated
institutions. Whilst Boyd-Franklin was, I think correctly, making explicit
the need to recognize how we as therapists symbolize in many clients'
eyes, the racial and cultural history of the institutions we work for,
I wish to go one step further and state that as Western trained clinicians,
we do represent Western white, middle-class institutions and their

values. Indeed we carry these values with us, mostly unconsciously, and our practices are steeped in the racial, cultural and class history of the Western trainings we have had to undertake. In order to work in our clinical establishments, we have all had to undergo training or a set of trainings in order for us to acquire the professional qualifications required by the governing authorities of our Western institutions. The trainings we do (such as psychiatry, psychology, social work, nursing, psychotherapy) teach us particular frameworks, each with their own, usually unspoken, value system that underpins their theoretical orientation. These frameworks then give us clinicians a methodology that we use to create particular meanings for the clinical problems we are then asked to deal with. As we in the mental health world are not dealing with 'rocket science', where we have at our finger tips, sophisticated tests, computer models, genetic analysis or any other ways of establishing an objective physical basis to our preferred theory, these trainings teach a particular ideology and cosmology through which to view childhood, child rearing and their problems. As these taught ideologies have been developed within modernist Western culture, they are deeply impregnated with many of the core assumptions of that culture. In a culture, which is built around values such as individualism, autonomy, cognitive and intellectual achievement, attaining power and superiority, cultural and racial dominance and a cosmology based on science and materialism, it is not surprising to find all these values reflected within the mental health theoretical frameworks we use (see for example Fernando, 1988; Timimi, 2002).

The history of colonization is written into our mental health trainings. For most trainees this is a problem they need never be aware of, for they will have grown up in the culture of the colonizer and the relative nature of the belief system they have absorbed never needs to become apparent. Others may be marched through these training systems only dimly aware of the extent to which the training is imposing a colonial view on them, feeling uneasy, but not having any access to materials and ideologies that challenge the dominance of the Western viewpoint. This can be a particularly difficult experience for those with an ethnic minority background. In order to work with their own communities, ethnic minority psychiatrists and therapists have to obtain the sanctioned qualifications from governing bodies through being trained in a Western ideologically colonial training scheme, in order to work in a recognized institution armed now with a 'superior' cultural framework for understanding the problems their communities face.

Transference and Counter-transference

Early on in Sigmund Freud's investigation of the mind through the medium of therapeutic work, he became aware that some of his patients were developing very powerful feelings about him (the therapist) – both positive and hostile – which seemed, to Freud at least, to relate little to what he had actually done. Initially Freud saw these powerful feelings towards him as a form of resistance on the part of the patient against the work of analysis and against the recovery of memory and phantasies from the past (Freud, 1912). A little later Freud began to realize that the patients' feelings towards him were part of an enactment on the part of the patient of a specific pattern of emotional responses that the patient had experienced in a previous important relationship, such as a reenactment of the patient's relationship with a parent (Freud, 1915). Patients' feelings towards the therapist were now termed 'transference' to imply that the patient was transferring feelings that first developed in a past relationship onto the therapist. From then on, identifying and interpreting the significance of a patient's feelings towards the therapist (transference interpretations) became an important cornerstone of the psychoanalytic therapeutic technique.

Later in the development of psychoanalytic theory the concept of counter-transference was developed and gained an important place in psychoanalytic therapeutic techniques. Counter-transference refers to the feelings that develop within the therapist towards the patient. Thus in the middle of the last century (1900–2000) a number of analysts began to write about the place of counter-transference in psychoanalytic psychotherapy (see for example Winnicott, 1947; Berman, 1949; Heinmann, 1950, 1960; Little, 1951; Gitelson, 1952; Reich, 1952; Rosenfeld, 1952; Weigart, 1952; Racker, 1953; Bion, 1955). As with transference, counter-transference was, and to some extent still is, conceptualized as both a potential hindrance and a vital tool to psychoanalytic psychotherapy. From the hindrance side of things, it is considered that a therapist's feelings towards a patient could be due to the therapist's own unresolved past relationship issues, which are thus interfering with the therapist's ability to act as an 'objective mirror' for their patient. On the usefulness side, it is hypothesized that counter-transference feelings of the therapist to the patient may well have resulted from feelings that the patient has been unable to deal with and which they have subsequently projected onto the therapist, who as a result feels them on the patient's behalf as it were. Often of course it is very difficult to distinguish in any counter-transference feeling whether the feeling is due to therapist issues or projections by their patients. For example a therapist struggling with a difficult patient may become aware of a strong feeling of impotence and failure with their patient. This counter-transference feeling could then be conceptualized as being due to unresolved feelings of failure and not being good enough in an important relationship in the therapist's past, or it could be that their patient is feeling a failure and, as they are unable to handle this unpleasant feeling, the patient has projected it onto their therapist and is giving covert signals to the therapist suggesting that it is the therapist and not them who is failing. Of course it could also be a bit of both, with a therapist who has struggled with the issue of failure in their life being in an ideal situation to pick up and accept such a projection from their patient. Whilst I have found the idea of counter-transference tremendously helpful, particularly in trying to understand the possible communications my clients are making by analysing the significance of the way I feel towards them, there is, it seems to me, a whole area of counter-transference that is ignored in this formulation.

Whilst this exploration of the personal history aspects of the therapist's unconscious is indeed helpful in trying to understand how counter-transference can interfere with therapy, its repeated failing is in the sparse attention given to context. There are many different types of unconscious. Just as we may be unconscious of how our personal history has shaped some of our future attitudes, feelings and behaviours towards clients, so we can be unconscious of how the beliefs and attitudes we have been exposed to in our social and cultural world has influenced our beliefs, thoughts, feelings and practice in our clinical relationships with clients. South Asian philosophies have for centuries had a wide-ranging and vibrant set of ideas on the nature of the unconscious. Theories of mind, personality and the human condition from these perspectives are familiar with notions of a many-layered unconscious affecting our perceptions of reality. Indeed for many South Asian theories (such as Buddhism and the Upanishads) our perceptions are always distortions of reality and recognizing this is the first step towards 'true' knowledge of the nature of reality (Goonatilake, 1998).

The Social and Cultural Unconscious in Professional Circles

Thus, in addition to the therapist's counter-transference-containing elements of unresolved personal issues they also contain a set of beliefs, attitudes and practices derived from those aspects of mainstream culture (in particular, those contained in their professional trainings) with which they have identified. Arguably, it is this socio-cultural unconscious which exerts the most influence on what happens in the clinical encounter, as our trainings, institutions, dominant theories and techniques are deeply embedded within the assumptions of the dominant culture.

All science is subject to such social conditioning. Disciplines develop within a particular social context and its knowledge base moves through a tunnel surrounded by its epistemological boundaries and guarded jealously by its members (Barnes, 1982). The scientist working at the frontier of the discipline crawls up through the historical tunnel of the discipline and glimpses only what is immediately ahead, unable to conceptualize what is outside this tunnel. The boundaries of this tunnel are made up by a set of fundamental assumptions about the nature and purpose of the subject being studied and these assumptions are often derived from the social history of that discipline and the culture that allowed that discipline to develop.

Putting science within its social and cultural context has allowed feminist thinkers to argue that through the predominance of male scientists, masculine metaphors dominate much of the scientific analysis of reality. From this perspective much of the intellectual history of science is shown to be patriarchal in origin with close ties to capitalism. According to this view the dominant perspectives implicitly focus on masculine matters such as the exploitation of nature and the stigmatization of motherhood. These unspoken gender dynamics have then become ingrained in the history of modern, Western science (Hallberg, 1990; Jansen, 1990). Science's patriarchal bias has also favoured biological explanations for inequalities in factors such as gender, class and race. A masculine worldview gives more primacy to controlling nature than to understanding and finding harmony with it. For example, according to one argument, when science searches for master molecules, it presupposes a hierarchical model of nature rather than an interactive one. Masculine science rests heavily on linear thinking, quantification and reductionism in preference to the many other ways of obtaining and organizing information (Keller, 1985; Witt *et al.*, 1989). Gender bias means that knowledge we take for granted as being apparently objective is deeply influenced by its gender relations and therefore can only ever be partial. The social position of the producer of knowledge effects how knowledge is constructed and investigated, thus all science can be thought of as having developed in a social field consisting of struggles, forces and relationships. These relationships determine what will be considered important problems, acceptable methods and correct knowledge that then govern the practices and results of that science (Harding, 1986, 1991; Vandana, 1988).

Just as knowledge is constructed from a primarily masculine perspective so it is also constructed from a primarily Western cultural perspective. Thus psychiatric ideology and its system of classification reflect Western values. Western concepts of mental health tend to emphasize a focus on individualism, autonomy, secular, efficient and consumerist orientations with a heavy bent on the use of biological conceptualizations and quantification to build up the knowledge base (Fernando, 1995; Waldegrave, 1997). Such an approach to knowledge in mental health fits the economic interests of Western, market economies (for example, the pharmaceutical industry) as well as confirming to the knowledge producers the perceived cultural superiority of Western culture. As a result, mainstream psychiatric ideology assumes that Western definitions of good mental health are the standards by which to compare other cultures (Kleinman, 1998).

In my last book (Timimi, 2002) I showed how our understanding of child mental health is similarly dominated by Western cultural assumptions. A debate on the cultural foundations of Western child psychiatric theory and practice is virtually absent from professional circles. In my last book (Timimi, 2002) I reviewed around one thousand six hundred articles that had been published over five years between 1996 and 2001, from the two leading academic child psychiatric journals, and could find only one article that had anything in it to suggest that culture was being considered by the authors as an important dimension. None of the articles questioned the cultural validity of the constructs and questionnaires they were using.

Similarly, class as a factor that influences our mental health and understanding of mental health has all but disappeared from psychiatric literature. The predominance of the middle classes amongst psychiatrists and therapists make it easier for them to ignore the harsh realities of living in adversity and also the potential, the strengths and resilience of working-class communities. As biological psychiatry continues to assert its authority, the effect of class dynamics are trivialized or dismissed. Issues such as the increased incidence of 'mental illness' amongst those suffering adversity is usually put down to the biological effect of the illness causing the person to suffer greater adversity despite considerable evidence that the reverse is also true, suggesting that more interactive models would take theory and practice further and necessitate the psychiatrist to understand and tackle the politics of social inequality (Cohen and Thompson, 1992; Cohen, 2000, 2002).

The result of all of this class, culture and gender dynamics is that the dominant professional mental health theories and practices promote a masculine, white, Western, middle-class, heterosexual view of the world, and other systems of potentially helpful knowledge are marginalized. On a global scale the problems go deeper. Since the end of the cold war many, including myself, feel that Western civilization in a triumphalist mood has at its heart a political project, which is that of the homogenization of the rest of the world – in other words it wants the rest of the world to copy Western society. Much of the rest of the world resents these arrogant and imperialist wishes, a fact that stunned many Americans following the terrible tragedy of September 11 when they began to realize the depth to which America is resented around the world. Unfortunately, since the events of September 11, the politics of 'you're either with us or against us' has meant that in addition to these imperial wishes being realized more than ever, there is an active dumbing down of democratic debate, a form of power politics that can be seen within some branches of mainstream Western mental health movements' (such as the confidence of the drug industry/psychiatry complex) newfound confidence in proclaiming their pet bio-babble theories as fact that should not be disputed.

The global, political aims of the West are simply unrealizable. The extension of the Western way of life with its huge appetite for consumerism, to the six billion plus inhabitants of the planet runs into ecological obstacles. The people of the world could not benefit from the high standards of living seen in the West without gigantic transformations at every level, which would require us, particularly in the West, to make significant sacrifices to our standards (materially) of living. The present Western value system based around free markets has absolutely no chance of equalizing the economic conditions in which different people live. Four centuries of capitalist expansion has already demonstrated this fact. The last half-a-century (1950–2000), during which the ideology of development (based on a Western vision of what development means) has not brought about even the smallest reduction of the North/South divide, rather the opposite (Amin, 1988).

Likewise, the wholesale export of Western concepts of childhood and child rearing (and their problems) will not work for other cultures. What we urgently need instead of the colonial export of Western ideology is a model based on a more productive exchange of knowledge and ideology that is likely to bring benefits to both North and South.

Mainstream child mental health theories and related practices must be challenged. The value system it represents is having a deeply negative impact not only on the children we see, but also on societies as a whole and arguably on the world as a whole. Our status and power as a professional group means that we are actively changing the way childhood and its problems are viewed. By divorcing children from their context and stifling diversity through insistence on narrow, reductionist, biomedical models, our cultural expectations of children have been transformed (for the worse).

Professionals working with naughty boys must be prepared to understand the value system their approach represents and serves. They must be prepared to explore the cultural origins of their professional ideology, in Western history where medicine has been an active participant in promoting the white, male, middle-class value system which spawned racist, sexist and classist societies (including the eugenic movement) and who, inspired by the belief in their 'scientific' superiority, colonized much of the rest of the world and in the process suppressed local culture, beliefs, ideologies and practices. They must be prepared to explore how Western, biomedical psychiatry serves the economic value system of capitalist, free market thinking and be happy to go along with the pharmaceutical industry's drive to open up new markets (children's mental health being one of their biggest growth areas), use short-term perspectives on problems and how to solve them and sign up to the mythical ideal that more production (e.g. of knowledge) means progress. They must also understand that their political function is in serving governments as one of the major agents of social control and be happy to go along with that society's definition of deviance and recognize the ethical conflicts involved in recommending and sometimes insisting on treatments with potentially addictive and mind debilitating drugs (Timimi, 2003).

Developing a Value System

This chapter (like the rest of the book) is not about providing a prescription of what values are required in order for the therapist to develop a more holistic attitude. By questioning many of the assumptions underpinning our theory and practice it is hoped that the reader is given some ideas through which an exploration of their own value system and how it impinges on their work (and their life more generally) can be undertaken. In a similar vein Bracken and Thomas (2001) have argued that psychiatry needs to rethink its goals and give greater importance to contexts (social, political and cultural), ethics and the politics of coercion.

Much of this may seem common sense, indeed who would argue with the idea that we need to take a more holistic approach to children's mental health. The reality, however, is that the opposite has been happening and childhood is being divorced from context, the ethics of our technical orientation goes un-debated (e.g. prescribing controlled drugs to children) and few seem to notice the social control agenda embedded in the current ideology with regard to the mental health of children. Yet, 'holistic' is still a word that I often hear used by professionals who are, to my mind, practising in a way that is far removed from my understanding of holistic. For example, it is often assumed that a holistic treatment means that a group of professionals are involved, each of whom is dealing with a little bit of the child's assumed pathology. There is a doctor who is prescribing medication and monitoring this, a psychologist carrying out a behaviour treatment programme, an occupational therapist doing social skills training and an emotional behavioural support service worker who is dealing with the child's school-based problems by doing sessions with the child in the school. These professionals may never talk to each other. Thus, under the guise of being holistic the child's experience has been carved up into little pieces as if they were all autonomous from each other. Furthermore, the pathological attitude (in other words focusing on deficit rather than strength) that usually runs through the focus of each of these person's work sends with it the message that the more people are involved, the more serious your problems must be (a potentially self-fulfilling prophesy).

For my part, as I have moved away from holding on to the exclusively Western ideologies I was trained with, I have turned towards post-modern philosophy and non-Western psychologies (see Chapter 8 in Timimi, 2002, 2003). Eastern psychologies are less concerned with mind/body splits and more with concepts such as mindfulness, balance and harmony. Eastern cultures have, in my view, a more mature attitude to the nature of our existence. They reflect on the sacredness of our relationships to each other, to the earth and indeed to the universe. In contrast, Western culture has majored on power, control and conquest (e.g. of nature) at the expense of an interest in relationships. In the West we are now paying the cost of our wish to tame nature and focus on matter as a thing rather than a dynamic.

One of the most hopeful things I have gained from a post-modernist perspective is the importance of noticing and amplifying people's strengths. By adhering to the dominant model of focusing on illness and deficit we lose our chance to empower children, families, teachers and others and create unnecessary dependence upon us as, the so-called, experts. In other words we distance people from their own knowledge, their own ways of solving problems because we wrongly believe that our technical knowledge must be superior.

My value system means that I can no longer collude with our cultural hostility and ambivalence towards children. As I argued in Chapter 4, children simply get in the way in Western culture. Western values of freedom and looking after number one, together with an economic system that demands mobility, have led to a breakdown of family ties resulting in separations, divorce, absent fathers and the death of the extended family. Likewise, local communities have become dispirited and fractured, leading to a loss of good social support networks. Despite many non-Western cultures suffering from similar problems of excessive patriarchy, the values of duty and responsibility that override those of individual aims and self-gratification has helped keep extended families and local communities together in many non-Western societies, giving a much more secure base for children to grow up in.

I carry these values of duty and responsibility into my work. I am no longer interested in how to classify children's behaviour and the rest of the mindless child psychiatry that I was taught but I am more interested in understanding children's context and how to help families develop their relationships more positively. Thus, rather than concentrate on teaching behavioural techniques to a single mother where the child's father has tried to absent himself from responsibility I will first try to see if I can first draw the father into the therapeutic process. In the same way that I give importance to the value of developing relationships within families, I also give value to developing my relationship with the children and families I see. Therefore I try to be natural, polite, respectful, truthful, open, curious and so on in an effort to help those I see feel welcomed and valued. I try to model my belief with regard to openness and honesty in relationships by expressing my honest feelings (without rejection), even if these are hostile, when opportunities present themselves.

I value diversity. This allows me to find genuinely positive aspects about the vast majority of clients and families I see. Of course, I do see families where there is an issue of persistent rejection or other forms of maltreatment that need to be confronted. However, my attitude and belief is that the vast majority of families I see are there because of a genuine concern from a parent(s) or carer(s) about their child and as a result this is indeed what I find. Our institutionalized intolerance, as professional bodies, for children mirrors the cultural vacuum for childhood in the West with the result that child psychiatrists and paediatricians have unwittingly absorbed the increasingly narrow blue print of cultural expectations for children, resulting in more and more children being stigmatized with a variety of pseudo-medical labels such as ADHD, Asperger's Syndrome and Autistic Spectrum Disorders. This problem is particularly acute for naughty boys. An attitude that is more accepting of diversity, not only in terms of children's behaviour but also in the chosen child rearing methods of the families we see, reduces the stigma by reducing the need for these pseudo-medical labels, medication and the sense of guilt, failure and blame many parents who seek our services feel.

Celebrating diversity also means diversity in us as professionals, both in our social and cultural backgrounds and in the approaches, ideas and creativity we use in our work. Experience has led me to discover that being a little bit dramatic at times can help the therapeutic process and the development of a deeper more complex relationship with families I see. This can push the boundaries of mainstream practice's ideas concerning acceptable therapeutic techniques. Yet, keeping the best interests of the patient in mind, careful use of the self of the therapist can have very powerful effects. For example the technique of being really challenging and sometimes even negative to a child or their parents (at a time carefully chosen) can dramatically and deliberately increase the tension in the session, then just when it feels like it could get no worse (perhaps when you sense someone is on the verge of walking out) the tension is released through some positive comments. For example I may choose to say that I had set the session up to carry out this very challenging test, of course I could not tell them that initially as the test needs to be done without them, knowing as I am trying to work out the child's (or families') capacity for tolerating extreme emotional states. Once I have explained this I can then comment and congratulate the child (or parents or family) quite genuinely on just how competent they showed themselves to be when it comes to dealing with strong emotion inside them. Exploring and utilizing such techniques requires a mindset that is prepared to challenge mainstream discourses (that often confuse empathy with sympathy) that would frown upon such methodology.

Celebrating diversity does not mean condoning anti-social behaviour. Indeed, on this score I again look to non-Western cultures where expectations with regard to social behaviour are lower during the early years but much higher following this, when compared to Western culture. In my opinion, much of popular Western culture has increasingly shied away from the question of enforcing effective discipline. We have competing discourses, one telling us that children are not given enough boundaries, the other that adults are routinely abusing and violating children's rights by smacking them or being too harsh on them in other ways. Both discourses are unhelpful particularly without being first situated within the context of the child having a secure set of relationships (family or otherwise) as found more consistently in non-Western cultures. The Children's rights discourse has been distorting power relationships within the family and frequently undermines parents. Smart children understand this and may unjustly complain to teachers or the police about their parents, resulting in further undermining of parents' authority. Professionals need to challenge assumptions of the child's rights movement that says that children and adolescents do not make up stories or that parents are often abusive to their children, sometimes without knowing it. We need to understand parents' intentions before judging their actions. Sometimes their actions are making the situation worse just as professionals' actions may make the situation worse despite the best intentions. I believe we should support parents in finding effective ways to enforce discipline in their children using their own parental value system providing we are happy with the level of security and love for that child in their family. The other major parent-blaming discourse is that of children not getting enough discipline. Many parents are caught in the above trap where they wish to enforce discipline but, scared by the child's rights discourse, they are afraid they may 'abuse' their child or they may be seen as abusing their child. In such situations these well-intentioned parents need our professional support, often as an advocate, to empower them in the face of criticism they are sometimes getting (or more often perceive they will get) from other agencies such as social services.

There are also more ancient systems of medicine that give useful frameworks. For example Ayurvedic medicine is a system to do with balance. Here retrospective evidence is most important. Each individual is given their own specially formulated mixture of medicines and thereafter experimentation with each patient's formula is carried out depending on the results (Goonatilake, 1998). In such a system randomized double blind control studies are not practical. I have similar approach to psychotherapy/therapy using an individualized mixture of family, individual, lifestyle, behaviour management, modernist and post-modern approaches that are changed on each occasion depending on results. Similarly Unani medicine's principles can be utilized. Unani medicine revolves around building the patient's own natural abilities to ward off illness. Likewise 'building health' as a principle in my therapeutic approach is very helpful. This means noticing, strengthening and amplifying abilities, as well as building a healthy lifestyle (through inclusion of diet, exercise, relaxation and family time – see Chapters 5 and 7).

Working with other professionals in a multi-disciplinary team in which a more traditional hierarchy (with diagnosis and drugs at the top of the hierarchy) is challenged is a particularly rewarding aspect of challenging mainstream practice. Generally speaking, most other non-psychiatric mental health professionals I have worked alongside are more sympathetic to my approach than other child psychiatrists. Whilst working in a non-traditional medical hierarchy style can sometimes be experienced as frustrating by other agencies who are used to psychiatrists who diagnose and prescribe medication (thereby shifting the problems out of their arena), and often takes other colleagues a little time to get used to, it does, I believe, mean other professionals are more enabled to value their own skills and abilities. This also means developing new ideas about the role of consultant as a team leader. A non-hierarchical and more democratic approach to leadership does not mean telling others what to do, nor does it mean having the final say. What it does mean is leading the search for shared values and philosophy, developing and advocating for the team's philosophy and model of service delivery, letting others get on with what they are good at doing, giving others in the team a voice and advocating for those who have no power (especially service users).

Taking a context-rich approach also means engaging in dialogue with other (non-child-and-adolescent mental health) local professionals such as paediatricians, social workers and teachers as well as non-statutory agencies. Many of these agencies already have a more context-rich discourse than child psychiatry and are therefore more open and interested in a context-embedded view of mental health. For example, there is an ongoing debate within education about the gendered nature of school environments and educational curricula. Feminist perspectives influenced education in Western schools of the past couple of decades through the equal opportunities discourse which led to the introduction of alternative and non-sexist images into teaching (Skelton, 2001). More recently the growing concern about boys' failure has led to men's rights movements describing schools as feminized institutions because of day-to-day practices that favour girls, low expectations of boys, the absence of male role models and a curriculum that favours girls' learning style (Delamont, 1999; Mason, 1999). Evidence that backs this up shows that girls prefer open-ended tasks that are related to real situations (as is popular in current school curricula), whereas boys prefer memorization of rules and abstract facts (Arnot *et al.*, 1998). In the United Kingdom the government seems to have been influenced by the men's rights discourse on this and having scared many men away from teaching (due to fears of being accused of child abuse) they are now trying to actively recruit more men back into teaching. There are, however, other perspectives from a more feminist viewpoint, which offer other ways of trying to deal with the problem of boys in education including drawing on more relational (rather than equal opportunity) ideas of gender to tackle stereotyped construction, such as through story telling (Yeoman, 1999), confronting stereotypical attitudes to school work (Whitelaw *et al.*, 2000) and encouraging boys to recognize their violent and aggressive actions starting during nursery years (MacNaughton, 2000). Furthermore agencies such as school usually have a lot more face-to-face contact with families and once teachers are moved away from expectations of a diagnosis, a dialogue that opens up new avenues of understanding is relatively easy to achieve.

On the Struggle to Become a Post-modern Practitioner

Culturally intrinsic in the West is the idea of external expertise that has a higher hierarchical status than the person's own knowledge, none more so than the doctor. In the post-modern world this status has been challenged (e.g. Muir-Gray, 1999). In the world of the mental health industry, the psychiatrist remains hierarchically privileged with their knowledge being viewed as somehow more expert than other professionals. Psychiatry has yet to be properly influenced by the multiple voices we can hear in the post-modern world. In adult psychiatry there is some evidence that other voices need to be taken into account (e.g. Bracken and Thomas, 2001), particularly with the growing strength of the user movement in recent years. Although these alternative voices have yet to make a serious impact on day-to-day clinical practice, at least it is a beginning, in child psychiatry there is just a vacuum. It seems that child psychiatric theory and practice has years of catching up to do before the profession can claim to be taking cross-disciplinary ideas seriously. Of course psychiatry's hierarchical status means that it is too powerful to incorporate ways of understanding that have the potential to challenge its hegemony, therefore this is unlikely to happen without it being in some way 'forced' to do so (as user movements are doing with adult psychiatry). How can those of us who can see 'the big picture' influence practice to incorporate other views and voices? First, we must challenge our own practice sufficiently to question those assumptions and cherished ideals that we take into our clinical encounters. First we must clarify our own values.

I can no longer subscribe to a value system that (as enshrined in the application of a traditional medical model to mental health) privileges notions of deficit and pathology. As Gergen (1991: 13) states, 'The vocabulary of human deficit has undergone enormous expansion within the present century [last century]. We have countless ways of locating faults within ourselves and others that were unavailable to even our great-grandfathers.' Or as Szasz (1970: 203) states, the impact on personal identity of the practice of pathologizing is most obvious in mindless application of psychiatric diagnoses: 'The diagnostic label imparts a defective personal identity to the patient; it will henceforth identify him to others and govern their conduct toward him, and his toward them. The psychiatric nosologist thus not only describes his patient's so-called illness, but also prescribes his future conduct.' The ramifications of this kind of therapeutic violence have been horrifying for many persons who have experienced the debilitating and totalizing effects of diagnostic labels in terms of self-blame, self-loathing and intense self-monitoring (Tomm, 1990).

'Making sense' is a social process; it is an activity that is always situated within a cultural and historical framework (Bruner and Haste, 1987). Through their social interactions with adults, children create accounts of their lives that become their worldview – a sort of social map of the world (Garbarino, 1993). When adults bring attention to children's failures and the ways they do not measure up to educational and/or behavioural expectations, children then enter into a worldview and self-narrative of incompetence. The educational and behavioural expectations being passed on are of course absorbed by adults and derived from dominant cultural discourses that are born out of Western capitalist machismo (see Chapter 4). The impact these discourses have on our everyday notions of childhood, boyhood, parenthood and mother–boy relationships in particular are very powerful. As doctors/therapists we can strengthen this discourse or practice with a value system that challenges it.

Since the therapist's attention is influential, she/he must carry both the moral and the social responsibility to examine the consequences of various choices they make, concerning what to attend to and what to focus on with the child and their family (Waldegrave, 1992; Lobovits *et al.*, 1995). Messages or therapeutic biases that remain invisible to the client are the ones with the greatest potential for harm (particularly as they tend to be given to clients in a manner to imply that what the doctor/therapist is saying is the only truth). In our sessions we should strive towards establishing transparency and being open about our particular biases.

As I have shown throughout this book, Western culture has an individualist orientation to selfhood, an orientation that is born of many factors including industrialization, market economy-based value system and an idealization of competitive, masculine ideology. For me, however, the metaphor of 'connection' is a better one than the metaphor of 'separation/individuation', particularly in relation to the experiences of marginalized groups such as women and ethnic minorities (Jordan *et al.*, 1991). I strive to place a positive value on caring and concern for others. Paradoxically, even this discourse can become problematic when mothers are influenced by the belief that they are only valuable through the extent to which they show concern for others. 'Looking after number one' and chasing personal preference to family or group aspirations is then viewed as pathological when a woman does it, with men who do it seemingly able to 'get away with it'. Similarly men who show an attitude that places the family/group interests over their individual ones are often seen as somehow 'special' or worthy of the sort of extra praise that a women who carries such a sense of social responsibility rarely receives. These gender biases are reflected in family law that assumes that it is the mother who should have automatic right to be the main (and often only) parent to a child when a marital or parental partnership has broken down. Father's love and capacity for responsibility is often ignored, resulting in deep unhappiness for many children whose devoted fathers are then marginalized or an easy route for the irresponsible father to follow in order to disappear from their children's lives.

The discourse of separation/individuation may also support depression in mothers (Gilligan *et al.*, 1991; Dickerson *et al.*, 1994). Parents can fall victim to parent-blaming (particularly mother-blaming) if they do not push their children to becoming independent. Boys may be particularly aware of their ambivalent position with regard to 'connection' in Western society and internalize the discourse that says 'boys don't cry' and 'don't be a mummy's boy/sissy'. Thus boys may be particularly vulnerable to the powerful effects of a cultural discourse that invites them and their parents to stigmatize feelings of dependence, belonging and connection. In my work I no longer give value to the discourse of autonomy and separation/individuation. Children can and should be encouraged to feel connected to their families, as can their parents/carers.

Striving towards a way of practising that challenges the notion that professional knowledge is the 'truth', or at least a good reflection of it, means finding new ways of conceptualizing clinical problems. The claim that there is no politically or socially neutral, objective way of giving meaning and therefore finding a way forwards with a problem is not the same as saying there is no way to find solutions to problems. On the contrary, by being mindful of the nature of socio-cultural and political discourse we can, through conversation and discussion, arrive at pragmatically helpful ways forwards, which are not dependent on pre-existing concrete therapist/doctor-derived notions of normality, progress and good outcome. This value challenges the notion of the doctor/therapist as the ultimate or only arbiter of the therapeutic process.

This style of practice has been called post-modern given that its theoretical routes lie in using a post-modern philosophical paradigm (e.g. Gergen and Kaye, 1992; Lax, 1992; Hare-Mustin, 1994). Although the idea of a more open and multiple construction of reality is attractive, in the pressure of the moment found in any therapeutic encounter, it is more difficult to sustain. Indeed even the above passages slip into a more 'modernist' tone through my own claims that such-and-such a value system is not helpful and the subsequent claim that a different value system *should* be adopted. Weingarten (1997a) describes this tension and the constant pull a therapist experiences to return to the more comfortable role of the modernist expert who possesses essential truths,

> I had moved out of a postmodern paradigm into a modernist one...I suspect that the reasons I moved from a postmodern to a modern paradigm at this point in the interview are similar to the reasons it happens to me on other occasions. I knew I was nearing the end of allotted time together, and I was silently reviewing whether or not I had 'done enough'. Critical self-evaluation told me that I had not- that I should have 'done' more. (Weingarten, 1997a: 325)

I think, however, it could be a 'modernist' mistake to construct an argument based on perfecting and purifying any therapeutic technique.

I think it disingenuous to propose that as therapists we hold no particular knowledge. When we challenge existing assumptions, we are questioning the absolutism as well as exploring the cultural impact of modernist systems of knowledge. Doing this in itself highlights that the questioner has acquired a particular sort of knowledge that allows them to look at things differently. Consequently, moving in and out of modernist and post-modernist styles can be potentially more rewarding, enriching and pragmatic than purifying the therapeutic technique. We can carry different systems of knowledge and utilize this diversity. As a doctor/therapist I can deconstruct, try to re-script a narrative, solve problem co-operatively, prescribe a clearly structured intervention, engage emotionally, choose my bias and be open about this, use my status to heighten the impact of an intervention, deconstruct my status to de-mystify an explanation, amplify a client's explanation, provide a new potential explanation and so on. I would be more concerned about what was happening to my practice if my practice were to become completely post-modern in the same way I would be concerned if my practice had remained completely modernist.

Putting the Cart Before the Horse?

Science develops in a social context. It is never a value-neutral enterprise. The values we hold frame the knowledge we choose to collect and the significance we choose to give this knowledge. For some areas of science (such as in mental health) the knowledge is based more on subjective belief than on hard evidence. Such branches of science have little to differentiate their process of knowledge construction from those seen in religious systems of knowledge (Timimi, 2002). As things stand we cannot answer questions about life, the universe and everything, we do not have a system of knowledge capable of giving us such unequivocal answers. What we have instead are systems of knowledge that develop within a social context and reflect the dynamics of that economic and social context. Power relationships then give a particular system of knowledge higher or lower status in any particular local culture at any particular point in time. These dynamics can be seen operating even within the physical and technical sciences. For example, a pressing problem that needs the attention of scientists and technicians is that of how to help much of the rural developing world develop local and sustainable supplies of basics such as power and water. Unfortunately, there is little profit to be found in such an endeavour, instead more effort goes into refining the combustion engine for faster, more efficient, quieter and smoother performance.

When it comes to children's mental health, the subjective nature of the constructions we use means that the socio-cultural and political context has a very powerful impact on the beliefs and values that we carry into our daily clinical practice. How much of what we do as child mental health practitioners has become a colonial exercise, that of prescribing for children, families and allied institutions ways of acting that are based on the best interests of capitalist society and not necessarily the best interests of our clients? The West's values may be good for adventure loving middle-class, white males who like having individual gratification, freedom and minimal responsibility, but is it good for children?

To me there is nothing radical in suggesting that if we truly wish to understand the nature of the problem of naughty boys (and what to do about it) then we must put cultural questions at the heart of our thinking. To put a system of knowledge (be this scientific or religious) ahead in theoretical importance than the social context out of which it evolved is to put the cart in front of the horse. Giving socio-cultural context a more prominent position in our theoretical (and consequently clinical) orientation will open our eyes, ears and hearts to see further a field.

We can start importing some of the value systems of developing world cultures, value systems that have served their children so much better than Western ones. Childhood, motherhood and fatherhood can begin to be understood as having a central place in social and economic arrangements.

Connection to each other rather than power, control and mastery can become guiding principles. Macho working practices can be challenged as bad for society. Free market thinking as a value system can be challenged as bad for society. We can promote Eastern ideals such as balance and harmony, such as learning to live with sequential rhythms of life that takes you through light and darkness, through suffering and joy, through humiliation and mastery. Governments' ideas on education can be challenged to provide more boy-friendly activity-based curricula and to enforce discipline without the use of medical labels or washing of hands from the problem through exclusion. Doctors can be challenged to stop the lunacy of addiction to medical labels and drug prescriptions. Parents can be urged to challenge such stigmatizing practice and to insist on non-psychotropic drug-based solutions. The cultural resistance of objectors can be fostered. Our professional trainings can be challenged; there needs to be debate, openness and transparency, we need to explore how the dynamics of cultural discourse and power influence our professional theory and practice. The voice of protest (despite the overwhelming odds against it) can make itself heard, however, dimly through writing, conferences, seminars, local consultations with other agencies and engaging media. For us as medical professionals to carry on blindly colluding with the instutionalization of our cultural hostility towards children is simply not acceptable.

Bibliography

Abu-Lughod, L. (1986) *Veiled Sentiments*. Berkley: UCLA Press.

Adrian, N. (2001) Explosive outbursts associated with methylphenidate. *Journal of the American Academy of Child and Adolescent Psychiatry* 40, 618–619.

Ainscow, M. and Tweddle, D.A. (1988) *Encouraging Classroom Success*. London: Fulton.

Akhtar, S. (1993) *The Muslim Parents' Handbook*. London: Ta-Ha publishers.

Alcock, P. and Harris, P. (1982) *Welfare, Law and Order: A Critical Introduction to Law for Social Workers*. London: MacMillan.

Alexander, J.F. and Parsons, B.V. (1982) *Functional Family Therapy*. Monterey, CA: Brooks-Cole.

Alexander, J.F., Waldron, H.B., Newberry, A.M. and Liddle, N. (1988) 'Family approaches to treating delinquents', in E.W. Nunnally, C.S. Chilman and F.M. Cox (eds) *Mental Illness, Delinquency, Addictions and Neglect*. Newbury Park, CA: Sage.

Alston, P. (1994) *The Best Interests of the Child: Reconciling Culture and Human Rights*. Oxford: Clarendon Press.

Althusser, L. (1969) *For Marx*. Harmondsworth: Penguin.

Amin, S. (1988) *Eurocentrism*. New York: Monthly Review Press.

Andersen, T. (1991) 'Guidelines for practice', in T. Andersen (ed.) *The Reflective Team: Dialogues and Dialogues About Dialogues*. New York: Norton.

—— (1993) 'See and hear and be seen and heard', in S. Friedman (ed.) *The New Language of Change: Constructive Collaboration in Psychotherapy*. New York: Guildford.

Anderson, H. and Goolishian, H. (1988) Human systems as linguistic systems: Preliminary and evolving ideas about the implications for clinical theory. *Family Process* 27, 371–393.

—— (1992) 'The client is the expert: A not-knowing approach to therapy', in S. McNamee and K.J. Gergen (eds) *Therapy as Social Construction*. Newbury Park, CA: Sage.

Angold, A., Erkanli, A., Egger, H.L. and Costello, E.J. (2000) Stimulant treatment for children: A community perspective. *Journal of the American Academy of Child and Adolescent Psychiatry* 39, 975–984.

American Academy of Pediatrics (1998) Committee on psychosocial aspects of child and family health guidance for effective discipline. *Pediatrics* 101, 723–728.

American Psychiatric Association (1952) *Diagnostic Statistical Manual of Mental Disorders*. Washington, DC: APA.

American Psychiatric Association (1966) *Diagnostic Statistical Manual of Mental Disorders, Second Edition (DSM-II)*. Washington, DC: APA.

—— (1980) *Diagnostic Statistical Manual of Mental Disorders, Third Edition (DSM-III)*. Washington, DC: APA.

—— (1987) *Diagnostic and Statistical Manual of Mental Disorders, Third Edition Revised (DSM-III-R)*. Washington, DC: APA.

—— (1994) *Diagnostic and Statistical Manual of Mental Disorders, Fourth Edition (DSM-IV)*. Washington, DC: APA.

Argyle, M. (1982) 'Inter-cultural communication', in S. Bochner (ed.) *Cultures in Contact: Studies in Cross-Cultural Interaction*. Oxford: Pergammon.

Aries, P. (1962) *Centuries of Childhood*. London: Jonathan Cape.

Armstrong, T. (1995) *The Myth of the ADD Child*. New York: Dutton.

Arnot, M., David, M. and Weiner, G. (1996) *Educational Reforms and Gender Equality in Schools*. Manchester: Equal Opportunities Commission.

Arnot, M., Gray, J., James, M. and Rudduck, J. (1998) *A Review of Recent Research on Gender and Educational Performance*. OFSTED Research Series. London: The Stationery Office.

Aronowitz, S. and Giroux, H. (1991) *Post-modern Education: Politics, Culture and Social Criticism*. Minneapolis: University of Minnesota Press.

Ayensu, E. (1983) 'Endangered plants used in traditional medicine', in R. Bannerman, J. Burton and W. Ch'en (eds) *Traditional Medicine and Health Care Coverage*. Geneva: World Health Organization.

Baistow, K. (1995) From sickly survival to realisation of potential: Child health as a social project. *Children in Society* 9, 20–35.

Baldessarini, R.J. (1985) *Chemotherapy in Psychiatry: Principles and Practice*. Cambridge, MA: Harvard University Press.

Baldwin, S. and Anderson, R. (2000) The cult of methylphenidate: Clinical update. *Critical Public Health* 10, 81–86.

Baldwin, S. and Cooper, P. (2000) How should ADHD be treated? *The Psychologist* 13, 598–602.

Ball, S.J. and Gerwitz, S. (1997) Girls in the education market: Choice, competition and complexity. *Gender and Education* 19, 207–222.

Barker, P. (1985) *Using Metaphors in Psychotherapy*. New York. Brunner-Mazel.

—— (1998) *Basic Family Therapy* (4th Edition). Oxford: Blackwell Scientific.

Barkley, R.A. (1981) *Hyperactive Children: A Handbook for Diagnosis and Treatment*. New York: Guilford Press.

—— (1987) *Defiant Children: A Clinicians' Manual for Parent Training*. New York: Guilford.

—— (1994) Attention Deficit Hyperactivity Disorder. Presentation at the Royal Society of Medicine. London, 1994.

—— (1997) *Defiant Children: A Clinicians' Manual for Assessment and Parent Training* (2nd Edition). New York: Guilford.

Barkley, R.A., McMurray, M.B., Edelbrock, C.S. and Robbins, K. (1990) Side-effects of methylphenidate in children with attention deficit hyperactivity disorder: a systematic, placebo-controlled evaluation. *Pediatrics* 86, 184–192.

Barkley, R. and 78 co-endorsers (2002) International Consensus Statement on ADHD. *Clinical Child and Family Psychology Review* 5, 89–111.

Barlow, G. and Hill, A. (1985) *Video Violence and Children*. London: Hodder and Stoughton.

Barnes, B. (1982) *T.S. Kuhn and Social Science*. London: MacMillan Press.

Battle, E.S. and Lacey, B. (1972) A context for hyperactivity in children over time. *Child Development* 43, 757–773.

Baughman, F.A. (2002) 'Malpractice and violation of informed consent', in *Documenting Psychiatry: Harming in the Name of Care*. USA: Citizens Commission on Human Rights.

Baumeister, A.A. and Hawkins, M.F. (2001) Incoherence of neuroimaging studies in attention deficit/hyperactivity disorder. *Clinical Neuropharmacology* 24, 2–10.

Baumgaertel, A., Wolraich, M.L. and Dietrich, M. (1995) Comparison of diagnostic criteria for Attention Deficit Disorders in a German elementary school sample. *Journal of the American Academy for Child and Adolescent Psychiatry* 34, 629–638.

Begley, S. (2000) The nature of nurturing. A new study finds that how parents treat a child can shape which of his genes turn on. *Newsweek* 135, 64–66.

Benn, C. and Chitty, C. (1996) *Thirty Years on: Is Comprehensive Education Alive and Well, or Struggling to Survive?* London: David Fulton.

Benson, G. (1984) Short-term hypnotherapy with delinquent and acting-out adolescents. *British Journal of Experimental and Clinical Hypnosis* 1, 19–27.

—— (1989) Hypnosis as a therapeutic technique for use by a school psychologist. *School Psychology International* 10, 113–119.

Berman, L. (1949) Counter-transference and attitudes of the analyst in the therapeutic process. *Psychiatry* 12, 159–166.

Bertalanffy, L. Von (1968) *General Systems Theory: Foundations, Development, Application.* New York: Braziller.

Biederman, J. (1999) Pharmacotherapy of attention deficit/hyperactivity disorder reduces the risk for substance use disorder. *Pediatrics* 104, e20–e30.

Biederman, J., Newcorn, J. and Sprich, S. (1991) Comorbidity of attention deficit disorder with conduct, depressive, anxiety and other disorders. *American Journal of Psychiatry* 148, 564–577.

Bion, W. (1955) 'Language and the schizophrenic', in M. Klein, P. Heimann and R. Money-Kyrle (eds) *New Directions in Psychoanalysis.* London: Tavistock.

Bleach, K. (1996) *What Difference Does it Make? An Investigation of Factors Influencing the Motivation and Performance of Year Eight Boys in a West Midland Comprehensive School.* Wolverhampton: University of Wolverhampton Educational Research Unit.

Bloom, F.E., Nelson, C.A. and Lazerson, A. (2001) *Brain, Mind and Behavior* (3rd Edition). New York: Worth Publications.

Boh, K., Bak, M., Clason, M.P., Qvortrup, J., Syritta, G.B. and Waerness, K. (1989) *Changing Patterns of European Family Life.* London: Routledge.

Borduin, C.M. (1999) Multisystemic treatment of criminality and violence in adolescents. *Journal of the American Academy of Child and Adolescent Psychiatry* 27, 171–174.

Boscolo, L., Cecchin, G., Hoffman, L. and Penn, P. (1987) *Milan Systemic Family Therapy.* New York. Basic books.

Bowlby, J. (1969) *Attachment and Loss, Volume 1, Attachment.* London: Hogarth Press.

—— (1973) *Attachment and Loss, Volume 2, Separation.* London: Hogarth Press.

Boyd-Franklin, N. (1989) *Black Families in Therapy: A Multi-Systems Approach.* New York: Guildford.

Boyden, J. (1997) 'Childhood and the policy makers: A comparative perspective on the globalization of childhood', in A. James and A. Prout (eds) *Constructing and Recon-structing Childhood.* London: Falmer Press.

Boyden, J. and Meyer, W. (1995) *Exploring Alternative Approaches to Combating Child Labour: Case Studies from Developing Countries.* Florence: Innocenti Occasion Papers; Child rights series, Number 8. Florence UNICEF International Child Development Centre.

Boyle, M.H. and Jadad, A.R. (1999) Lessons from large trials: The MTA study as a model for evaluating the treatment of childhood psychiatric disorder. *Canadian Journal of Psychiatry* 44, 991–998.

Bracken, P. (2002) *Trauma: Culture, Meaning and Philosophy.* London: Whurr Publishers.

Bracken, P. and Thomas, P. (2001) Post psychiatry: a new direction for mental health. *British Medical Journal* 322, 724–727.

Bradley, B.S. (1989) *Visions of Infancy: A Critical Introduction to Child Psychology.* Cambridge: Polity Press.

Bradley, C. (1937) The behaviour of children receiving Benzedrine. *American Journal of Psychiatry* 94, 577–585.

Bradshaw, J. (1990) *Child Poverty and Deprivation in the United Kingdom*. London: National Children's Bureau.

Breggin, P. (1991) *Toxic Psychiatry*. New York: St Martins Press.

Breggin, P.R. (1994) *The War Against Children: How the Drugs Programmes and Theories of the Psychiatric Establishment are Threatening America's Children with a Medical 'Cure' for Violence*. New York: St Martin's Press.

Breggin, P. (1997) *The Heart of Being Helpful: Empathy and the Creation of a Healing Presence*. New York: Springer Publishing Company.

—— (1999) Psycho-stimulants in the treatment of children diagnosed with ADHD: Part II – Adverse effects on brain and behavior. *Ethical Human Sciences and services* 1, 213–241.

—— (2000) The NIMH multimodal study of treatment for attention deficit/ hyperactivity disorder: A critical analysis. *International Journal of Risk and Safety in Medicine* 13, 15–22.

—— (2001a) *Talking Back to Ritalin: What Doctors Aren't Telling You about Stimulants for Children* (revised edition). Cambridge, MA: Perseus Publishing.

—— (2001b) *The Antidepressant Fact Book: What Your Doctor Won't Tell You About Prozac, Zoloft, Paxil, Celexa and Luvox*. Cambridge: Perseus Publishing.

—— (2002) *The Ritalin Fact Book*. Cambridge, MA: Perseus Publishing.

Breggin, P. and Breggin, G. (1994) *Talking Back to Prozac*. New York: St Martins Press.

—— (1998) *The War Against Children of Color*. Maine: Common Courage Press.

Brimblecombe, F. (1980) *Child Rearing: Fashion or Science*. Exeter: University of Exeter Press.

Brink, J.H. (1995) 'Changing child-rearing patterns in an Egyptian village', in E.W. Fernea (ed.) *Children in the Muslim Middle East*. Austin: University of Texas Press.

British Medical Journal News (1995) *British Medical Journal* 310, 1429.

British Psychological Society (1996) *Attention Deficit Hyperactivity Disorder (ADHD): A Psychological Response to an Evolving Concept, Report of a Working Party of the BPS*. London: British Psychological Society.

Brod, H. (1987) 'A case for men's studies', in M. Kimmel (ed.) *Changing Men*. Newbury Park, LA: Sage.

Bronfenbrenner, U. (1992) 'Child care in Anglo-Saxon mode', in M.E. Lamb, K. Sternberg, C.P. Hwang and A.G. Broberg (eds) *Child Care in Context: Cross-cultural Perspectives*. Hillsdale, NJ: Erlbaum.

—— (1993) 'The ecology of cognitive development: Resarch models and fugitive findings', in R.H. Wozniak and K. Fischer (eds) *Specific Environments: Thinking in Contexts*. Hillsdale, NJ: Erlbaum.

—— (1994) 'Foreword', in R.A. Levine, S. Dixon, S. Le Vine, A. Richman, P.H. Leiderman, C.H. Keefer, and T.B. Brazelton, *Childcare and Culture: Lessons from Africa*. Cambridge: Cambridge University Press.

Brooks, R. (1993) 'Creative characters', in C.E. Schaefer and D.M. Langelosi (eds) *Play Therapy Techniques*. Nothvale NJ: Jason Aronson.

Broughton, J. (1986) 'The psychology, history and ideology of the self', in K. Larsen (ed.) *Dialectics and Ideology in Psychology*. Norwood, NJ: Ablex.

Bruner, J. and Haste, H. (1987) *Making Sense: The Child's Construction of the World*. London: Methuen.

Buck-Morss, S. (1977) *The Origin of Negative Dialectics: Theodor W. Adorno, Walter Benjamin and the Frankfurt Institute*. Hassocks: The Harvester Press.

—— (1987) 'Piaget, Adorno and dialectical operations', in J. Broughton (ed.) *Critical Theories of Psychological Development*. New York: Plenum.

Burlingame, E.W. (1991) *Bhuddist Parables*. Delhi: Motilal Banarasidas.

Burman, E. (1994) *Deconstructing Developmental Psychology*. London: Routledge.

Burton, B. and Rowell, A. (2003) Unhealthy spin. *British Medical Journal* 326, 1205–1207.

Calvert, K. (1992) *Children in the House: The Material Culture of Early Childhood, 1600–1900*. Boston: Northeastern University Press.

Campbell, M., Cohen, I.L. and Small, A.M. (1982) Drugs in aggressive behaviour. *Journal of the American Academy Child and Adolescent Psychiatry* 21, 107–117.

Campbell, M., Rapoport, J.L. and Simpson, G.M. (1999) Antipsychotics in children and adolescents. *Journal of the American Academy of Child and Adolescent Psychiatry* 38, 537–545.

Cantwell, D.P. (1972) Psychiatric illness in the families of hyperactive children. *Archives of General Psychiatry* 27, 414–417.

—— (1975) 'Genetic studies of hyperactive children: Psychiatric illness in biologic and adopting parents', in R. Fieve, D. Rosenthal and H. Brill (eds) *Genetic Research in Psychiatry*. Baltimore: John Hopkins University Press.

Cantwell, N. (1989) 'A tool for the implementation of the UN convention', in R. Barnen (ed.) *Making Reality of Children's Rights*. New York: UNICEF.

Carey, W.B. and McDevitt, S.C. (1995) *Coping With Children's Temperament: A Guide for Professionals*. New York: Basic Books.

Caron, C. and Rutter, M. (1991) Comorbidity in child psychopathology: concepts, issues and research strategies. *Journal of Child Psychology and Psychiatry* 32, 1063–1080.

Carpenter, M. (1853) *Juvenile Delinquents: Their Condition and Treatment*. London: Cash.

Carrel, A. (1935) *Man the Unknown*. New York: Harper and Brothers.

Carstairs, G.M. (1957) *The Twice Born*. London: Hogarth.

Chaney, S.E. and Piercy, F.P. (1988) A feminist family behaviour therapy checklist. *American Journal of Family Therapy* 16, 305–318.

Charles, L. and Schain, R. (1981) A four year follow up study of the effects of methyl-phenidate on the behaviour and academic achievement of hyperactive children. *Journal of Abnormal Child Psychology* 9, 495–505.

Charlton, B.G. (1998) Psychopharmacology and the human condition. *Journal of Research into Social Medicine* 91, 699–701.

Chase, A. (1980) *The Legacy of Malthus*. Illinois: University of Illinois Press.

Cherland, E. and Fitzpatrick, R. (1999) Psychotic side effects of psycho-stimulants: A five year review. *Canadian Journal of Psychiatry* 44, 811–813.

Chess, S. and Thomas, A. (1996) *Temperament Theory and Practice*. New York: Brunner Mazel.

Children's Defence Fund (1994) *The State of America's Children Yearbook: 1994*. Washington, DC: Children's Defence Fund.

Christie, D., Lieper, A.D., Chessells, J.M. and Vergha-Khadem, F. (1995) Intellectual performance after presymptomatic cranial radiotherapy for leukaemia: effects of age and sex. *Archives of Disease in Childhood* 73, 136–140.

Chu, G.C. (1985) 'The emergence of a new Chinese culture', in W. Tseng and D. Wu (eds) *Chinese Culture and Mental Health*. New York: Academic Press.

Clarke, J., Hall, S., Jefferson, T. and Roberts, B. (1975) 'Subcultures, culture and subcultures', in S. Hall and T. Jefferson (eds) *Resistance Through Rituals: Youth Subcultures in Post-War Britain*. London: Hutchinson.

Clarke-Stewart, K.A. (1973) Interaction between mothers and their young children: Characteristics and consequences. *Monographs for the Society for Research in Child Development* 38, 132–153.

Cohen, C. (1997) The political and moral economy of mental health. *Psychiatric Services* 48, 768–774.

—— (2000) overcoming social amnesia: The role for a social perspective in psychiatric research and practice. *Psychiatric Services* 51, 72–79.

—— (2002) Social inequality and health: Will psychiatry assume center stage? *Psychiatric Services* 53, 937–940.

Cohen, C. and Thompson, K. (1992) Homeless mentally ill or mentally ill homeless? *American Journal of Psychiatry* 149, 816–823.

Cohen, M. (1998) 'A habit of healthy idleness: Boys underachievement in historical perspective', in D. Epstein, J. Elwood, V. Hey and J. Maw (eds) *Failing Boys? Issues in Gender and underachievement*. Buckingham: Open University Press.

Coles, R. (1986) *The Political Life of Children*. Boston: Atlantic monthly press.

Comaroff, J. and Comaroff, J. (1991) 'Africa observed: Discourses of the imperial imagination', in J. Comaroff and J. Comaroff (eds) *Of Revelation and Revolution: Christianity, Colonialism and Consciousness in South Africa*, Vol. 1. Chicago: University of Chicago Press.

Connell, R.W. (1989) Cool guys, swots and wimps: The interplay of masculinity and education. *Oxford Review of Education* 15, 291–303.

—— (1995) *Masculinities*. Cambridge: Polity Press.

Connor, D.F. (2002) *Aggression and Antisocial Behaviour in Children and Adolescents: Research and Treatments*. New York: Guildford.

Connor, D.F., Ozbayrak, K.R., Harrison, R.J. and Melloni, R.H. Jr (1998) Prevalence and patterns of psychotropic medication and anti-convulsant medication use in children and adolescents referred to residential treatment. *Journal of Child and Adolescent Psychopharmacology* 8, 27–38.

Cooper, P., Upton, G. and Smith, C. (1991) Ethnic minority and gender distribution among staff and pupils in facilities for pupils with emotional and behavioural difficulties in England and Wales. *British Journal of the Sociology of Education* 12, 77–94.

Copeland, L., Wolraich, M., Lindgren, S., Milich, R. and Woolson, R. (1987) Pediatricians reported practices in the assessment and treatment of Attention Deficit Disorders. *Journal of Developmental and Behavioural Pediatrics* 8, 191–197.

Corvin, A. and Gill, M. (2003) Psychiatric genetics in the post-genome age. *British Journal of Psychiatry* 182, 95–96.

Cramond, B. (1994) Attention Deficit Hyperactivity Disorder and creativity: What is the connection? *Journal of Creative Behaviour* 28, 193–210.

Cunningham, H. (1991) *The Children of the Poor: Representations of Childhood Since the Seventeenth Century*. Oxford: Basil Blackwell.

—— (1995) *Children and Childhood in Western Society Since 1500*. London: Longman.

Cunningham, L., Cadoret, R., Loftus, R. and Edwards, J.E. (1975) Studies of adoptees from psychiatrically disturbed biological parents. *British Journal of Psychiatry* 126, 534–539.

Curt, B. (1994) *Textuality and Tectonics: Troubling Social and Psychological Science*. Buckingham: Open University Press.

Dale, P.S., Dionne, G., Eley, T.C. and Plomin, R. (2000) Lexical and grammatical development: A behavioural genetic perspective. *Journal of Child Language* 27, 619–642.

Daniels, H., Hey, V., Leonard, D. and Smith, M. (1998) Difference, difficulty and equity: Gender race and SEN. *Management in Education* 12, 5–8.

Davidoff, L. and Hall, C. (1987) *Family Fortunes: Men and Women of the English Middle Class 1788–1850*. London: Hutchinson.

Davis, L. (1992) School power cultures under economic constraint. *Educational Review* 43, 127–136.

Davis, S.S. and Davis, D.A. (1989) *Adolescence in a Moroccan Town*. New Brunswick, NJ: Rutgers University Press.

De Grandpre, R. (1999) *Ritalin Nation*. New York: W.W. Norton.

De Mause, L. (1984) *Reagan's America*. New York: Creative Roots.

Delamont, S. (1989) 'Both sexes lose out: Low achievers and gender', in A. Ramasuk (ed.) *Whole School Approaches to Special Needs*. London: Falmer.

—— (1999) Gender and the discourse of derision. *Research Papers in Education* 14, 3–21.

Department of Health (1999) *Prescription Cost Analysis*. London: Department of Health.

De Shazer, S. (1985) *Keys to Solutions in Brief Therapy*. New York: Norton.

—— (1988) *Clues: Investigating Solutions in Brief Therapy*. New York: Norton.

—— (1991) *Putting Difference to Work*. New York: Norton.

—— (1994) *Words were Originally Magic*. New York: Norton.

Dickerson, V.C., Zimmerman, J.L. and Berndt, L. (1994) Challenging developmental 'truths': Separating from separation. *Dulwich Centre Newsletter* 4, 2–12.

Diller, L.H. (1998) *Running on Ritalin*. New York: Bantam.

—— (2002) ADHD: real or an American myth. Presented at the 14th Annual Conference of the Associazone Cultural Pediatri. Rome: 10 October 2002.

Donnelly, M. and Rapoport, J.L. (1985) 'Attention Deficit Disorders', in J.M. Weiner (ed.) *Diagnosis and Psychopharmacology of Childhood and Adolescent Disorders*. New York: Wiley.

Donovan, S.J., Stewart, J.W., Nunes, E.V., Quitkin, F.M., Parides, M., Daniel, W., Susser, E. and Klein, D.F. (2000) Diralproex treatment of youth with explosive temper and mood lability: A double-bind, placebo-controlled crossover design. *American Journal of Psychiatry* 157, 818–820.

Donzelot, J. (1979) *The Policing of Families*, trans. R. Hurley. New York: Pantheon.

Dorsky, S. and Stevenson, T.B. (1995) 'Children and Education in Highland North Yemen', in E.W. Fernea (ed.) *Children in the Muslim Middle East*. Austin: University of Texas Press.

Dosanji, J.S. and Ghuman, P.A.S. (1996) *Child Rearing in Ethnic Minorities*. Clevedon: Multilingual Matters Ltd.

Double, D. (2002) The limits of psychiatry. *British Medical Journal* 324, 900–904.

Douglas, V.I. (1972) Stop, look and listen: the problems of sustained attention and impulse control in hyperactive and normal children. *Canadian Journal of Behavioural Science* 4, 254–282.

—— (1983) 'Attention and cognitive problems', in M. Rutter (ed.) *Developmental Neuropsychiatry*. New York: Guildford.

Draeger, S., Prior, M. and Sanson, A. (1986) Visual and auditory attention performance in hyperactive children: competence or compliance. *Journal of Abnormal Child Psychology* 14, 411–424.

Drug Enforcement Administration (1994) *ARCOS (Automation of Reports and Consolidated Orders Systems) Data Base 1981–1992*. Washington, DC: US Department of Justice.

Duncan, B., Hubble, M. and Miller, S. (1997) Stepping off the throne. *Family Therapy Networker* 21, 22–33.

Durkheim, E. (1925) *Moral Education: A Study in the Theory and Application of the Sociology of Education*. Translated by E.K. Wilson and H. Schnurer. New York: Free Press of Glancoe (1961).

Dwivedi, K.N. (1993) 'Coping with unhappy children from ethnic minorities', in V.P. Varma (ed.) *Coping with Unhappy Children*. London: Cassell.

—— (1996) 'Culture and Personality', in K.N. Dwivedi and V.P. Varma (eds) *Meeting the Needs of Ethnic Minority Children*. London: Jessica Kingsley.

—— (1997) 'Management of anger and some Eastern stories', in K.N. Dwivedi (ed.) *Therapeutic Use of Stories*. London: Routledge.

Dwivedi, K. and Gardner, D. (1997) Theoretical perspectives and clinical approaches', in K. Dwivedi (ed.) *Therapeutic Use of Stories*. London: Routledge.

Earls, F. (1991) 'A developmental approach to understanding and controlling violence', in H.E. Fitzgerald, B.H. Lester and M.W. Yogman (eds) *Theory and Research in Behavioral Pediatrics*. New York: Plenum Press.

Eaves, L.J., Silberg, J.L., Hewitt, J.K., Myer, J.M., Rutter, M.L., Simonoff, E., Neale, M.C. and Pickles, A. (1993) 'Genes, personality and psychopathology. A latent class analysis of liability to symptoms of attention deficit hyperactivity disorder in twins', in R. Plomin and G.E. McClearn (eds) *Nature, Nurture and Psychology*. Washington, DC: American Psychological Association.

Eley, T.C. (1999) Behavioural genetics as a tool for developmental psychology: Anxiety and depression in children and adolescents. *Clinical Child and Family Psychology Review* 2, 21–36.

Elias, N. (1939) *The Civilizing Process*. New York: Blackwell, 1978.

Emslie, G.J., Walkup, J.T., Pliszka, S.R. and Ernst, M. (1999) Nontricyclic anti-depressants: Current trends in children and adolescents. *Journal of the American Academy of Child and Adolescent Psychiatry* 38, 517–528.

Erasmus, D. (1985) *The Collected Works of Erasmus*, Vol. 25. Toronto: University of Toronto Press.

Erickson, M.H. (1980a) *The Nature of Hypnosis and Suggestion* (collected papers, Vol. I, edited by E.L. Rossi). New York: Irvington.

—— (1980b) *Hypnotic Alteration of Sensory, Perceptual and Psychological Processes* (collected papers, Vol. II, edited by E.L. Rossi). New York: Irvington.

—— (1980c) *Hypnotic Investigation of Psychodynamic Processes* (collected papers, Vol. III, edited by E.L. Rossi). New York: Irvington.

—— (1980d) *Innovative Psychotherapy* (collected papers, Vol. IV, edited by E.L. Rossi). New York: Irvington.

—— (1985) *Conversations with Milton H. Erickson* (Vol. III, Changing Children and Families, edited by J. Haley). New York: Norton.

Erny, P. (1981) *The Child and His Environment in Black Africa*. Translated by G.J. Wanjohi. Oxford: Oxford University Press.

Farmer, A. and Owen, M.J. (1996) Genomics: The next psychiatric revolution? *British Journal of Psychiatry* 169, 135–138.

Feingold, B. (1975) *Why Your Child is Hyperactive*. New York: Random House.

Fergusson, D.M. and Horwood, L.J. (1993) The structure, stability and correlations of the trait components of conduct disorder, attention deficit disorder and anxiety withdrawal reports. *Journal of Child Psychology and Psychiatry* 34, 749–766.

Fernando, S. (1988) *Race And Culture in Psychiatry*. London: Croom Helm.

—— (1995) 'Social realities and mental health', in S. Fernando (ed.) *Mental Health in a Multi-Ethnic Society*. London: Routledge.

Fernea, E.W. (1965) *Guests of the Sheik: An Ethnography of an Iraqi Village*. New York: Doubleday & Co.

—— (1995) 'Childhood in the Muslim Middle East', in E.W. Fernea (ed.) *Children in the Muslim Middle East*. Austin: University of Texas Press.

Fernea, E.W. and Fernea, R. (1981) 'A look behind the veil', in *Annual Editions Anthropology 80/81*. Guildford Conn. Dushkin Publishing Group.

Fineman, J.A. (1995) 'Loss, aggression and violence: Two groups of traumatized children', in T.B. Cohen, M.H. Etezady and B.L. Pacella (eds) *The Vulnerable Child*, Vol. 2. Madison: International University Press.

Fisher, S.L., Francks, C., McCracken, J.T., McGough, J.J., Marlow, A.J., MacPhie, I.L., Newbury, D.F., Palmer, C.G, Woodward, J.A., Del Homme, M., Cantwell, D.P., Nelson, S.F., Monaco, A.P. and Smalley, S.L. (2002). A genomewide scan for loci involved in Attention Deficit/Hyperactivity Disorder (ADHD). *American Journal of Human Genetics* 70, 1183–1196.

Ford, J.D., Racusin, R., Davis, W.B., Ellis, C.G., Thomas, J., Rogers, K., Reiser, J., Schiffman, J. and Sengupta, A. (1999). Trauma exposure among children with oppositional defiant disorder and attention deficit-hyperactivity disorder. *Journal of Consulting and Clinical Psychology* 67, 786–789.

Ford, J.D., Racusin, R., Ellis, C.G., Davis, W.B., Reiser, J., Fleischer, A. and Thomas, J. (2000). Child maltreatment, other trauma exposure, and posttraumatic symptomatology among children with oppositional defiant and attention deficit hyperactivity disorders. *Child Maltreatment* 5, 205–217.

Forehand, R. and McMahon, R.J. (1981) *Helping The Non-Compliant Child: A Clinician's Guide to Parent Training*. New York: Guildford Press.

Forgatch, M.S. and Patterson, G.R. (1989) *Parents and Adolescents Living Together: Part 2. Family Problem Solving*. Eugene, O.R.: Castilia.

Foucault, M. (1977) *Discipline and Punish: The Birth of Prison*. New York: Pantheon.

—— (1981) *The History of Sexuality: An Introduction*, Vol. 1. Harmondsworth: Pelican.

Fox, N.A., Rubin, K.H., Calkins, S.D., Marshall, T.R., Coplan, P.J., Porges, S.W., Long, J.M. and Stewart, S. (1995) Frontal activation asymmetry and social competence at four years of age. *Child Development* 66, 1770–1784.

Freeman, M.D.A. (1983) *The Rights and Wrongs of Children*. London: Francis Pinter Publishers.

Freeman, J., Epston, D. and Lobovits, D. (1997) *Playful Approaches to Serious Problems: Narrative Therapy with Children and their Families*. New York: Norton.

Freemantle, N. (2002) Medicalisation, limits to medicine or never enough money to go round? *British Medical Journal* 324, 864–865.

Freud, S. (1912) 'The dynamics of transference', in *The Standard Edition of the Complete Psychological Works of Sigmund Freud*. London: Hogarth.

—— (1915) 'Remembering, repeating and working through', in *The Standard Edition of the Complete Psychological Works of Sigmund Freud*. London: Hogarth.

—— (1922) *Beyond The Pleasure Principle*. London: The Psychoanalytical Press.

—— (1930) 'Civilisation and its discontents', in *Civilisation, Society and Religion*. London: Penguin, 1985.

Frosh, S., Phoenix, A. and Pattman, R. (2002) *Young Masculinities: Understanding Boys in Contemporary Society*. Basingstoke: Palgrave.

Fyfe, A. (1989) *Child Labour*. Cambridge: Polity Press.

Gadow, K.D. (1983) Effects of stimulant drugs on academic performances in hyperactivity and learning disabled children. *Journal of Learning Disabilities* 16, 290–299.

Garbarino, J. (1993) Childhood: What do we need to know. *Childhood* 1, 3–10.

Garbarino, J. Dubrow, N, Kostelny, K. and Pardo, C. (1992) *Children in Danger: Coping with the Consequences of Community Violence.* San Francisco: Jossey-Bass Publishers.

Garber, S.W., Garber, M.D. and Spizman, R.F. (1996) *Beyond Ritalin.* New York: Harper Perennial.

Gardner, R.A. (1993) *Story Telling in Psychotherapy with Children.* London: Jason Aronson.

Gardner, C.G. and Olness, K. (1981) *Hypnosis and Hypnotherapy with Children.* New York: Grune and Stratton.

Geertz, C. (1983) *Local Knowledge.* New York: Basic Books.

Geller, B., Reising, D., Leonard, H.L., Riddle, M.A. and Walsh, B.T. (1999) Critical review of tricyclic anti-depressant use in children and adolescents. *Journal of the American Academy of Child and Adolescent Psychiatry* 38, 513–516.

Gergen, K. (1985) The social constructionist movement in modern psychology. *American Psychologist* 40, 266–275.

—— (1991) *The Saturated Self: Dilemmas of Identity in Contemporary Life.* New York: Basic Books.

—— (1992) 'Toward a post modern psychology', in S. Kuale (ed.) *Psychology and Post-Modernism.* London: Sage.

Gergen, K. and Kaye, J. (1992) 'Beyond narrative in the negotiation of therapeutic meaning', in S. McNamee and K. Gergen (eds) *Therapy as Social Construction.* Newbury Park, CA: Sage.

Gersie, A. and King, N. (1990) *Story Making in Education and Therapy.* London: Jessica Kingsley.

Ghuman, P.A.S. (1980) Punjab parents and English education. *Educational Research* 22, 121–130.

—— (1994) *Coping with Two Cultures: A Study of British Asians and Indo-Canadian Adolescents.* Clevedon: Multilingual matters.

Gibson, M. (1984) Hypnosis with children. *British Journal of Experimental and Clinical Hypnosis* 1, 31–34.

Gil'adi, A. (1992) *Children of Islam: Concepts of Childhood in Medieval Muslim Society.* Oxford: MacMillan.

Gilberg, I.C. (1987) *Deficits in Attention, Motor Control and Perception: From Preschool to Early Teens* (MD Thesis). Uppsala: Uppsala University Press.

Gilberg, I.C., Gillberg, C. and Groth, J. (1989) Children with preschool minor neuro-developmental disorders, V: Neurodevelopmental profiles at age 13. *Developmental Medicine and Child Neurology* 31, 14–24.

Gilligan, C., Rogers, A. and Tolman, D. (eds) (1991) *Women, Girls and Psychotherapy: Reframing Resistance.* New York: Haworth Press.

Gillis, J.J., Gilger, J.W., Pennington, B.F. and DeFries, J.C. (1992) Attention deficit disorder in reading-disabled twins: evidence for genetic etiology. *Journal of Abnormal Child Psychology* 20, 303–315.

Giroux, H. (1998) 'Stealing innocence', in H. Jenkins (ed.) *Children's Culture Reader.* New York: New York University Press.

Gitelson, M. (1952) The emotional position of the analyst in the psychoanalytic situation. *International Journal of Psychoanalysis* 33, 1–10.

Goldin, S. (1998) 'Unlearning black and white', in H. Jenkins (ed.) *Children's Culture Reader.* New York: New York University Press.

Goodman, R. (1997) An over extended remit. *British Medical Journal* 314, 813–814.

Goodman, R. and Stevenson, J. (1989) A twin study of hyperactivity II: The aetiological role of genes, family relationships and perinatal adversity. *Journal of Child Psychology and Psychiatry* 30, 691–709.

Goonatilake, S. (1998) *Mining Civilizational Knowledge.* Bloomington: Indiana University Press.

Gordon, D.A., Graves, K. and Arbuthnot, J. (1995) The effect of functional family therapy for delinquents on adult criminal behaviour. *Criminal Justice and Behaviour* 22, 60–73.

Gordon, N., Burke, S., Akil, H., Watson, S. and Panksepp, J. (2003) Socially-induced brain 'fertilization': Play promotes brain derived neurotrophic factor transcription in the amygdale and dorsolateral frontal cortex in juvenile rats. *Neuroscience Letters* 341, 17–20.

Gottlieb, S. (2002) 1.6 elementary school children have ADHD says report. *British Medical Journal* 324, 1296.

Graham, P. and Stevenson, J. (1985) A twin study of genetic influences on behavioural deviance. *Journal of the American Academy of Child and Adolescent Psychiatry* 24, 33–41.

Green, C. and Chee, K. (1997) *Understanding ADHD: A Parents' Guide to Attention Deficit Hyperactivity Disorder in Children.* London: Vermilion.

Green, M., Wong, M., Atkins, D., Taylor, J. and Feinleib, M. (1999). *Diagnosis of Attention Deficit Hyperactivity Disorder.* Rockville MA: Agency for Healthcare Policy and Research.

Greenblatt, J. (1999) Nutritional supplements in ADHD. *Journal of the American Academy for Child and Adolescent Psychiatry* 38, 1209–1211.

Greenhill, L. (1998) 'Childhood ADHD: Pharmacological treatments', in P. Nathan and J. Gorman (eds) *A Guide to Treatments that Work.* Oxford: Oxford University Press.

Greenough, W.T., Black, J.E. and Wallace, C.S. (1987) Experience and brain development. *Child Development* 58, 539–559.

Guevara, J.P. and Stein, M.T. (2001) Evidence based management of attention deficit hyperactivity disorder. *British Medical Journal* 323, 1232–1235.

Hackett, L. and Hackett, R. (1994) Child rearing practices and psychiatric disorder in Gujarati and British children. *British Journal of Social Work* 24, 191–202.

Haigh, R. (2003) 'The Role and Value of Therapeutic Communities', in *Towards Emotional Health.* Proceedings of the fifth annual conference of the James Naylor Foundation. New York, March 2003.

Haley, J. (1973) *Uncommon Therapy: The Psychiatric Techniques of Milton H. Erickson.* New York: Norton.

—— (1976) *Problem Solving Therapy.* San Francisco: Jossey-Bass.

—— (1980) *Leaving Home.* New York: McGraw-Hill.

Hallberg, M. (1990) Science and feminism. *Sociologisk-Forskning* 27, 27–34.

Hamilton, A. (1980) *Nature and Nurture: Aboriginal Child Rearing in North-Central Arnhem Land.* Canberra: Australian Institute of Aboriginal Studies.

Hamilton, C. (2003) *Growth Fetish.* Crows Nest: Allen & Unwin.

Hanf, C. (1969) A two-stage programme for modifying maternal controlling during mother–child interaction. Paper Presented at the Meeting of the Western Psychological Association. Canada: Vancouver.

Harding, S. (1986) *The Science Question in Feminism.* Ithaca NY: Cornell University Press.

—— (1991) *Whose Science? Whose Knowledge?* Ithaca NY: Cornell University Press.

Hardyment, C. (1995) *Perfect Parents: Baby-Care Advise Past and Present.* Oxford: Oxford University Press.

Hare-Mustin, R. (1975) Treatment of temper tantrums by a paradoxical intervention. *Family Process* 14, 481–485.

—— (1994) Discourses in the mirrored room: A postmodern analysis of therapy. *Family Process* 33, 19–35.

Harper, P. and Clarke, A. (1997) *Genetics, Society and Clinical Practice*. London: Bios Scientific Publications.

Harper, P. and Gray, M. (1997) 'Maps and meaning in life and healing', in K. Dwivedi (ed.) *Therapeutic Use of Stories*. London: Routledge.

Harre, R. (1983) *Personal Being: A Theory for Individual Psychology*. Oxford: Blackwell.

—— (1986) 'The step to social constructionism', in M. Richards and P. Light (eds) *Children of Social Worlds*. Cambridge: Polity Press.

Harris, G.G. (1978) *Casting out Anger: Religion Among the Taita of Kenya*. Cambridge: Cambridge University Press.

Hart, O. (1983) *Rituals in Psychotherapy: Transition and Continuity*. New York: Irvington.

Hartman, T. (1996) *Beyond ADD: Hunting for Reasons in the Past and Present*. Grass Valley, CA: Underwood Books.

Harvey, D. (1990) *The Condition of Postmodernity*. Oxford: Blackwell.

Hasan, A.H. and Al-Quattami, L. (1995) 'Early education in Kuwait: A brief description of the nursery curriculum translated by A. Sweity', in Fernea, E.W. (ed.) *Children in the Muslim Middle East*. Austin: University of Texas Press.

Hazell, P. (1997) The overlap of attention deficit hyperactivity disorder with other common mental disorders. *Journal of Paediatric Child Health* 33, 131–137.

Healy, D. (1999) *The Antidepressant Era*. Cambridge, MA: Harvard University Press.

Healy, J.M. (1998) *Failure to Connect*. New York: Simon & Schuster.

Heasman, K. (1962) *The Evangelicals in Action*. London: Geoffrey Bles.

Heinmann, P. (1950) On counter-transference. *International Journal of Psychoanalysis* 31, 81–84.

—— (1960) Counter-transference. *British Journal of Medical Psychology* 33, 9–15.

Hendrick, H. (1992) Changing attitudes to children 1800–1914. *Genealogists Magazine* 24, 41–49.

—— (1994) *Child Welfare England 1870–1989*. London: Routledge.

—— (1997) 'Constructions and reconstructions of British childhood: An interpretive survey, 1800 to the present', in A. James and A. Prout (eds) *Constructing and Reconstructing Childhood: Contemporary Issues in the Sociological Study of Childhood*. London: Falmer Press.

Hengeller, S.W. and Borduin, C.M. (1990) *Family Therapy and Beyond: A Multi-Systemic Approach to Treating the Behaviour Problems of Children and Adolescents*. Pacific Grove, CA: Brooks-Cole.

Herxheimer, A. (2003) Relationships between pharmaceutical industry and patients organizations. *British Medical Journal* 326, 1208–1210.

Hetchman, L., Weis, G. and Perlman, T. (1984) Young adult outcome of hyperactive children who received long term stimulant medication. *Journal of the American Academy of Child and Adolescent Psychiatry* 23, 261–269.

Hey, V., Leonard, D., Daniels, H. and Smith, M. (1998) 'Boys' underachievement, special needs practices and questions of equity', in D. Epstein, J. Elwood, V. Hey and J. Maw (eds) *Failing Boys? Issues in Gender and Underachievement*. Buckingham: Open University Press.

Heyman, R. (1994) Methylphenidate (Ritalin): Newest drug of abuse in schools. *Ohio Pediatrics* Spring, 17–18.

Hill, C. (1997) *Society and Puritanism in Pre-revolutionary England*. London: St Martins Press.

Hill, P. and Cameron, M. (1999) Recognising Hyperactivity: A guide for the cautious clinician. *Child Psychology and Psychiatry* 4, 50–60.

Hinshaw, S.P. (1987) On the distinction between attention deficits/hyperactivity and conduct problems/aggression in child psychopathology. *Psychological Bulletin* 101, 443–463.

—— (1994) *Attention Deficit Disorders and Hyperactivity in Children*. Thousand Oak, CA: Sage.

Hoch, E. (1960) A pattern of neurosis in India. *American Journal of Psychoanalysis* 20, 87–97.

Hofstede, G. (1994) *Cultures and Organisations: Software of the Mind*. London: HarperCollins.

Holman, B. (1995) *The Evacuation*. London: The Lion Press.

Holme, J. (1984) Growing up in Hinduism. *British Journal of Religious Education* 15, 19–28.

—— (2002) All you need is cognitive behaviour therapy? *British Medical Journal* 324, 288–294.

Homans, G.C. (1993) 'Behaviourism and after', in A. Giddens and J. Turner (eds) *Social Theory Today*. Cambridge: Polity Press.

Hooten, E. (1937) *Apes, Men and Morons*. New York: G. Putman and Sons.

Horne, G. (2001) Race backwards: Genes, violence, race and genocide. *Journal of Human Behaviour in the Social Environment* 4, 155–166.

Horvath, A. and Symonds, D. (1991) Relationship between working alliance and outcome in psychotherapy: a meta-analysis. *Journal of Counselling Psychology* 38, 139–149.

Hsu, F.L. (1983) *Rugged Individualism Reconsidered*. Knoxville: University of Tennessee Press.

Hsu, J. (1985) 'The Chinese family: Relations, problems and therapy', in W. Tseng and D. Wu (eds) *Chinese Culture and Mental Health*. New York: Academic Press.

Humphries, S. (1981) *Hooligans or Rebels? An Oral History of Working Class Childhood and Youth, 1889–1939*. Oxford: Blackwell.

Huyuh, H., Luk, S.L., Singh, R., Pavaluri, M. and Mathai, J. (1999) Medium-term outcome of children given stimulants for attention deficit hyperactivity disorder. *Child Psychology and Psychiatry Review* 4, 610–617.

Hynd, G.W. and Hooper, S.R. (1995) *Neurological Basis of Childhood Psychopathology*. London: Sage Publications.

Illich, I. (1990) *Limits to Medicine*. London: Penguin.

Ingleby, D. (1985) 'Professionals as socialisers: The "Psy Complex"', in S. Spitzer and A.T. Scull (eds) *Research in the Law, Deviance and Social Control: A Research Annual*, Vol. 7. London: JAI Press.

Inglis, R. (1990) *The Children's War: Evacuation 1939–45*. London: Fontana.

Jackson, D. (1998) 'Breaking out of the binary trap: Boy's underachievement, schooling and gender relations', in D. Epstein, J. Elwood, V. Hey and J. Maw (eds) *Failing Boys? Issues of Gender and Underachievement*. Buckingham: Open University Press.

Jacobson, M. and Schardt, D. (1999) *Diet, ADHD and Behavior: A Quarter-Century Review*. Washington: Center for Science in the Public Interest.

Jansen, S. (1990) Is science a man? New feminist epistemologies and the reconstruction of knowledge. *Theory and Society* 19, 235–246.

Jenhs, C. (1996) *Childhood*. London: Routledge.

Jenkins, H. (1998) 'Introduction: Childhood Innocence and Other Modern Myths', in H. Jenkins (ed.) *The Children's Culture Reader*. New York: New York University Press.

Jordan, J., Kaplan, A., Miller, J.B., Stiver, I. and Surrey, J. (1991) *Women's Growth in Connection: Writings from the Store Center*. New York: Guilford Press.

Joseph, J. (2003) *The Gene Illusion: Genetic Research in Psychiatry and Psychology Under the Microscope*. Ross-on-Wye: PCCS Books.

Joughin, C. and Zwi, M. (1999). *Focus on the Use of Stimulants in Children with Attention Deficit Hyperactivity Disorder. Primary Evidence-Base Briefing No.1*. London: Royal College of Psychiatrists Research Unit.

Kagitcibasi, C. (1989) 'Child rearing in Turkey: Implications for immigration and intervention', in J. Kloprogge (ed.) *Different Cultures Same School: Ethnic Minority Children in Europe*. Lisse: Swets & Zeitlinger.

—— (1996) *Family and Human Development Across Cultures. A View from the Other Side*. Hove: Lawrence Earlbaum.

Kakar, S. (1978) *The Inner World: A Psychoanalytic Study of Childhood and Society in India*. Delhi: Oxford University Press.

—— (1979) Childhood in India. *International Social Science Journal* 31, 444–456.

—— (1982) *Shamans, Mystics and Doctors: A Psychological Inquiry into India and its Healing Traditions*. New York: Knopf.

—— (1994) *The Inner World of the Indian Child*. New Delhi: Oxford University Press.

Kallman, F. (1938) Heredity, reproduction and eugenic procedure in the field of schizophrenia. *Eugenic News* 23, 105.

Karmiloff-Smith, A. (1992) *Beyond Modularity: A Developmental Perspective on Cognitive Science*. Cambridge, MA: MIT Press.

Karon, B.P. (1994) Problems of psychotherapy under managed care. *Psychotherapy in Private Practice* 2, 55–63.

Kaufman, M. (1994) 'Men, feminism and men's contradictory experiences of power', in H. Brod and M. Kaufman (eds) *Theorising Masculinities*. Newbury Park, CA: Sage.

Kazdin, A.E. (1987) Treatment of antisocial behaviour in children: Current status and future directions. *Psychological Bulletin* 102, 187–203.

—— (1996) *Conduct Disorder in Childhood and Adolescents* (2nd Edition). Thousand Oaks, CA: Sage.

—— (1997) Practitioner review: Psychosocial treatments for conduct disorder in children. *Journal of Child Psychology and Psychiatry* 38, 161–178.

Kazdin, A.E. and Wassell, D. (2000) Therapeutic changes in children, parents and families resulting from treatment of children with conduct problems. *Journal of the American Academy of Child and Adolescent Psychiatry* 39, 414–420.

Keir, G. (1952) A history of child guidance. *British Journal of Educational Psychology* 22, 5–29.

Keller, E. (1985) *Gender and Science*. New Haven: Yale University Press.

Kelves, D.J. (1985) *In the Name of Eugenics*. California: University of California Press.

Kelves, D.J. (1999) Eugenics and human rights. *British Medical Journal* 319, 435–438.

Kendall, P.C. (1985) Toward a cognitive-behavioural model of child psychopathology and a critique of related interventions. *Journal of Abnormal Psychology* 13, 357–372.

Kennedy, J.G. (1977) *Struggle for Change in a Nubian Community*. Palo Alto: Marfield Publishing Co.

Kenway, J. and Fitzclarence, L. (1997) Masculinity, violence and schooling: Challenging 'poisonous pedagogies'. *Gender and Education* 9, 117–133.

Kessen, W. (1979) The American child and other cultural inventions. *American Psychologist* 34, 815–820.

Kewley, G.D. (1998) Attention Deficit Hyperactivity Disorder is under diagnosed and under treated in Britain. *British Medical Journal* 316, 1594–1595.

—— (1999) The relevance of ADHD for Paediatricians. *BACCH News* Summer, 18–21.

Khan, I. (1965) *Maxims of Mohammed*. Karachi: Umma Publishing House.

Kimmel, M. (1987) 'The contemporary crisis of masculinity in historical perspective', in H. Brod (ed.) *The Making of Masculinities*. Boston: Allen & Unwin.

Kincheloe, J. (1998) 'The new childhood; Home alone as a way of life', in H. Jenkins (ed.) *Children's Culture Reader*. New York: New York University Press.

Kindlon, D. and Thompson, M. (1999) *Raising Cain: Protecting the Emotional Life of Boys*. Harmondsworth: Penguin.

King, A. and Bond, M. (1985) 'The Confucian paradigm of man: A sociological view', in W. Tseng and D. Wu (eds) *Chinese Culture and Mental Health*. New York: Academic Press.

Kirschner, D.A. and Kirschner, S. (1986) *Comprehensive Family Therapy: An Integration of Systemic and Psychodynamic Models*. New York: Brunner-Mazel.

Klein, D.N. and Riso, L.P. (1994) 'Psychiatric disorders: problems of boundaries and comorbidity', in C.G. Costello (ed.) *Basic Issues in Psychopathology*. New York: Guildford Press.

Klein, R.G. and Mannuzza, S. (1991) Long-term outcome of hyperactive children: A review. *Journal of American Academy of Child and Adolescent Psychiatry* 30, 383–387.

Kleinman, A. (1988) *Rethinking Psychiatry: From Cultural Category to Personal Experience*. New York: The Free Press.

Kohn, A. (1989) Suffer the restless children. *Atlantic Monthly* November, 90–100.

Kojima, H. (1984) A significant stride towards the comparative study of control. *American Psychologist* 39, 972–973.

Konner, M.J. (1972) 'Aspects of developmental ethology of a foraging people', in N.G. Blurton-Jones (ed.) *Ethological Studies of Child Behaviour*. Cambridge: Cambridge University Press.

Kotlowitz, A. (1991) *Are There no Children Here: The Story of Two Boys Growing up in the Other America*. New York: Double Day.

Kovel, J. (2002) *The Enemy of Nature: The End of Capitalism or the End of the World?* New York: Zed Books.

Kryger, N. (1998) 'Teachers understanding and emotions in relation to the creation of boys masculine identity', in Y. Katz and I. Menezes (eds) *Affective Education: A Comparative View*. London: Cassell.

Kumar, K.T. (1992) To children with love. *British Medical Journal* 305, 1582–1583.

La Fontaine, J.S. (1979) *Sex and Age as Principles of Social Differentiation*. London: Academic Press.

Lahey, B.B., Applegate, B., McBurnett, K. and Biederman, J. (1994) DSM-IV field trials for Attention Deficit Hyperactivity Disorder in Children and Adolescents. *American Journal of Psychiatry* 151, 1673–1658

Lambert, N.M., and Hartsough, C.S. (1998) Prospective study of tobacco smoking and substance dependence among samples of ADHD and non-ADHD participants. *Journal of Learning Disabilities* 31, 533–544.

Langford, J. (1995) Ayurvedic interiors: Person, space and episteme in three medical practices. *Cultural Anthropology* 10, 330–366.

Lasch, C. (1980) *The Culture of Narcissism*. London: Norton (Abacus).

Lau, A. (1996) 'Family therapy and ethnic minorities', in K.N. Dwivedi and V.P. Varma (eds) *Meeting the Needs of Ethnic Minority Children*. London: Jessica Kingsley.

Law, I. (1997) 'Attention deficit disorder-therapy with a shoddily built construct', in C. Smith and D. Nyland (eds) *Narrative Therapies with Children And Adolescents.* New York: The Guildford Press.

Lax, W.D. (1992) 'Postmodern thinking in clinical practice', in S. McNamee and K. Gergen (eds) *Therapy as Social Construction.* Newbury Park, CA: Sage.

LeFever, G.B., Dawson, K.V. and Morrow, A.D. (1999) The extent of drug therapy for attention deficit hyperactivity disorder among children in public schools. *American Journal of Public Health* 89, 1359–1364.

Lenzer, J. (2004) Bush plans to screen whole US population for mental illness. *British Medical Journal* 328, 1458.

Leo, J. (2002) American preschoolers on Ritalin. *Society* 39, 52–60.

Leo, J.L. and Cohen, D.A. (2003) Broken brains or flawed studies? A critical review of ADHD neuroimaging research. *The Journal of Mind and Behavior* 24, 29–56.

LeVine, R.A., Dixon, S., LeVine, S., Richman, A., Leiderman, P.H., Keefer, C.H. and Brazelton, T.B. (1994) *Child Care and Culture: Lessons from Africa.* Cambridge: Cambridge University Press.

Leuchter, A.F., Cook, L.A. and Witte, E.A. (2002) Changes in brain function of depressed patients during treatment with placebo. *American Journal of Psychiatry* 159, 122–129.

Libow, J.A., Raskin, P.A. and Caust, B.L. (1982) Feminist and family systems therapy: Are they irreconcilable? *American Journal of Family Therapy* 10, 3–12.

Lieberman, A.F. and Pawl, J.H. (1990) 'Disorders of attachment and secure base behaviour in the second year of life', in M.T. Greenberg, D. Cicchetti and E.M. Cummings (eds) *Attachment in the Preschool Years.* Chicago: University of Chicago Press.

Linde, C. (1993) *Life Stories: The Creation of Coherence.* New York: Wiley.

Lindgren, S., Wolraich, M., Stromquist, A., Davis, C., Milich, R. and Watson, D. (1994) Reexamining Attention Deficit Disorder. Presented at the 8th Annual Meeting of the Society for Behavioural Pediatrics. Denver.

Lipsky, D. and Abrams, A. (1994) *Late Bloomers: Coming of Age in Today's America.* New York: Times Books.

Litchman, R. (1987) 'The illusion of maturation in an age of decline', in J. Broughton (ed.) *Critical Theories of Psychological Development.* New York: Plenum.

Little, M. (1951) Counter-transference and patients response to it. *International Journal of Psychoanalysis* 32, 32–40.

Lobovits, D.H., Maisel, R. and Freeman, J.C. (1995) 'Public practices: An ethic of circulation.', in S. Friedman (ed.) *The Reflecting Team in Action: Collaborative Practice in Family Therapy.* New York: Guilford Press.

Lochman, J.E. (1992) Cognitive-behavioural intervention with aggressive boys: Three year follow-up and preventive effects. *Journal of Consulting and Clinical Psychology* 60, 426–432.

Lochman, J.E., Lampron, L.B., Gemmer, T.C. and Harris, S.R. (1987) 'Anger coping intervention with aggressive children: A guide to implementation in school settings', in P.A. Keller and S.R. Heyman (eds) *Innovations in Clinical Practice: A Source Book,* Vol. 6. Sarasota, Fl.: Professional Resource Exchange.

Lochman, J.E. and Wells, K.C. (1996) 'A social cognitive intervention with aggressive children: Prevention effects and contextual implementation issues', in R.D. Peters and R.J. McMahon (eds) *Preventing Childhood Disorders, Substance Abuse and Delinquency.* Thousand Oaks, CA: Sage.

Locke, J. (1989) *The Clarendon Edition of the Works of John Locke* (edited by J.W. Yolton and J.S. Yolton). Oxford: Clarendon.

Long, N. (1996) Parenting in the USA: growing adversity. *Clinical Child Psychology and Psychiatry* 1, 483–496.

Luk, S.L. and Leung, P.W.L. (1989) Connors teachers rating scale – a validity study in Hong Kong. *Journal of Child Psychology and Psychiatry* 30, 785–794.

Lynch, O.M. (1990) 'The social construction of emotion in India', in O.M. Lynch (ed.) *Divine Passions: The Social Construction of Emotion in India*. California: The University of California Press.

Mac An Ghaill, M. (1994) *The Making of Men: Masculinities, Sexualities and Schooling*. Buckingham: Open University Press.

MacIntyre, A. (1980) 'Epistemological curse, dramatic narrative, and the philosophy of science', in G. Gutting (ed.) *Paradigms and Revolutions*. Indiana: University of Notre Dame Press.

—— (1985) *After Virtue*. Indiana: University of Notre Dame Press.

MacNaughton, G. (2000) *Rethinking Gender in Early Childhood Education*. London: Paul Chapman.

MacNicol, J. (1986) 'The effect of the evacuation of school children on official attitudes to state intervention', in H.L. Smith (ed.) *War and Social Change: British Society in the Second World War*. Manchester: Manchester University Press.

Madanes, C. (1981) *Strategic Family Therapy*. San Francisco: Jossey-Bass.

Malinowski, B. (1963) *The Family Among the Australian Aborigines*. New York: Schocken.

Malone, R.P., Delaney, M.A., Luebbert, J.F., Cater, J. and Campbell, M. (2000) A double-bind, placebo-controlled study of Lithium in hospitalized, aggressive children and adolescents with conduct disorder. *Archives of General Psychiatry* 57, 649–654.

Mandelbaum, D. (1970) *Society in India*. Berkley: University of California Press.

Mandoki, M.W. (1995) Risperidone treatment of children and adolescents: Increased risk of extra-pyramidal side effects? *Journal of Child and Adolescent Psychopharmacology* 5, 49–67.

Mann, E.M., Ikeda, Y., Mueller, C.W., Takahashi, A., Tao, K.T., Humris, E., Li, B.L. and Chin, D. (1992) Cross-cultural differences in rating hyperactive-disruptive behaviours in children. *American Journal of Psychiatry* 149, 1539–1542.

Manton, J. (1976) *Mary Carpenter and the Children of the Street*. London: Heinemann.

Mason, R. (1999) Giant steps for mankind. *Times Educational Supplement* 14, May 19.

May, M. (1973) Innocence and experience in the evolution of the concept of juvenile delinquency in the mid-nineteenth century. *Victorian Studies* 17, 7–29.

Mazaide, M. (1989) 'Should adverse temperament matter to the clinician? An empirically based answer', in G.A. Khonstaum, V.E. Bates and M.K. Rothbart (eds) *Temperament in Childhood*. New York: Wiley.

McGee, R., Feehan, M., Williams, S. and Anderson, J. (1992) DSM-III disorders from age 11 to age 15 years. *Journal of the American Academy for Child and Adolescent Psychiatry* 31, 50–59.

McGee, R., Williams, S. and Anderson, J. (1990) Hyperactivity and serum and hair zinc levels in 11-year-old children from the general population. *Biological Psychiatry* 28, 165–168.

McGinnis, J. (1997) Attention Deficit Disaster. *The Wall Street Journal* 18 September.

McGuiness, D. (1989) 'Attention Deficit Disorder, the Emperor's new clothes, Animal "Pharm" and other fiction', in S. Fisher and R. Greenberg (eds) *The Limits of Biological*

Treatments for Psychological Distress: Comparisons with Psychotherapy and Placebo. Hillsdale, NJ: Lawrence Erlbaum Associates.

McGuire, S. and Clifford, J. (2000) Genetic and environmental contributions to loneliness in children. *Psychological Science* 11, 487–491.

McGuire, S., Manke, B., Savdino, K.J., Reiss, D., Hetherington, E.M. and Plomin, R. (1999) Perceived competence and self-worth during adolescence: A longitudinal behavioural genetic study. *Child Development* 70, 1283–1296.

McMahon, R.J. and Wells, K.C. (1998) 'Conduct problems', in E.J. Mash and R.A. Barkley (eds) *Treatment of Childhood Disorders* (2nd Edition). New York: Guildford.

Mednick, S.A. and Christiansen, K.D. (1977) *Biosocial Basis of Criminal Behaviour.* New York: Gardner Press.

Melzer, D. and Zimmern, R. (2002) Genetics and medicalisation. *British Medical Journal* 324, 863–864.

Meredith, W.H. and Abbott, D.A. (1985) 'Chinese families in later life', in B.B. Ingoldsby and S. Smith (eds) *Families in Multicultural Perspective.* New York: Guildford Press.

Merrow, J. (1995) 'ADHD – A dubious diagnosis', Public Broadcasting Service (USA) 5 November.

Miller, S., Duncan, B. and Hubble, M. (1997) *Psychotherapy with Impossible Cases.* New York: Norton.

Miller, S., Hubble, M. and Duncan, B. (1995) *Escape from Babel: Toward a Unifying Language for Psychotherapeutic Practice.* New York: Norton.

Mills, J. and Crowley, R. (1986) *Therapeutic Metaphors for Children and the Child Within.* New York: Brunner-Mazel.

Mintzes, B. (2002) Direct to consumer advertising in medicalizing normal human experience. *British Medical Journal* 324, 908–909.

Minuchin, S. (1974) *Families and Family Therapy.* Cambridge, MA: Harvard University Press.

Miringolt, M. (1994) *Monitoring the Social Well-Being of the Nation: The Index of Social Health.* Tarytown, N.Y: Fordham Institute for Social Policy.

Moll, G., Hause, S., Ruther, E., Rothenberger, A. and Huether, G. (2001) Early methylphenidate administration to young rats causes a persistent reduction in the density of striatal dopamine transporters. *Journal of Child and Adolescent Psychopharmacology* 11, 15–24.

Morgan. P. (1987) *Delinquent Fantasies.* London: Temple Smith.

Morrell, R. (ed.) (2001) *Changing Men in South Africa.* London: Zed Books.

Morss, J.R. (1990) *The Biologising of Childhood: Developmental Psychology and the Darwinian Myth.* Hove: Lawrence Erlbaum Associates.

—— (1995) The developmental complex. *Psychoculture* 1, 16–17.

—— (1996) *Growing Critical: Alternatives to Developmental Psychology.* London and New York: Routledge.

Moynihan, R. (2003) The making of a disease: female sexual dysfunction. *British Medical Journal* 326, 45–47.

Moynihan, R., Heath, I. and Henry, D. (2002) Selling sickness: The pharmaceutical industry and disease mongering. *British Medical Journal* 324, 886–891.

Moynihan, R. and Smith, R. (2002) Too much Medicine? *British Medical Journal* 324, 859–860.

MTA Co-operative Group (1999a) A 14 month randomized clinical trial of treatment strategies for attention deficit/hyperactivity disorder. *Archives of General Psychiatry* 56, 1073–1086.

—— (1999b) Moderators and mediators of treatment response for children with attention deficit/hyperactivity disorder. *Archives of General Psychiatry* 56, 1086–1096.

Muir-Gray, J.A. (1999) Postmodern medicine. *Lancet* 354, 1550–1553.

Muller-Hill, B. (1991) 'Psychiatry in the Nazi era', in S. Block and P. Chodoff (eds) *Psychiatric Ethics*. New York: Oxford University Press.

Murphy-Berman, V., Levesque, H.L. and Berman, J.J. (1996) U.N. convention on the rights of the child. *American Psychologist* 51, 1257–1261.

Murray, T.H. (1997) 'Genetic exceptionalism and "future diaries". Is genetic information different from other medical information?', in M.A. Rothstein (ed.) *Genetic Secrets: Protecting Privacy and Confidentiality in the Genetic Era*. New Haven and London: Yale University Press.

National Institutes of Health (1998) *Consensus Statement: Diagnosis and Treatment of Attention Deficit Hyperactivity Disorders*. Rockville, MD: National Institute of Mental Health.

Nemzer, E.D., Arnold, L.E., Votolato, N.A. and McConnell, H. (1986) Amino acid supplementation as therapy for attention deficit disorder. *Journal of the American Academy for Child and adolescent Psychiatry* 25, 509–513.

Neven, R.S., Anderson, V., Goodbar, T. (2002) *Rethinking ADHD – Integrated Approaches to Helping Children at Home and at School*. Crows Nest, New South Wales: Allen & Unwin.

Newman-Black, M. (1989) 'How can the convention be implemented in developing countries', in R. Barnen (ed.) *Making Reality of Children's Rights*. New York: UNICEF.

Novick, K.K. and Novick, J. (1987) 'The essence of Masochism', in *The Psychoanalytic Study of the Child Series – Number 42*. New Haven, C.T.: Yale University Press.

Oas, P. (2001) *Curing ADD/ADHD Children*. Raleigh, NC: Pentland Press.

Obeyesekere, G. (1977) The theory and practice of psychological medicine in Ayurvedic tradition. *Culture, Medicine and Psychiatry* 1, 155–181.

Offord, E. (1998) Wrestling with the whirlwind: An approach to the understanding of ADD/ADHD. *Journal of Child Psychotherapy* 24, 253–266.

O'Hanlon, W.H. and Weiner-Davis, N. (1989) *In Search of Solutions, A New Direction in Psychotherapy*. New York: Norton.

Olfson, M., Marcus, S.C., Weissman, M.M. and Jensen, P.S. (2002) National trends in the use of psychotropic medications by children. *Journal of the American Academy of Child and Adolescent Psychiatry* 41, 514–521.

O'Meara, P. (2003) Putting power back in parental hands. *Insight Magazine*. 28 April 2003.

Organisation of African Unity (1990) 'The African Charter on the rights and welfare of the child', adopted by the 26th ordinary session of the assembly of heads of state and government of the OAU. Addis Ababa: July 1990.

Palazzoli, M.S., Boscolo, L., Lecchin, G and Prata, G. (1978) *Paradox and Counter Paradox*. New York: Jason Aronson.

Panksepp, J. (1998a) A critical analysis of ADHD, psychostimulants and intolerance of childhood playfulness: A tragedy in the making? *Current Directions in Psychological Sciences* 7, 91–97.

—— (1998b) The quest for long term health and happiness: To play or not to play that is the question. *Psychological Inquiry* 9, 56–65.

Panksepp, J., Burgdorf, J., Turner, C. and Gordon, N. (2003) Modeling ADHD-type arousal with unilateral frontal cortex damage in rats and beneficial effects of play therapy. *Brain and Cognition* 52, 97–105.

Papolos, D. and Papolos, J. (1999) *The Bipolar Child*. New York: Broadway Books.

Parker, I. (1992) *Discourse Dynamics*. London: Routledge.

Patterson, G.R. (1975) *Families: Application of Social Learning to Family Life*. Campaign, II: Research Press.

—— (1976) *Living with Children: New Methods for Parents and Teachers*. Campaign, IL: Research Press.

Patterson, G.R. and Forgatch, M. (1987) *Parents and Adolescents Living Together: Part I. The Basics*. Eugene, O.R.: Castilia.

Payer, L. (1992) *Disease Mongers*. New York: John Wiley.

Pearson, G. (1983) *Hooligan: A History of Respectable Fears*. London: MacMillan.

Penzer, N.M. (1968) *The Ocean of Story*. Translated by C.H. Tawny. Delhi: Motilal Banarsidas.

Peristiany, J.G. (1965) *Honor and Shame: The Values of Mediterranean Society*. London: Weidenfeld & Nicolson.

Perry, B.D., Pollard, R.A., Blackeley, T.L., Baker, W.L. and Vigilante, D. (1995) Childhood trauma, the neurobiology of adaptation and the use-dependent development of the brain, how states become traits. *Infant Mental Health Journal* 16, 20–33.

Pettengill, S.M. and Rohner, R.P. (1985) 'Korean-American adolescents' perceptions of parental control, parental acceptance/rejection and parent/adolescent conflict', in I.R. Lagunes and Y.H. Poortinga (eds) *From a Different Perspective: Studies of Behaviour Across Cultures*. Lisse: Swets & Zeitlinger.

Phillips, K. (1990) *The Politics of Rich and Poor*. New York: Random House.

Pilgrim, D. (1997) *Psychotherapy and Society*. London: Sage.

Pinchbeck, I. and Hewitt, M. (1973) *Children in English Society*. London: Routledge & Kegan Paul.

Pollock, L. (1983) *Forgotten Children*. Cambridge: Cambridge University Press.

Pollack, W. (1998) *Real Boys: Rescuing our Sons from the Myths of Boyhood*. New York: Henry Holt.

Popenoe, P. (1935) Public opinion on sterilization in California. *Eugenic News* 20, 73.

Postman, N. (1983) *The Disappearance of Childhood*. London: W.H. Allen.

Prendergast, M., Taylor, E., Rapoport, J.L., Bartko, J., Donnelly, M., Zametkin, A., Ahearn, M.B., Dunn, G. and Weiselberg, H.M. (1988) The diagnosis of childhood hyperactivity: A U.S.–U.K. cross-national study of DSM-III and ICD-9. *Journal of Child Psychology and Psychiatry* 29, 289–300.

Prior, M. and Sanson, A. (1986) Attention Deficit Disorder with hyperactivity: a critique. *Journal of Child Psychology and Psychiatry* 27, 307–319.

Proctor, R. (1988) *Racial Hygiene: Medicine Under the Nazis*. Cambridge MA: Harvard University Press.

Prout, A. and James, A. (1997) 'A new Paradigm for the sociology of childhood? Provenance, promise and problems', in A. James and A. Prout (eds) *Constructing and Re-constructing Childhood: Contemporary Issues in the Sociological Study of Childhood*. London: Falmer Press.

Qvortrup, J. (1985) 'Placing children in the division of labour', in P. Close and R. Collins (eds) *Family and Economy in Modern Society*. London: Macmillan.

Rabin, L. (1994) *Families on the Frontline: American Working Class Speaks About the Economy, Race and Ethnicity*. New York: HarperCollins.

Racker, H. (1953) A contribution to the problem of counter-transference. *International Journal of Psychoanalysis* 34, 313–324.

Rahman, A. (1993) *People's Self-Development.* London: Zed Press.

Ramchandani, P. (2004) Treatment of major depressive disorder in children and adolescents. *British Medical Journal* 328, 3–4.

Rapp, D.J. (1996) *Is this Your Child's World?* New York: Bantam Books.

Rappaport, J. (2003) Cornell improves the brain. Stratiawire.com. February 2003.

Rapoport, J.L., Buchsbaum, M.S., Zahn, T., Weingartner, H., Ludlow, C. and Mickkelsen, E.J. (1978) Dextroamphetamine: cognitive and behavioural effects in normal prepubertal boys. *Science* 199, 560–563.

Rapoport, J.L., Buchsbaum, M.S., Zahn, T., Weingarten, H., Ludlow, C. and Mickkelsen, E.J. (1980) Dextroamphetamine: Its cognitive and behavioural effect in normal and hyperactive boys and normal men. *Archives of General Psychiatry* 37, 933–943.

Rappley, M.D., Gardiner, J.C., Jetton, J.R. and Howang, R.T. (1995) The use of Methylphenidate in Michigan. *Archives of Paediatric and Adolescent Medicine* 149, 675–679.

Rapport, M.D. (1995) 'Attention Deficit Hyperactivity Disorder', in M. Hersen and R.T. Ammerman (eds) *Advances in Abnormal Child Psychology.* Hillsdale, NJ: Lawrence Erlbaum Associates.

Ravenel, D.B. (2002) A new behavioral approach for ADD/ADHD and behavioral management without medication. *Ethical Human Sciences and Services* 4, 93–106.

Read, T. (1990) The therapeutic use of self in constructionist/systemic theory. *Family Process* 29, 255–272.

Reiss, A. and Roth, J. (1993) *Understanding and Preventing Violence.* Washington, DC: National Academy Press.

Reich, A. (1952) On counter-transference. *International Journal of Psychoanalysis* 32, 25–31.

Reynolds, P. (1996) *Traditional Healers and Childhood in Zimbabwe.* Athens, Ohio: Ohio University Press.

Rhee, S.H., Waldman, I.D., Hay, D.A. and Levy, F. (1995) Sex differences in genetic and environmental influences on DSM-III-R Attention Deficit Hyperactivity Disorder (ADHD). *Behaviour Genetics* 25, 285.

Richards, B. (1989) Visions of freedom. *Free associations* 16, 31–42.

Richards, M. (2001) How distinctive is genetic information. *Studies in History, Philosophy and Biomedical science* 32, 663–687.

Riddell, S. (1996) 'Gender and special educational needs', in G. Lloyd (ed.) *Knitting Progress Unsatisfactory: Gender and Special Issues in Education.* Edinburgh: Moray House Institute of Education.

Rie, H., Rie, E., Stewart, S. and Anbuel, J. (1976) Effects of Ritalin on underachieving children: A replication. *American Journal of Orthopsychiatry* 45, 313–332.

Rifkin, A., Karajgi, B., Dicker, R., Perl, E., Boppana, V., Hasan, N. and Pollack, S. (1997) Lithium treatment of conduct disorders in adolescents. *American Journal of psychiatry* 154, 554–555.

Robin, A.L. and Barkley, R.A. (1998) *ADHD in Adolescents: Diagnosis and Treatment.* New York: Guildford.

Robinson, T.E. and Kolb, B. (2001) Persistent structural modifications in nucleus accumbens and prefrontal cortex neurons produced by previous experience with amphetamine. *Journal of Neuroscience* 17, 8491–8497.

Rogers, A., Pilgrim, D. and Lacey, R. (1993) *Experiencing Psychiatry: Users Views of Services.* London: MacMillan.

Rosanhoff, A. (1938) *Manual of Psychiatry and Mental Hygiene.* New York: John Wiley & Sons.

Rose, N. (1985) *The Psychological Complex: Psychology, Politics and Society in England 1869–1939.* London: RKP.

Rose, N. (1990) *Governing the Soul: The Shaping of the Private Self.* London: Routledge.

Rose, S. (1998) Neuro genetic determinism and the new eugenics. *British Medical Journal* 317, 1707–1708.

Rosemond, J.K. (2001) 'Foreword', in D. Stein (ed.) *Unravelling the ADD/ADHD Fiasco.* Kansas City: Andrew McMeel.

Rosen, S. (ed.) (1982) *My Voice Will Go With You: The Teaching Tales of Milton H. Erickson, M.D.* New York: Norton.

Rosenfeld, H. (1952) Notes on the psychoanalysis of the superego conflict in an acute catatonic schizophrenic. *International Journal of Psychoanalysis* 33, 111–131.

Rosman, D. (1984) *Evangelicals and Culture.* London: Croom Helm.

Rousseau, J.J. (1762) *Emile (edited by P.D. Jimack).* London: Everyman Library Series, 1992.

Ruesch, H. (1992) *Naked Empress or the Great Medical Fraud.* Massagne and Lugano: CIVIS Publication.

Rutter, M. (1982) Syndromes attributed to minimal brain dysfunction in childhood. *American Journal of Psychiatry.* 139, 21–33.

Rutter, M., Tizard, J. and Whitmore, K. (1970) *Education, Health and Behaviour.* London: Longman.

Sachs, W. (1992) *The Developmental Dictionary.* London: Zed Press.

Said, H.K. (1983) 'The Unani system of health and medicare', in R.H. Bannerman, J. Burton and L. Wen-Chieh (eds) *Traditional Medicine and Healthcare.* Geneva: World Health Organization.

Saks, M.J. (1996) The role of research in implementing the U.N. convention on the rights of the child. *American Psychologist* 51, 1262–1266.

Sandberg, S. (1996) Hyperkinetic or Attention Deficit Disorder. *British Journal of Psychiatry* 169, 10–17.

Sannerud, C. and Feussner, G. (2000) 'Is Ritalin an abused drug? Does it meet the criteria of a schedule II substance?' in L.L. Greenhill and B.B. Osman (eds) *Ritalin: Theory and Practice.* New York: Mary Ann Liebert.

Sarbin, T.R. and Kitsuse, J.I. (1994) *Constructing the Social.* London: Sage.

Sax, S. (2000) Living through better chemistry? *The World and I* 15, 287–299.

Schachar, R.J. (1991) Childhood hyperactivity. *Journal of Child Psychology and Psychiatry* 32, 155–191.

Schachar, R. and Tannock, R. (1997) Behavioural, situational and temporal effects of treatment of ADHD with methylphenidate. *Journal of American Academy of Child and Adolescent Psychiatry* 36, 754–763.

—— (2002) 'Syndromes of hyperactivity and attention deficit', in M. Rutter and E. Taylor (eds) *Child and Adolescent Psychiatry* (4th Edition). Oxford: Blackwell.

Schachter, H., Pham, B., King, J., Langford, S. and Moher, D. (2001). How efficacious and safe is short-acting methylphenidate for the treatment of attention-deficit disorder in children and adolescents? A meta-analysis. *Canadian Medical Association Journal* 165, 1475–1488.

Schaffer, H.R. (1990) *Making Decisions About Children: Psychological Questions and Answers.* Oxford: Blackwell.

Scheper-Hughes, N. and Stein, H.F. (1987) 'Child abuse and the unconscious in American popular culture', in N. Scheper-Hughes (ed.) *Child Survival.* New York: D. Reidel Publishing.

Schmidt, M.H., Esser, G., Allehoff, W., Geisel, B., Laught, M. and Woerner, W. (1987) Evaluating the significance of minimal brain dysfunction – results of an epidemiological study. *Journal of Child Psychology and Psychiatry* 28, 803–821.

Schneider, B.H. (1992) Didactic methods for enhancing children's peer relations: A quantative review. *Clinical Psychology Review* 12, 363–382.

Schneider, B.H., Smith, A., Poisson, S.E. and Kwan, A.B. (1997) 'Cultural dimensions of children's peer relations', in S.W. Duck (ed.) *Handbook of Personal Relationships: Theory, Research and Interventions* (2nd Edition). Chichester: John Wiley.

Schwartz, J.M., Stoessel, P.W., Baxter, L.R. and Karron, M. (1996) Systematic changes in cerebral glucose metabolic rate after successful behaviour modification treatment of obsessive compulsive disorder. *Archives of General Psychiatry* 53, 109–113.

Scott, S., Spender, Q., Doolan, M., Jacobs, B. and Aspland, H. (2001) Multicentre controlled trail of parenting groups for childhood antisocial behaviour in clinical practice. *British Medical Journal* 323, 194.

Seabrook, J. (1982) *Working Class Childhood: An Oral History.* London: Gollancz.

Segal, A.U. (1991) Cultural variables in Asian Indian families. *Families in Society. The Journal of Contemporary Human Services* 72, 233–242.

Seidler, V. (1989) *Rediscovering Masculinity: Reason, Language and Sexuality.* London: Routledge.

Selleck, R.J.W. (1985) Mary Carpenter: A confident and contradictory reformer. *History of Education* March, 101–115.

Sells, S. (2001) *Parenting Your Out of Control Teenager: Seven Steps to Re-Establishing Authority and Reclaim Love.* New York: St Martin's Press.

Sewell, T. (1995) 'A phallic response to schools: Black masculinity and race in an inner-city comprehensive', in M. Griffiths and B. Troyna (eds) *Anti-Racism, Culture And Social Justice In Education.* Stoke-on-Trent: Trentham Books.

Shamasundar, C. (1997) 'Psychotherapeutic paradigms from Indian mythology', in K.N. Dwivedi (ed.) *Therapeutic Use of Stories.* London: Routledge.

Sharry, J. (1999) *Bringing up Responsible Children.* Dublin: Veritas.

Shen, Y.C., Wong, Y.F. and Yang, X.L. (1985) An epidemiological investigation of minimal brain dysfunction in six elementary schools in Beijing. *Journal of Child Psychology and Psychiatry* 26, 777–788.

Shotter, J. (1974) 'The development of personal powers', in M.P.M. Richards (ed.) *The Integration of a Child into a Social World.* Cambridge: Cambridge University Press.

Shweder, R.A. (1991) *Thinking Through Cultures: Expeditions in Cultural Psychology.* Cambridge, MA: Harvard University Press.

Silberg, J., Rutter, M., Meyer, J., Maes, H., Hewitt, J., Simonoff, E., Pickles, A., Loeber, R. and Eaves, L. (1996) Genetic and environmental influences on the covariation between hyperactivity and conduct disturbance in juvenile twins. *Journal of Child Psychology and Psychiatry* 37, 803–816.

Simeon, J.G., Carrey, N.J., Wiggins, D.M. Milin, R.P. and Hosenbocus, S.N. (1995) Risperidone effects in treatment resistant adolescents: Preliminary case reports. *Journal of Child and Adolescent Psychopharmacology* 5, 69–79.

Skelton, C. (2001) *Schooling the Boys: Masculinities and Primary Education.* Buckingham: Open University Press.

Solanto, M.V. and Wender, E.H. (1989) Does Methylphenidate constricts cognitive functioning? *Journal of the American Academy of Child Adolescent Psychiatry* 28, 897–902.

Sommerville, J. (1982) *The Rise and Fall of Childhood*. London: Sage.

Sonuga-Barke, E.J.S., Houlberg, K. and Hall, M. (1994) On dysfunction and function in psychological models of childhood disorder. *Journal of Child Psychology and Psychiatry* 35, 1247–1253.

Sonuga-Barke, E.J.S., Minocha, K., Taylor, E.A. and Sandberg, S. (1993) Inter-ethnic bias in teachers' ratings of childhood hyperactivity. *British Journal of Developmental Psychology* 11, 187–200.

Speltz, M.C. (1990) 'The treatment of preschool conduct problems', in M.T. Greenberg, D. Cicchetti, and E.M. Cummings (eds) *Attachment in the Preschool Years*. Chicago: University of Chicago Press.

Spencer, T., Biederman, J., Wilens, T., Harding, M., O'Donnell, D. and Griffin, S. (1996) Pharmacotherapy of attention deficit hyperactivity disorder across the life cycle. *Journal of the American Academy of Child and Adolescent Psychiatry* 35, 409–432.

Sprague, S.L. and Sleator, E.K. (1977) Methylphenidate in hyperkinetic children: Differences in dose effects on learning and social behaviour. *Science* 198, 1274–1276.

Sproson, E.J., Chantrey, J., Hollis, C., Marsden, C.A. and Fonel, K.C. (2001) Effect of repeated methylphenidate administration on presynaptic dopamine and behavior in young adult rats. *Journal of Psychopharmacology* 15, 67–75.

Stainton-Rogers, R. and Stainton-Rogers, W. (1992) *Stories of Childhood: Shifting Agendas of Child Concern*. Hassocks: Harvester.

Stein, D.B. (1999) A medication, free parent management program for children diagnosed as ADHD. *Ethical Human Sciences and Services* 1, 61–79.

—— (2001) *Unraveling the ADD/ADHD Fiasco: Successful Parenting Without Drugs*. Kansas City: Andrews McMeel.

Stein, T.P. and Sammaritano, A.M. (1984) Nitrogen metabolism in normal and hyperkinetic boys. *American Journal of Clinical Nutrition* 39, 520–524.

Steinhausen, H.C. and Erdin, A. (1991) A comparison of ICD-9 and ICD-10 diagnosis of child and adolescent disorders. *Journal of Child Psychology and Psychiatry* 32, 909–920.

Stephens, S. (1995) 'Children and the politics of culture in "Late Capitalism"', in S. Stephens (ed.) *Children and the Politics of Culture*. Princeton: Princeton University Press.

Stevens, L., Zentall, S. and Deck, J. (1995) Essential fatty acid metabolism in boys with attention-deficit hyperactivity disorder. *American Journal of Clinical Nutrition* 62, 761–768.

Stevenson, J. and Graham, P. (1988) Behavioural deviances in 13 year old twins: an item analysis. *Journal of the American Academy of Child and Adolescent Psychiatry* 27, 791–797.

Stewart, M.A., De Blois, S. and Cummings, C. (1980) Psychiatric disorder in the parents of hyperactive boys and those with conduct disorder. *Journal of Child Psychology and Psychiatry* 21, 283–292.

Stiefle, I. (1997) Can disturbance in attachment contribute to attention deficit hyperactivity disorder? A case discussion. *Clinical Child Psychology and Psychiatry* 2, 45–64.

Still, G.F. (1902) Some abnormal psychiatric conditions in children. *Lancet* I, 1008–1012, 1077–1082, 1163–1168.

Stone, R. (1993) Panel finds gaps in violence studies. *Science* 260, 1584–1585.

Strauss, A. and Lehtinen. L. (1947) *Psychopathology and Education of the Brain Injured Child*. New York: Grune and Stratton.

Survivors Speak Out (1987) *Charter of Needs*. London: Survivors Speak Out.

Sutherland, G. (1984) *Ability, Merit and Measurement Mental Testing and English Education*. Oxford: Clarendon Press.

Suvannathat, C., Bhanthumnavin, D., Bhuapirom, L. and Keats, D.M. (eds) (1985) *Handbook of Asian Child Development and Child Rearing Practices*. Bangkok: Srina Kharinwirot University, Behavioural Science Research Institute.

Szasz, T. (1970) *Ideology and Insanity*. New York: Doubleday-Anchor.

Szatmari, P., Boyle, M. and Offord, D.R. (1989a) ADDH and conduct disorder: degree of diagnostic overlap and differences among correlates. *Journal of the American Academy of Child and Adolescent Psychiatry* 28, 865–872.

Szatmari, P., Offord, D.R. and Boyle, M.H. (1989b) Ontario child health study: prevalence of Attention Deficit Disorder with Hyperactivity. *Journal of Child Psychology and Psychiatry* 30, 219–230.

Taylor, E. (1988) 'Attention deficit and conduct disorder syndromes', in M. Rutter, A.H. Tuma and I.S. Lann (eds) *Assessment and Diagnosis in Child Psychopathology*. New York: Guildford Press.

—— (1994) 'Syndromes of attention deficit and overactivity', in M. Rutter, E. Taylor and L. Hersov (eds) *Child and Adolescent Psychiatry, Modern Approaches* (3rd Edition). Oxford: Blackwell Scientific Publications.

Taylor, E. and Hemsley, R. (1995) Treating hyperkinetic disorders in childhood. *British Medical Journal* 310, 1617–1618.

Taylor, E., Sandberg, S., Thorley, G. and Giles, S. (1991) *The Epidemiology of Childhood Hyperactivity, Maudsley Monographs No. 33*. Oxford: Oxford University Press.

Taylor, E., Schachar, R., Thorley, G., Weiselberg, H.M., Everitt, B. and Rutter, M. (1987) Which boys respond to stimulant medication? A controlled trial of Methylphenidate in boys with disruptive behaviour. *Psychological Medicine* 17, 121–143.

Thapar, A., Hervas, A. and McGuffin, P. (1995) Childhood hyperactivity scores are highly heritable and show sibling competition effects: twin study evidence. *Behavioural Genetics* 25, 537–544.

Thomas, A. and Chess, S. (1977) *Temperament and Development*. New York: Brunner-Mazel.

Timimi, S. (1995) Adolescence in immigrant Arab families. *Psychotherapy* 32, 141–149.

—— (2002) *Pathological Child Psychiatry and the Medicalization Of Childhood*. London: Brunner, Routledge.

—— (2003) The new practitioner. *Young Minds* 62, 14–16.

Timimi, S. and 33 co-endorsers (2004) A critique of the international consensus statement on ADHD. *Clinical Child and Family Psychology Review* 7, 59–63.

Timimi, S. and Taylor, E. (2004) ADHD is best understood as a cultural construct. *British Journal of Psychiatry* 184, 8–9.

Tomm, K. (1990) A critique of DSM. *Dulwich Center Newsletter* 3, 5–8.

Toone, B. and Van Der Linden, G.J.H. (1997) Attention deficit hyperactivity disorder or hyperkinetic disorder in adults. *British Journal of Psychiatry* 170, 489–491.

Trawick, M. (1990) 'The ideology of love in a Tamil family', in O.M. Lynch (ed.) *Divine Passions: The Social Construction of Emotion in India*. Berkley: University of California Press.

—— (1991) An Ayurvedic theory of cancer. *Medical Anthropology* 13, 121–136.

Triandis, H.C. (1995) *Individualism and Collectivism*. Boulder Co: Westview Press.

Trommsdorf, G. (1985) 'Some comparative aspects of socialization in Japan and Germany', in I.R. Lagunes and Y.H. Poortinga (eds) *From a Different Perspective: Studies of Behaviour Across Cultures*. Lisse: Swets & Zeitlinger.

Tronick, E.Z., Morelli, G.A. and Ivey, P.K. (1992) The Efe forager infant and toddler's pattern of social relationships: Multiple and simultaneous. *Developmental Psychology* 28, 568–577.

Tuthill, R.W. (1996) Hair lead levels related to children's classroom attention-deficit behavior. *Archives of Environmental Health* 51, 214–220.

Tyrer, P. (1996) Co-morbidity or consanguinity. *British Journal of Psychiatry* 168, 669–671.

UNICEF (1994) *The Progress of Nations*. New York: UNICEF.

United Nations (1959) 'Declaration of the rights of the child', in *Resolution 1386 (xiv), Yearbook of the United Nations*. New York: United Nations.

United Nations Development Programme (1992) *Human Development Report*. New York: Oxford University Press.

United Nations General Assembly (1989) Adoption of a convention on the rights of the child. *U.N. Doc. A/Res/44/25. Nov.1989*. New York: United Nations.

United States Department of Education (1991) *Memorandum September 16th: Clarification of Policy to Address the Needs of Children with Attention Deficit Disorders*. Washington, DC: United States Dept. of Education.

Valenstein, E.S. (1998) *Blaming the Brain*. New York: The Free Press.

Vandana, S. (1988) *Staying Alive: Women, Ecology and Development*. London: Zed Books.

Van Der Meere, J.J. (1996) 'The role of attention', in S.T. Sandberg (ed.) *Monographs in Child and Adolescent Psychiatry: Hyperactive Disorders of Childhood*. Cambridge: Cambridge University Press.

Van Praag, H.M. (1996) Comorbidity (psycho)analysed. *British Journal of Psychiatry* 168 (Supplement 30), 129–134.

Vittachi. A. (1989) *Stolen Childhood: In Search of the Rights of the Child*. Cambridge: Polity Press.

Volkow, N.D., Ding, Y.S., Fowler, J.S., Wang, G.J., Logan, J., Gatley, J.S., Dewey, S., Ashby, C., Liebermann, J., Hitzemann, R. and Wolf, A.P. (1995) Is Methylphenidate like Cocaine. *Archives of General Psychiatry* 52, 456–463.

Waldegrave, C. (1992) Psychology, politics and the loss of the welfare state. *New Zealand Psychological Bulletin* 74, 14–21.

—— (1997) 'The challenges of culture to psychology and post modern thinking', in M. McGoldrick (ed.) *Re-visioning Family Therapy: Multicultural Systems Theory and Practice*. New York: Guildford Press.

Walkerdine, V. (1984) 'Developmental psychology and the child-centred pedagogy', in J. Henriques, W. Holloway, C. Urwin, C. Venn and V. Walkerdine (eds) *Changing the Subject: Psychology, Social Regulation and Subjectivity*. London: Methuen.

—— (1993) Beyond developmentalism? *Theory and Psychology* 3, 451–469.

—— (1996) 'Popular culture and the eroticization of little girls', in J. Curran, D. Morley and V. Walkerdine (eds) *Cultural Studies and Communications*. London: Arnold.

Wasserman, R.C., Kelleher, K.J., Bocian, A., Baber, A., Childs, C.E., Indacochea, F., Stulp, C. and Gardner, W.P. (1999) Identification of attentional and hyperactivity problems in primary care: A report from pediatric research in office settings and the ambulatory sentinel practice network. *Pediatrics* 103, E38.

Watson, J.B. (1928) *Psychological Care of Infant and Child*. New York: W.W. Norton.

Watson, J. (2003) *DNA: The Secret of Life*. London: William Heinemann.

Watzlawick, P., Weakland, J. and Fisch, R. (1974) *Change: Principles of Problem Formation and Problem Resolution*. New York: Norton.

Webster-Stratton, C. (1996) 'Early intervention with videotape modeling: Programmes for families of children with oppositional defiant disorder or conduct disorder', in

E.S. Hibbs and P.S. Jensen (eds) *Psychosocial Treatments for Child and Adolescent Disorders: Empirically Based Strategies for Clinical Practice*. Washington, DC: American Psychological Association.

Weigart, E. (1952) Contribution to the problem of terminating psychoanalysis. *Psychoanalytic Quarterly* 21, 465–480.

Weingarten, K. (1995) *Cultural Resistance: Challenging Beliefs about Men, Women and Therapy*. New York: Haworth Press.

—— (1997a) *The Mother's Voice: Strengthening Intimacy in Families*. New York: Guilford Press.

—— (1997b) 'From cold care to warm care', in C. Smith and D. Nylund (eds) *Narrative Therapies with Children and Adolescents*. New York: Guilford Press.

Weis, G., Kruger, E., Danielson, U. and Elman, M. (1975) Effect of long term treatment of hyperactive children with methylphenidate. *Canadian Medical Association Journal* 112, 159–165.

Welner, Z., Welner, A., Stewart, M., Palkes, H. and Wish, E. (1977) A controlled study of siblings of hyperactive children. *Journal of Nervous and Mental Disease* 165, 110–117.

Werry, J.S., Elkind, G.S. and Reeves, J.C. (1987a) Attention deficit, conduct oppositional and anxiety disorders in children. III. Laboratory differences. *Journal of Abnormal Child Psychology* 15, 409–428.

Werry, J.S., Reeves, J.C. and Elkind, G.S. (1987b) Attention Deficit, conduct oppositional and anxiety *disorders* in children. 1. A review of research on differentiating characteristics. *Journal of the American Academy of Child and Adolescent Psychiatry* 26, 133–143.

White, M. (1989) *Selected Papers*. Adelaide: Dulwich Centre Publications.

White, M. and Epston, D. (1990) *Narrative Means to Therapeutic Ends*. New York: Norton.

Whitelaw, S., Milosevic, L. and Daniels, S. (2000) Gender, behaviour and achievement: a preliminary study of pupil perceptions and attitudes. *Gender and Education* 12, 87–113.

Whittaker, R. (2002) *Mad in America*. Cambridge MA: Perseus.

Winn, M. (1984) *Children Without Childhood*. Harmondsworth: Penguin.

Winnicott, D.W. (1971) *Playing and Reality*. London: Tavistock Publications.

—— (1947) 'Hate in the counter-transference', in D.W. Winnicott (ed.) Collected Papers: Through Paediatrics to Psychoanalysis. London: Hogarth, 1958.

Witt, P., Barnerle, C., Deroven, D., Kamel, F., Kelleher, P., McCarthy, M., Namenworth, M., Sabatini, L. and Voytovich, M. (1989) The October 29th group: Defining a feminist science. *Women's Studies International Forum* 12, 253–259.

Wolf, R. (1996) *Marriages and Families in a Diverse Society*. New York: HarperCollins.

Wolfenstein, M. (1955) 'Fun morality: An analysis of recent child-training literature', in M. Mead and M. Wolfenstein (eds) *Childhood in Contemporary Cultures*. Chicago: The University of Chicago Press.

Wolin, S.J. and Bennett, L.A. (1984) Family rituals. *Family Process* 23, 401–420.

Wolraich, M., Windgren, S., Stromquist, A., Milich, R., Davis, C. and Watson, D. (1990) Stimulant medication use by primary care physicians in the treatment of Attention Deficit Hyperactivity Disorder. *Paediatrics* 86, 95–101.

Wooldridge, A. (1995) *Measuring the Mind*. Cambridge: Cambridge University Press.

World Health Organization (1990) *International Classification of Diseases*, 10th edition. Geneva: World Health Organization.

Wright, O. (2003) Ritalin use and abuse fears. *The Times (UK)* 28, July 3.

Wurtzel, E. (2002) *More, Now, Again*. London: Virago.

Xantian, L. (1985) 'The effect of family on the mental health of the Chinese people', in W. Tseng and D. Wu (eds) *Chinese Culture and Mental Health*. New York: Academic Press.

Yamani, M.A. (1995) 'Teach your children the love of God's messenger' translated by F. Ghannam, in E.W. Fernea (ed.) *Children in the Muslim Middle East*. Austin: University of Texas Press.

Yeoman, E. (1999) How does it get into my imagination? Elementary school children's intertextual knowledge and gendered storylines. *Gender and Education* 11, 427–440.

Zachary, G.P. (1997) Male order: Boys used to be boys, but do some now see boyhood as a malady? *The Wall St. Journal* 2 May.

Zahn, T.P., Rapoport, J.L. and Thompson, C.L. (1980) Autonomic and behavioural effects of dextroamphetamine and placebo in normal and hyperactive pre-pubertal boys. *Journal of Abnormal Child Psychology* 8, 145–160.

Zeig, J.K. (1980) *A Teaching Seminar with Milton H. Erickson, M.D.* New York: Brunner-Mazel.

Zelizer, V.A. (1985) *Pricing the Priceless Child: The Changing Social Value of Children.* New York: Basic Books Inc.

Zimmerman, F. (1987) *The Jungle and the Aroma of Meats: An Ecological Theme in Hindu Medicine*. Berkley: University of California Press.

Zito, J.M., Safer, D.J., Dosreis, S., Gardner, J.F., Boles, J. and Lynch, F. (2000) Trends in prescribing of psychotropic medication in pre-schoolers. *Journal of the American Medical Association* 283, 1025–1030.

Zwi, M., Ramchandani, P. and Joughlin, C. (2000) Evidence and belief in ADHD. *British Medical Journal* 321, 975–976.

Index